IB STUDY GUIDES

Economics

FOR THE IB DIPLOMA

Standard and Higher Level

Constantine Ziogas

OXFORD
UNIVERSITY PRESS

OXFORD
UNIVERSITY PRESS

Great Clarendon Street, Oxford OX2 6DP

Oxford University Press is a department of the University of Oxford.
It furthers the University's objective of excellence in research, scholarship,
and education by publishing worldwide in

Oxford   New York

Auckland   Cape Town   Dar es Salaam   Hong Kong   Karachi
Kuala Lumpur   Madrid   Melbourne   Mexico City   Nairobi
New Delhi   Shanghai   Taipei   Toronto

With offices in

Argentina   Austria   Brazil   Chile   Czech Republic   France   Greece
Guatemala   Hungary   Italy   Japan   Poland   Portugal   Singapore
South Korea   Switzerland   Thailand   Turkey   Ukraine   Vietnam

British Library Cataloguing in Publication Data

Data available

ISBN-13: 9780-19-915228-5

10 9 8 7 6 5 4

Printed in China by Prosperous

Paper used in the production of this book is a natural, recyclable product made
from wood grown in sustainable forests. The manufacturing process conforms to
the environmental regulations to the country of origin.

Acknowledgments
The Publisher would like to thank the following for permission to reproduce photographs:
Cover image: Mark Karrass/Corbis

Dedication
To my darlings, Daphne, Myrto and Elias

Introduction and acknowledgments

Introduction for the student

- This book has been written specifically for the student studying Higher or Standard Level Economics for the International Baccalaureate Diploma.

- It may prove helpful to any student of Introductory Economics, especially in the area of understanding the construction and use of diagrams.

- The study guide is organized in boxes and bullet points and also includes 'tips' to facilitate your work. Explanations are provided for all points presented.

- It is possible, but not advisable, to ignore a bullet point if your instructor has not focused on it or if you face a severe time constraint.

- The importance of diagrams in Economics in general and in the IB examination process in particular cannot be overemphasized. This guide has been written to help you realize that diagrams are not just 'pictures' for you to remember and 'paste' onto your answer sheets but perfectly logical constructions that once you understand you will never forget.

- Essay questions from past IB Higher and Standard Level examinations have been included to help you ensure that you have covered all the material.

- Questions that involve 'using an appropriate diagram' have also been included to ensure that you master most if not all necessary diagrams.

- A glossary is also available as well as advice on how to become better at evaluation, a necessary higher-order skill for Economics students.

Acknowledgments

I would like to thank Manuel Fernandez as well as all of my past and present students for helping me become a better teacher, and my Kris, for always making sure I keep things in perspective. I am indebted to all of them and many more.

Constantine H. Ziogas

Contents

Introduction

Scarcity

The fundamental problem all societies face is that of **scarcity**, defined as the excess of human wants over what can actually be produced to fulfil these wants. Human wants are unlimited. On the other hand the *means* of fulfilling these human wants are limited because the world has only a limited amount of resources.

As a result, choices have to be made. The **opportunity cost** of a choice is defined as the value of the next best alternative sacrificed.

Resources (factors of production)

- **Land and raw materials (natural resources)**
These are inputs into production that are provided by nature, e.g. unimproved land and mineral deposits in the ground, forests, pastures, etc. The world's land area and raw materials are limited. Some resources are non-renewable. If they are used now, they will not be available in the future, e.g. oil, coal deposits. Other resources are renewable, e.g. forests (timber), the stock of fish.
- **Labour (human resources)**
This is all forms of human input, both physical and mental, into current production. The labour force is, at any point in time, limited both in number and in skills. The total number of people available for work is referred to collectively as the labour force or working population. Note that the term **human capital** refers to the education, training and skills embodied in the labour force of a country.

- **Capital**
Physical capital includes manufactured resources, in other words, produced means of production (or goods used to produce other goods). The world has a limited stock of capital: limited supply of factories, machines, tools and other equipment. Note that the meaning of capital in economics is different from that used in ordinary speech where people refer to money as capital.
- **Entrepreneurship**
A term that is related but not identical to management. When a new venture is being considered, *risks* exist. They involve the unknown future. Someone must assess these risks and make judgements about whether or not to undertake them. The people who do so are called entrepreneurs. Entrepreneurship refers to the willingness and ability to take risks and mobilize the remaining factors of production.

Useful introductory terms

- **Normative economic statements:** they are value judgements, opinions, statements that cannot be falsified, or proven right or wrong; statements that cannot be tested against fact (data), e.g. 'inflation is rising *too fast*' or 'the income distribution is not *fair*'. Key words in normative statements include: ought to be, should be, too much, too little, fair, unfair.
- **Positive economic statements:** statements that can be falsified, or proven, at least in principle, right or wrong. They can be tested against facts (data), e.g. 'a minimum wage policy will increase unemployment among unskilled workers'.
- **Economic goods:** goods and services that require scarce resources to be sacrificed in order for them to be produced.

- **Free goods (in contrast to economic goods):** goods that have a zero opportunity cost of production (there are very few real-world examples, perhaps sea water and air). Note that goods available at a zero price are not free in the economist's sense if scarce resources may have been used up.
- **Competitive market:** a market is considered competitive if there are very many small firms, the good is homogeneous (it is considered identical across firms by consumers) and nothing prevents a new firm from entering the market.
- **Factor endorsements:** the quantity and quality of factors of production available.

The fundamental questions of economics

Economic choices

Scarcity necessitates choice. As a result, all societies, independently of their level of economic development or the economic system adopted, face and must answer the following three questions:

- What (i.e. which goods) will be produced and in what quantities?
- How will each good be produced (using, say, a labour-intensive or capital-intensive technology)?
- For whom? (How will income be distributed?)

How a society goes about answering these questions depends on the economic system it adopts. An economic system can be broadly defined as the institutional framework within which economic activity takes place. It is easy to distinguish two extreme cases but in the real world the variations are very many. Countries historically develop their own set of institutions that answer these questions. The current Chinese experience is a case in point. The two extremes are market economies and command economies, with mixed economies being in between.

- A **market economy** is an economy where households and firms each acting in their own self-interest determine answers to the three questions above through their interaction in markets.
- A **command economy** is one where the state provides the answers.
- A **mixed economy** is one where both markets and the state are responsible for the answers.

The production possibilities frontier

- A production possibilities frontier (PPF) refers to an economy endowed with a fixed amount of resources, is characterized by a given level of technology as well as some institutional framework, and producing only two goods. It shows for every amount produced of good X, the maximum amount of good Y that it *can* produce, if it fully utilizes its limited resources using the available technology. For example, referring to Fig. 1.1, if the economy decides to produce X1 units of good X then it *can* produce *at the most* Y1 units of good Y, assuming that it fully utilizes its limited resources with the available technology. A PPF is a technological relationship and it provides us no information about choices. It shows what an economy *can* do, not what it chooses to do.
- The mere existence of a PPF reflects scarcity: an economy is constrained in production to only some combinations of output. It follows that points *outside* a PPF (such as point A in Fig. 1.1) denote output combinations of the two goods that are unattainable given the amount of resources available and the present level of technology. Points *inside* the PPF (such as point B in Fig. 1.1) denote attainable but inefficient output combinations in the sense that resources are not fully utilized, e.g. unemployment is present. Points *on* the PPF (such as points F and H) denote attainable and efficient combinations as no waste of scarce resources is present and it is not possible to produce more of one good without sacrificing some of the other.
- The negative slope of the PPF reflects that in order to produce *more* of one good, resources have to be diverted away from the production of the other good so that less of the latter *can now be at most produced*: there is thus an 'opportunity cost' involved in producing an extra unit of a good. It is the amount of the other good that has to be sacrificed.
- Because scarce resources are *not* equally well suited for the production of all goods (in other words, because

Figure 1.1 The production possibilities frontier

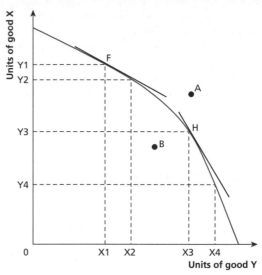

resources tend to be specialized) the PPF is bowed towards the origin. The slope (the tangent at each point, such as at points F and H) becomes steeper and steeper, reflecting that the opportunity cost of producing more and more of good X (the good on the horizontal axis) is increasing. In Fig. 1.1, the opportunity cost of producing X1X2 *extra* units of good X is the sacrifice of Y1Y2 units of good Y. The opportunity cost of X3X4 *extra* units of X (where X3X4 = X1X2) is thus bigger and equal to Y3Y4 units of good Y. This is the law of increasing costs. The typical shape of the production possibilities curve shows that it becomes more and more costly to produce ever-increasing quantities of a good as resources tend to be specialized. If, on the other hand, resources were perfectly substitutable then the PPF would be a negatively sloped straight line reflecting constant opportunity costs.

The production possibilities frontier continued

Growth

Growth of an economy can be illustrated through an outward shift of the PPF. We can distinguish between:

- **Actual growth:** this refers to an increase in the amounts of goods and services actually produced. It refers to an increase in total output. It is illustrated with a movement from a point inside the PPF to another point towards the northeast with more of at least one good. Real GDP (the term used later to refer to the total output produced in an economy) has increased.
- **Potential growth:** the term refers to the rate at which a country's economy *could* grow if all its resources were fully employed. Potential growth is illustrated with an outward shift of the PPF.
- In Fig.1.2a, actual growth is illustrated as a movement from point A1 to point A2 where output mix A1 contains X1 and Y1 units of the two goods while output mix A2 contains *more of both* goods (X2 units of good X and Y2 units of good Y). Actual growth can thus be achieved by better utilization of existing resources. Figure 1.2b illustrates potential growth as the production possibilities of the economy have increased (expanded) from FF′ to HH′. This economy is now *able* to produce combinations of output that were initially unattainable. Potential growth is the result of an increase in resources (more labour and more capital) and/or better technology being available (which may also refer to improved institutions).

More specifically growth occurs if there is an increase in:

- **Land (natural resources):** e.g. if new metal deposits/minerals are discovered.
- **Labour:** labour can increase if: population increases (through a natural increase or through migration); if there is an increase in the number of people of working age; if there is an increase in the participation rate of some population group (e.g. more women decide to join the labour force, or more teenagers).
- **Human capital:** the skills, education and training embodied in the labour force of an economy.
- **Capital:** if the stock of capital (i.e. of machines, tools, equipment, buildings, etc.) increases. An increase in the stock of capital is defined as investment.
- Technology and institutions improve (as the ability of all factors to produce will be enhanced).

Figure 1.2 (a) Actual growth (b) potential growth

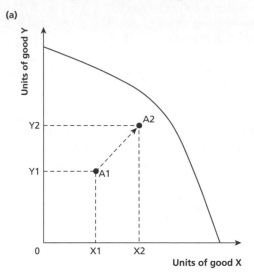

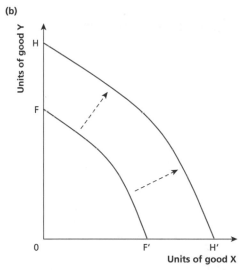

Tips

Make sure that the PPF you draw touches the two axes and is not 'floating' in mid-air. Draw it bowed (concave) towards the origin unless you are using it to illustrate constant opportunity costs. Also note that the axes may be labelled 'consumption goods' and 'capital goods' in order to illustrate the opportunity cost of investment. In this case, the opportunity cost of producing more capital goods (i.e. the opportunity cost of investment) is the sacrifice of present levels of consumption.

Microeconomics

Microeconomics is concerned with the individual parts of the economy. It is concerned with the demand and supply of *particular* goods, services and resources. It focuses in other words on individual markets.

Markets

- A market can be defined as a process or an institution in which producers and consumers interact in order to sell and buy a good or a service. A **market economy** is one where market forces alone provide answers to the three fundamental questions and in which private property rights are well defined and enforced. In a pure market economy there is no government intervention beyond setting and enforcing **property rights**.

- The participants in a market economy are **consumers** and **producers**. The interaction of consumers and producers (firms) in markets determine the market price of each product. Changes in market conditions thus result in market price changes which set off a chain of events leading to more or less of the good being produced and thus to a change in the allocation of scarce resources. Analysis of how markets function requires examination of the behaviour of consumers and producers.

The behaviour of consumers

Demand

- The concept of demand is a way of summarizing the behaviour of buyers. Specifically, we define demand as the relationship between various possible prices of a good and the corresponding quantities that consumers are willing and able to purchase per time period, ceteris paribus (i.e. all other factors affecting demand remaining constant).
- This relationship is inverse (negative), meaning that if the price per unit of the product decreases consumers will be willing and able to buy more per period (ceteris paribus). The inverse relationship between price and quantity demanded is referred to as the **law of demand**. The law of demand asserts that if the price per unit of a good rises then quantity demanded per period of time will fall, ceteris paribus.
- A demand curve now shows this inverse relationship between the price per unit of a good and the quantity of the good demanded per time period. Price per unit is measured on the vertical axis; quantity demanded per time period is measured on the horizontal axis.
- For example in Fig. 2.1, if the price per unit is P then consumers will be willing and able to buy Q units per period, whereas if price decreased to P' per unit then consumers will be willing and able to buy Q' units per

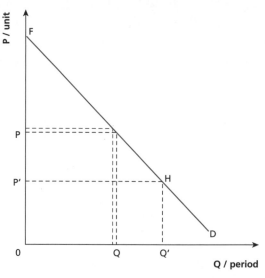

Figure 2.1 The demand curve (and consumer surplus)

period, ceteris paribus. A demand curve can be for an individual consumer or for the whole market. The market demand curve is diagrammatically derived by the horizontal summation of the individual demand curves.

The law of demand holds because of   HL

- **The substitution effect:** if the price of good X rises, all other goods *automatically* become *relatively* cheaper; thus, people will tend to substitute other goods for X. The size of the substitution effect depends primarily on the number and closeness of available substitute goods.

- **The income effect**: if the price per unit of good X rises, consumers' *real* income (the purchasing power of income) drops; thus, people will tend to buy less. The size of the income effect depends primarily on the proportion of income spent on the good.

Goal of the typical consumer

It is assumed that the typical consumer tries to *maximize his or her* **utility**, defined as the satisfaction derived from consuming a good or a bundle of goods. She will thus choose that bundle of goods which maximizes her satisfaction and which she can afford, given her income and the prices she faces in the market.

Consumer surplus

- Note that a demand curve can also be read 'vertically'. Unit Q in Fig. 2.1 is worth to consumers P as they would be willing to pay *at the most* P to buy it, not a cent more: if the price was even *slightly* higher (say at the level of the red dotted line) then they would not have been willing to buy *that last unit Q*. Unit Q' is worth to consumers P' as that is *the most* they would be willing to pay to acquire it.
- To consume greater and greater amounts per period, the market price must decrease as consumption of more and more units per period is worth less and less to consumers. This reflects the law of diminishing **marginal utility**, namely that the extra satisfaction derived from the consumption of greater amounts per period typically decreases.
- Given that the vertical distance reflects how much each extra unit is worth to consumers then the area (0Q'HF) in Fig. 2.1 measures how much *all* units Q' are worth to the consumer, i.e. how much she would be willing *at the most* to pay to enjoy *all* these units. If the market price is P' then she will be willing and able to consume all units up until unit Q' for which they would spend (P') times (Q') = area (0Q'HP'). Area (P'HF) is the difference between what the consumer would at the most be willing to pay to enjoy units Q' and what she will end up paying for them in the market and is known as the **consumer surplus**.

Tips

Demand curves can be linear or curved; they may or they may not touch the axes; just make sure that they are negatively sloped (unless you want to illustrate some special case). If you wish to illustrate the notion of the consumer surplus it is easier to have the demand curve touch the axes. Note that the above discussion refers to the demand for a product: the demand for a factor of production ('derived demand'; say, for labour services by firms) is similar but not identical. Also, be careful about the meaning of the term 'quantity demanded'. It refers to the amount that consumers are willing and able to purchase at a given price over a given time period. It does not refer to what people would simply *want* to consume. Note that 'willingness' reflects preferences whereas 'ability' reflects the income constraint people face

Other factors affecting demand ('shift' factors)

- **Changes in consumers' income**
  As income rises, demand for most goods will rise and the demand curve will shift to the right. Such goods are called **normal goods**. There are exceptions to this general rule, however. As people get richer, they spend less on **inferior goods**, such as low-quality food or low-quality clothing, and switch to better-quality goods. The demand for inferior goods decreases when incomes increase and thus the demand curve for inferior goods will shift to the left. If the per capita level of income in an economy rises through time, the *pattern* of demand will change. This has important implications for production, unemployment, etc.
- **Changes in the distribution of income**
  If the income distribution becomes less skewed and more equal, demand for certain luxuries may drop and for certain basic goods and services may rise. Thus a policy of redistributing income through taxes and transfers may alter the patterns of demand.
- **Changes in preferences (tastes)**
  The more desirable people find a good, the more they will demand it. Tastes are affected by advertising, by fashion, by observing other consumers, by considerations of health, etc.
- **Changes in the price of other goods**
  Two cases are distinguished:
  a **Case of complements:** defined as goods that are consumed together ('jointly consumed'), such as peanut butter and jelly, shoes and shoe polish, coffee and sugar, etc. When the price of a complement of good X rises, demand for X will drop (shift left; e.g. if the price of coffee rises then demand for sugar will drop).
  b **Case of substitutes:** defined as goods in competitive consumption, such as coffee and tea. When the price of a substitute of good X rises, demand for X will rise (will shift right; e.g. if coffee becomes more expensive then demand for tea will increase).
- **Size of the market, i.e. number of consumers**
  As the size of a market (the number of consumers) increases, demand for most products will tend to rise.
- **Age distribution of the population**
  A change in the age distribution would affect the *pattern* of demand. The classic example refers to an ageing population (where the average age is rising) where demand for false teeth will rise and for chewing gum will drop.

Other factors affecting demand ('shift' factors) continued

- **Expectations** (of changes in market prices or in income) For example, if people think that the price of a good is going to rise in the future, they are likely to buy more of it now before prices go up, shifting its demand curve to the right.

Shifts of demand versus movements along a demand curve

This is the source of a typical mistake. A shift in the demand curve occurs when a determinant other than the price changes: we then say that a change in demand has occurred. A movement along the demand curve occurs when there is a change in price: we then say there is a change in quantity demanded.

Tips

Never say that demand shifts up or down as it increases the chance of getting confused and making a mistake. Always use the expression demand shifts right (when it increases) and shifts left (when it decreases). Also note that the new demand curve does not have to be parallel to the initial one.

Exceptions to the law of demand

- The law of demand is almost universal. It is very rare for a higher price to lead to an increase in quantity demanded per period. Giffen goods and Veblen goods are two exceptions where a rise in the price leads to more of the good being consumed per period.

Figure 2.2 Positively sloped demand curves: Giffen and Veblen goods

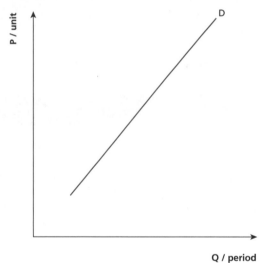

Giffen goods

Giffen goods have the following *three* characteristics:

- they are very strongly inferior goods;
- they are consumed by the very poor;
- expenditure on these goods must represent a very significant proportion of total consumer expenditures.

- Being very strongly inferior goods, the income effect runs in the opposite direction of the substitution effect and dominates it, leading to the perverse result described. All Giffen goods are inferior goods but not all inferior goods are Giffen goods.
- Giffen goods were first mentioned in 1895 by Alfred Marshall in his *Principles*. The original example was bread, which in Sir Robert Giffen's time (19th century) was consumed by the very poor in London. The typical textbook example has since been potatoes, consumed by very poor Irish farmers during the 1845 famine. Both examples have been refuted by analysis of historical data. Recent research using detailed panel data has shown that in China, where 30% of the population still survives on less than a dollar a day per person, noodles in the north and rice in the south exhibit such Giffen behaviour.

Veblen goods

- Veblen goods are the other exception to the law of demand. These are goods viewed as status symbols. They are valued because their high price is beyond the reach of other individuals.
- Beluga caviar and Franck Muller watches selling for $750,000 may be good examples. Increasing the price for these goods may not decrease quantity demanded. Veblen goods should obviously not be confused with inferior goods.

Tip

Remember that inferior goods (unless they are also Giffen goods) have typical, negatively sloped, demand curves.

Exceptions to the law of demand continued

The role of expectations

A further exception to the law of demand is the case when the quantity demanded of a product rises as the price rises, because of **expectations** that the price will rise even more in the future. This is known as the 'bandwagon' effect, with buyers 'jumping on the bandwagon'. Not all economists agree about this. It is perhaps preferable to treat expectations of a future price increase as a shift factor of a typical downward slopeing demand curve (see page 10).

The behaviour of producers

Supply

- Supply is a way to analytically summarize the behaviour and the goals of firms.
- It is defined as the relationship between various possible prices and the corresponding quantities that firms are willing to offer per time period, ceteris paribus.
- The supply curve is a graph showing the relationship between the price per unit of a good and the quantity that a firm (or firms) is willing to offer per period of time.
- Typically, supply is upward sloping, meaning that if the price per unit of a product increases then a firm will be willing to offer a greater quantity per period of time, ceteris paribus.
- In Fig. 2.3, if the price is P then producers will be willing to offer Q units per period, whereas if the price increased to P′ then producers will be willing to offer Q′ units per period.
- The question is why? A simplistic answer is that at higher prices, a firm's profit margin is greater, thus it will be willing to offer more of the good per period. Also, since it becomes more and more difficult for a firm to produce more per period *using existing capacity*, it will be willing to do so only if price per unit rises.

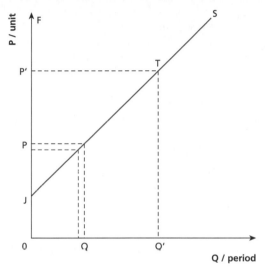

Figure 2.3 The supply curve (and producer surplus)

Producer surplus

- Note that the supply curve in Fig. 2.3 can also be read 'vertically': a firm would be willing to offer unit Q only if the price in the market is *at least* P. P is *the minimum price the firm would be willing to accept*.
- Even if the price was *slightly* lower (at the red dotted line level) the firm would not be willing to offer unit Q. Why? Because it would not cover the extra cost of producing that unit. The vertical distance thus reflects how much *each extra* unit costs the firm to produce.

- Thus area (0Q′TJ) measures how much *all units* Q′ cost the firm to produce. It represents the minimum amount it requires in order to offer all these Q′ units. If the market price is P′ per unit then the firm will be willing to offer all units up until unit Q′ for which they would earn (P′) times (Q′) = area (0Q′TP′).
- Area (JTP′) represents the difference between what the firm earns when producing and selling Q′ units and the minimum amount of money it requires to be willing to offer these units. This is the 'producer surplus'.

Other factors affecting supply ('shift' factors)

- **Changes in input prices**
  If, for example, wages or raw material prices decrease then a firm at each price will be willing to offer more per period as production is now less costly. The supply curve will shift to the right.
- **Changes in technology**
  Improvements in technology lower the costs of production since they permit less to be spent on inputs. Supply will thus increase and shift to the right.
- **Change in productivity**
  Productivity of a factor is defined as output per unit of input. If, for example, labour becomes more experienced, better trained or healthier then labour productivity will increase, meaning that output per worker will be greater. It follows that supply will increase and shift to the right.
- **Changes in government policy**
  Government subsidies (per unit of output payments to firms) will lower production costs, while imposing indirect taxes will increase production costs. The supply decision is thus in both cases affected.
- **Size of the market**
  The market supply will be affected if the number of firms in the market changes. As, for example, more firms are lured into a market the market supply will tend to rise.

- **Expectations**
  The expectation that a price will be higher in the future may cause supply of the product to decrease now.
- **Other factors**
  Weather conditions for obvious reasons affect the supply of farm products; a terrorist act or a war may affect the supply of oil, etc.

Tips

Supply curves may be straight lines or curves; they may or may not start from the vertical (or horizontal) axis. Just make sure they are (in the general case) upward sloping. To illustrate the producer surplus it is easier to have your supply curve start from the vertical axis. The supply of a factor of production (say of labour services by 'workers') is similar but not identical to the supply of a good. Also an increase or a decrease in supply should always be referred to as a shift to the right or to the left, respectively. Using 'up' or 'down' may lead to confusion as, for example, a shift down on the diagram reflects an increase in supply. It is a shift to the right.

Equilibrium

Price and output determination in a competitive market

- The price at which a good will be sold in a competitive market will be determined by the interaction between consumers and producers, in other words by the interaction of demand and supply.
- If at some price excess supply exists (if quantity supplied per period exceeds quantity demanded) then the price will tend to drop.

- If at some price excess demand exists (if quantity demanded per period exceeds quantity supplied) then the price will tend to rise.
- It follows that there will be no tendency for the price to change if there is neither excess supply nor excess demand in the market. This requires that quantity demanded per period at that price is equal to quantity supplied. This price is the **equilibrium price** (or **market clearing price**) and the corresponding quantity is the **equilibrium quantity**.

Price and output determination in a competitive market continued

- Referring to Fig. 2.4, could P1 be the 'equilibrium' price? At P1 consumers are willing to buy Qd1 units per period while firms are willing to offer Qs1 units per period. Quantity supplied *per period* is greater than quantity demanded. There is excess supply (a surplus) equal to Qs1–Qd1 = HF units per period which will create pressure for the price to fall. Since the excess supply creates a tendency for the market price to fall it follows that P1 is not an 'equilibrium' price.
- Could P2 be the 'equilibrium' price? At P2 consumers are willing to buy Qd2 units per period while firms are willing to offer Qs2 units per period. Quantity demanded *per period* is greater than quantity supplied. There is excess demand (a shortage) equal to Qd2–Qs2 = JV units per period which will create pressure for the price to rise. Since the excess demand creates a tendency for the market price to rise (to change) it follows that P2 is not an 'equilibrium' price.
- Quantity demanded per period is equal to quantity supplied only at price P. At P there is no excess demand or excess supply so the market 'clears'. Price P is thus the equilibrium price.

Figure 2.4 The determination of equilibrium price in a competitive market

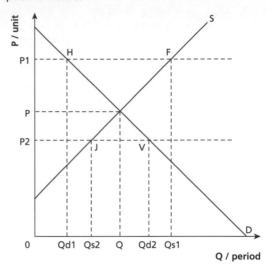

Tip

A shortage (or a surplus) is *not* an area but the horizontal distance between the quantity demanded and the quantity supplied at some price.

The question of resource allocation

The allocation of scarce resources in a market economy

- A problem any society faces is how much to produce of each good, and thus how many resources should be allocated in the production of each. To illustrate the problem, think of a society endowed with two resources, labour and land, wishing to produce two goods, say apples and oranges. The problem it faces is how many apples to produce and how many oranges and, consequently, how much land and how much labour to allocate in the production of apples and how much to oranges. Since resources are scarce, producing more apples implies that fewer oranges can be produced.
- Figure 2.5 incorporates all the necessary information to determine the answer. The demand curve drawn reflects how much each extra unit of apples is valued by consumers and more generally by society. The supply curve reflects how much each extra unit of apples costs to produce (as it shows the minimum price required for the unit to be offered). In this simple setup it should be clear that producing an extra unit of apples requires more resources allocated in apple production, so the cost of each extra unit of apples produced are the oranges that need to be sacrificed.

Figure 2.5 The allocation of scarce resources (a)

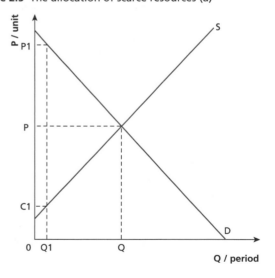

The allocation of scarce resources in a market economy continued

- Should unit Q1 be produced from society's point of view? The answer will be yes, if it is valued more than what it costs to produce it. The demand curve for apples informs us that unit Q1 is valued by society at P1 dollars (or yuan), as that is how much consumers would *at the most* be willing to pay.
- The supply curve for apples informs us that it costs C1 dollars (or yuan) to produce unit Q1 as that is the *minimum suppliers would be willing to accept to offer that unit*. Since unit Q1 is valued more than what it costs, the answer is that it should be produced.
- Thus, more units of apples (in general, more of any good 'x') should be produced as long as the valuation of the extra unit (what people would be at the most willing to pay) exceeds the extra cost of producing it.
- It follows that the very last unit of apples society would want to be produced is that unit which is valued as much

as it costs to produce it. In Fig. 2.5 this would be unit Q. Stopping short of that unit (producing a tiny bit less than unit Q) would beg the question why not produce a 'tiny bit' more.
- The startling result of *competitive* markets is that even though each consumer and each producer is looking after his own self-interest (consumers aiming at maximizing utility and producers aiming at maximizing profit) the market outcome is precisely the best possible from society's point of view; this idea was first expressed by the famous economist Adam Smith. In a competitive market, price will indeed gravitate to P dollars (or yuan) per unit and output will be exactly Q units per period, so all units worth more than what they cost to produce are indeed produced.

The power of relative price changes

- Assume now that preferences in this society change and that, for example, more apples are in demand. Why and how will more apples be produced and thus additional scarce resources attracted and employed in apple production? What mechanisms will come into play to guarantee that these changed preferences of society will be satisfied?
- Focusing on Fig. 2.6, let the price of apples initially be P1 per unit and the output of the apple industry Q1 units per period. A greater demand for apples can be shown as a shift of the demand for apples to the right to D2. Of course, no one in the market sees the shift but now there will be excess demand for apples equal to HF units per period. As a result P1 is no longer an equilibrium price. There is pressure for the price to rise.
- The rise in the price of apples is visible and it initiates changes in the behaviour of both firms and consumers. Changing relative prices thus have 'signalling power'. Some consumers will drop out of the market or will cut down on their purchases. On the other side, higher prices mean increased profits for existing firms and an opportunity for other firms to enter the market and partake in these profits. As a result quantity supplied per period rises but it should be realized that for this to happen more resources will have to shift into apple production.

Figure 2.6 The allocation of scarce resources (b)

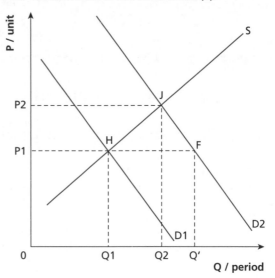

- The price mechanism thus leads to a change in resource allocation as rising relative prices and profits provide the signal and the incentive for firms to produce more. Eventually, the extension of supply (from H to J) and the contraction of demand (from (F to J) will stop when the new equilibrium price P2 per unit is reached and industry output is higher at Q2 units per period.

Elasticity

In general, **elasticity** is defined as the *responsiveness* of some economic variable, when another economic variable changes.

Price elasticity of demand

Definition: The responsiveness of quantity demanded to a change in price.

Symbol: PED

Measure: The percentage change in quantity demanded divided by the percentage change in price:

PED = $\%\Delta Q_d / \%\Delta P$. Thus PED = $(\Delta Q/Q1)/(\Delta P/P1)$ = $(\Delta Q/\Delta P)*(P1/Q1)$

- PED is thus the **ratio of the changes** of two variables (price and quantity demanded) that move in opposite directions: if the price of the good goes up, then the quantity demanded goes down and vice versa, implying that if the denominator has a plus sign (the price increased) then the numerator will have a negative sign (the quantity demanded will have decreased).
- As a result PED is always a *negative* number. Note that often the minus sign is ignored. *But* in any calculation questions *never forget to use the minus sign* even if it is not provided.

Ranges of price elasticity of demand

- Demand is **elastic** (for small changes around the initial price) if the percentage change in quantity demanded is larger than the percentage change in price (PED >1). Alternatively we can say that if a change in price leads to a *proportionately* greater change in quantity demanded then demand for the product is price elastic.
- Demand is **inelastic** (for small changes around the initial price) if the percentage change in quantity demanded is smaller than the percentage change in price (0< PED <1). Alternatively we can say that if a change in price leads to a *proportionately* smaller change in quantity demanded then demand for the product is price inelastic.
- Demand is **unit elastic** if the percentage change in quantity demanded is equal to the percentage change in price (PED = 1).
- Demand is **perfectly elastic** if a small change in price leads to an infinitely large change in quantity demanded (PED → ∞). This means that if, for example, the price of a product rises *even slightly*, nothing will be bought by consumers. A demand curve of infinite price elasticity is a line parallel to the quantity axis.
- Demand is **perfectly inelastic** if a small change in price leads to no change in the quantity demanded (PED = 0). Price changes have no effect on the amount purchased per period. A demand curve of zero price elasticity is a line parallel to the price axis.

Note that the minus sign is ignored.

Price elasticity of demand varies along a typical demand curve

Note that even along a linear, negatively sloped, demand curve PED continuously varies, taking on all values from infinity to zero.

- Referring to Fig. 2.7, at the midpoint M of the demand curve AB that corresponds to price Pm (located at the midpoint of segment 0A), PED = 1.
- Within line segment AM corresponding to prices higher than Pm within the segment APm, demand is price elastic (PED >1).
- Within line segment MB corresponding to prices lower than Pm within the segment PmB, demand is price inelastic (0< PED <1).
- Lastly, at point A price elasticity of demand tends to infinity while at point B price elasticity of demand is zero.

Figure 2.7 PED along a negatively sloped linear demand curve

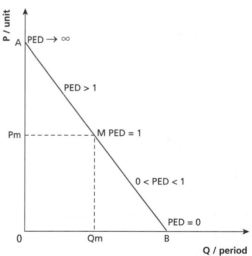

Tips

A common mistake is to consider the price elasticity of demand for a linear demand curve that is at a 45 degree angle to both axes as constant and equal to 1. This is not the case. Price elasticity for such a demand curve *also* varies from infinity to zero. The slope of such a curve is 1 but slope is *not* elasticity. Strictly speaking it is incorrect to characterize any linear demand as price elastic if it is flat, and as price inelastic if it is steep. But, since for two intersecting linear demand curves, the flatter one is indeed more price elastic, then, *for small price changes around the intersection price*, it is accepted to claim that a flatter demand curve is relatively price elastic whereas a relatively steep one is relatively price inelastic.

Demand curves with constant PED

- The case of a perfectly inelastic demand curve: PED = 0
  The demand curve (Fig. 2.8) is thus vertical at some quantity. Any change in price will lead to no change in quantity demanded.

Figure 2.8 Perfectly price-inelastic demand curve

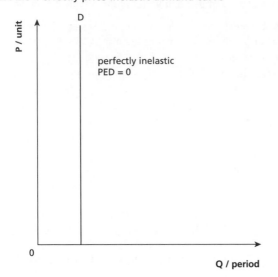

Often used to describe the case of highly addictive goods such as drugs or to describe the individual demand for pharmaceutical products for which no substitutes exist.

- The case of a perfectly elastic demand curve: PED → ∞
  The demand curve (Fig. 2.9) is horizontal at some price. It is used to describe the demand that a perfectly competitive firm faces. Such a firm is so 'tiny' in size compared to the market that it can sell any amount at the going market price. It is as if it is facing a perfectly elastic demand at the market price.

Figure 2.9 Perfectly price-elastic demand curve

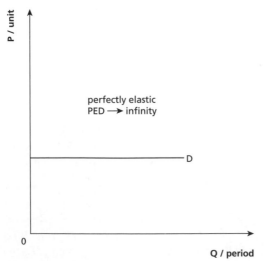

- The case of a unitary elastic demand curve: PED = 1
  The demand curve (Fig. 2.10) in this case is asymptotic to both axes, i.e. it never touches either. The demand curve is a rectangular hyperbola.

Figure 2.10 Unitary elastic demand curve

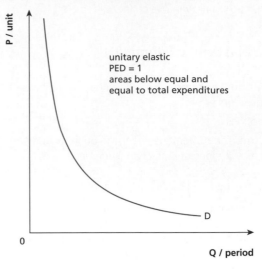

All areas below the curve represent firm revenues and are equal in size. In other words in a unitary elastic demand curve a change in price does not change total firm revenues.

Relationship between PED and total revenues

- What will happen to firms' revenues (and hence to consumer expenditures) if there is a change in price? The answer depends on the price elasticity of demand. Total revenues (TR) which a firm collects are the product of the price per unit and the quantity sold (TR = PQ). It is not the same as profits which are the difference between the total revenues collected and the total costs incurred.

Three cases can be distinguished:

- Case 1: Price changes when PED >1 (demand is price elastic)
  A change in price leads to a change in the *opposite* direction in quantity demanded. When demand is price elastic, quantity demanded changes *proportionately* more than price. Thus the change in quantity has a bigger effect on revenues than does the change in price. Thus, if demand is elastic, total expenditure changes in the same direction as quantity demanded. If P rises then Q *falls* proportionately more. Thus TR will *fall*. But if P falls, then Q *rises* proportionately more and thus TR will *rise*.
- Case 2: Price changes when 0< PED <1 (demand is price inelastic)
  In this case, price rises *proportionately* more than quantity. Thus, the change in price has a bigger effect on total revenue than does the change in quantity. Total revenues change in the same direction as price. If P *rises* then Q falls proportionately less, thus TR *rises*. But if P *falls*, Q rises proportionately less, thus TR *falls*.
- Case 3: Price changes when PED = 1 (demand is unitary elastic)
  In this case, price and quantity change in exactly the same proportion. The demand curve is a 'rectangular hyperbola'. A change in price will have no effect on total revenues. On a graph of *total revenues* against Q, the function will be a straight line parallel to the horizontal axis.

Demand curves with constant PED continued

PED and the shape of the TR curve

It follows from the above that there is a close relationship between price elasticity of demand and the shape of the total revenues curve a firm faces.

Focusing on Fig. 2.11a which illustrates the typical, linear, negatively sloped demand curve:

- At zero quantity (at the origin) total revenues are zero and at zero price (point H) total revenues are also zero.
- As price decreases (think of 'walking down' the price axis) from point F to Pm, quantity demanded increases from 0 to Qm. Since demand for that price range is price elastic the resulting increase in quantity demanded is proportionately greater so total revenues rise.
- Now, skip to the midpoint price Pm. If price continues to decrease past Pm all the way down to zero, quantity demanded increases from Qm to H. Since demand is now price inelastic, the resulting increase in quantity demanded is proportionately smaller, so total revenues decrease.
- Since we established that revenues rise all the way to the midpoint Qm and then, right after Qm, they decrease, it necessarily follows that at Qm they are at a maximum. Thus, right below the midpoint of the linear demand curve where PED is equal to 1, total revenues are maximized.

- *(HL only)* Define marginal revenue as the extra revenue from selling one more unit of output. MR is thus the change in TR because of a change in Q so it is the slope of the TR curve. At Qm where TR is maximum it follows that MR is zero. If demand is a negatively sloped line then MR has double the slope. In Fig. 2.11a it will thus go through output Qm.

Focusing on Fig. 2.11b which illustrates a unitary elastic demand curve:

- The percentage increase in quantity demanded is equal to the percentage decrease in price. As a result total revenues remain unchanged (constant). In the bottom diagram TR is thus drawn as a straight line parallel to the quantity axis illustrating that total revenues do not change as output varies.

Focusing on Fig. 2.11c which illustrates the case of a perfectly elastic demand curve:

- Here the firm is so tiny that it can sell all it wants at the price P', say, for example, £3.00 per unit. It follows that the total revenue curve is a rising straight line starting from the origin as the revenues from one unit sold will be £3.00, the revenues from two units sold will be £6.00, the revenues from three units sold will be £9.00 etc.

Figure 2.11 Price elasticity of demand and the shape of the total revenues curve

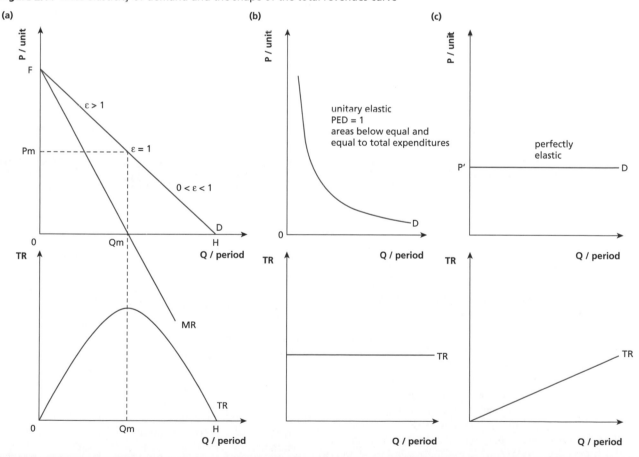

Determinants of price elasticity of demand

- **The number and closeness of available substitutes**
  The more substitutes there are for a good, and the closer these are, the more easily people will switch to these alternatives when the price of the good rises; the greater therefore will be the price elasticity of demand. (Also think of how broadly or narrowly the good is defined – e.g. Pepsi vs. soft drinks – the broader the definition, the fewer the substitutes available to the consumer and thus the more price inelastic demand is expected to be for small price changes.)
- **The proportion of income spent on the good**
  The higher the proportion of income spent on a good, the more consumers will be forced to lower consumption when its price rises (the bigger will be the income effect) and the more elastic will be the demand. If we spend a small proportion of our income on a good (if it is 'insignificant') then a change in price will not affect our spending behaviour; demand will be price inelastic.

- **The time period involved**
  When price of a product rises it takes some time for people to find alternatives and adjust their consumption patterns. It follows that the longer the time period after a price change, the more price elastic demand is likely to be.
- **The nature of the good, i.e. whether or not it is addictive**
  Demand for addictive products is relatively price inelastic (cigarettes, alcohol etc.). This has profound implications on the decision of governments to impose a tax on such products.

Tip

Students often confuse the factors affecting the demand for a product with the factors affecting the price elasticity of demand for a product.

Uses of price elasticity of demand

- It permits a firm to predict the direction of change of its total revenues given a price change. For example a firm wishing to increase its revenues will lower the price if demand is thought to be price elastic and it will increase the price if its demand is price inelastic.
- It allows comparison of *quantity* changes with *monetary* (i.e. price) changes.
- *(HL only)* It permits a firm to employ price discrimination. The higher price will be charged in the market with the relatively inelastic demand.

- *(HL only)* It helps a firm determine what proportion of an indirect tax can be passed on to the consumer.
- It permits a government to estimate the size of the necessary tax required to decrease consumption of a 'demerit' good, such as cigarettes or alcoholic beverages.
- *(HL only)* It permits the government to determine the incidence of an indirect tax.
- It helps a government predict the effect of currency devaluation on the **trade balance** of the country.

Income elasticity of demand

Definition: The responsiveness of demand when consumer income changes

Symbol: YED

Measure: The percentage change in quantity demanded divided by the percentage change in income:

$$YED = \%\Delta Q_d/\%\Delta Y, \text{ thus } YED = (\Delta Q/Q_1)/(\Delta Y/Y_1) = (\Delta Q/\Delta Y)*(Y_1/Q_1)$$

- Since income elasticity of demand is the ratio of the percentage changes in demand and income levels it follows that if both *changes* are positive (plus sign) or if both are negative (minus sign) then YED is a positive number. If one change is positive (plus sign) and the other is negative (minus sign) then YED is a negative number. For example if an increase in income leads to a decrease in quantity demanded then YED is a negative number. We

can thus distinguish between normal and inferior goods based on whether YED is positive or negative:
- If YED >0: the good is a **normal good** since demand increases (decreases) as consumer income increases (decreases).
- If YED <0: the good is an **inferior good** since demand decreases (increases) as consumer income increases (decreases).

Focusing now on normal goods:

- YED >1: this implies that $\%\Delta Q_d > \%\Delta Y$ therefore we say that demand is income elastic as a rise in income leads to a faster rise (a *proportionately* greater increase) in demand. **Luxury goods** (as well as most services) usually are considered income elastic, for example demand for plastic surgery or for spa therapy or for haute couture clothing.

Income elasticity of demand continued

- 0< YED <1: this implies that %ΔQ_d < %ΔY therefore we say that demand is income inelastic as a rise in income leads to a slower rise (a *proportionately* smaller increase) in demand. Basic goods (everyday goods; 'staple' goods) are usually income inelastic (e.g. demand for food as a broad category is income inelastic).

Lastly:

- If YED = 0 then demand for the good is not affected by a change in income.
- If YED = 1 then the percentage change in income is equal to the percentage change in quantity demanded.

Engel curves

Graphs that show how quantity demanded varies with the level of consumer income are known as Engel curves. Income is usually on the vertical axis.

- In Fig. 2.12a three Engel curves are depicted. All three represent normal goods as all three are positively sloped illustrating that as income levels rise, quantity demanded per period also rises. But, income elasticities differ. Engel curve 1 which has a vertical intercept at point F is income elastic throughout its length (without YED being constant); Engel curve 2 which goes through the origin 0 has an income elasticity of demand equal to one throughout its length; lastly, Engel curve 3 which has a horizontal intercept at point H is income inelastic throughout its length (without YED being constant).
- In Fig. 2.12b the probable effect of rising income levels on the demand for a product is shown: starting from

low levels of income and up to some income level Y1 the Engel curve is AB illustrating that the good is normal as demand is rising with YED positive (and as there is a vertical intercept greater than one). As incomes rise more from level Y1 all the way to some level Y2 the quantity demanded per period stays constant so YED is zero; and, if incomes rise further past Y2 per period then demand for this good starts to shrink signifying that the good behaves as an inferior product and that YED is negative.

Tips

Remember that elasticity and slope are not the same thing so even if three Engel curves are parallel their elasticities differ as in Fig. 2.12a. Also, Engel curves need not be linear. In this case judging whether at some point they are income elastic or inelastic becomes a bit more complicated.

Some industries are considered 'cyclical' and some 'acyclical' as a result of their income elasticity of demand: as overall economic activity fluctuates in the short run (this fluctuation of economic activity is known as the 'trade' or 'business' cycle), sales in the construction, the car and the furniture industries are significantly affected whereas sales in the food industry are not affected as much. The former industries are 'cyclical' whereas the latter is 'acyclical'.

Figure 2.12 Income elasticity of demand: Engel curves

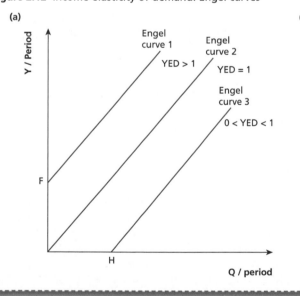

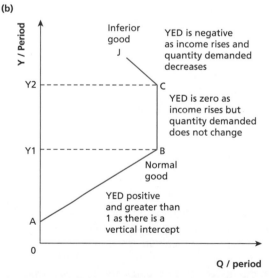

Determinants of income elasticity of demand

- **The degree of 'necessity' of the good**
  In a developed country, the demand for luxury goods and services expands rapidly as people's incomes rise further, whereas the demand for basic goods, such as bread and most food products in general, rises slowly. **Engel's law** states that as incomes increase, a declining *proportion* is spent on *food* because of the 'fixed capacity' of the human stomach. Demand for food is therefore income inelastic. Furthermore, certain basic foodstuffs may behave as inferior goods, meaning that their income elasticities are negative. Thus, as incomes increase, people may substitute basmati rice and multigrain bread for low-quality rice or white sliced bread. As their incomes rise further, total expenditure on food may even increase but it takes a declining *proportion* of their income.
- **The living standards of the economy**
  Whether market demand for a good is income elastic or income inelastic is not within its 'nature' but is a function of the living standards of the market participants. The same good may behave as an inferior good with negative YED in a highly developed country and as a highly income-elastic one in a least developed country.

Uses of income elasticity of demand

- Firms would like to know whether demand for their product is highly income elastic or rather income inelastic to help them better plan their investments. If an economy is growing and incomes are increasing fast then firms producing highly income-elastic products may have to invest now in expanding their capacity to be able to meet the increased demand. Conversely, farmers growing, say, potatoes may think of switching to kiwi fruit (this explains why in Ethiopia coffee growers are switching to chat, a narcotic) or to agro-tourism which have a higher income elasticity of demand.

- A government may also be interested in knowing income elasticity of demand in various sectors in order to plan ahead training for displaced workers: the economic significance and viability of income-inelastic sectors will shrink in the long run so some workers in these sectors may lose their jobs and will need retraining. In this sense, a growing economy may suffer from increased (structural) unemployment and move away from full employment. Also, as sectors producing highly income-elastic products (e.g. services) will grow fast, employment needs will also grow fast so governments should plan ahead changes in school curricula and vocational schools. Employment bottlenecks will thus be avoided.

Cross price elasticity of demand

Definition: The responsiveness of demand for one good (x) to a change in the price of another good (y).

Symbol: XPE or CPE

Measure: The percentage change in the quantity demanded of good x divided by the percentage change in the price of good y:

$$XPE = \%\Delta Q_x / \%\Delta P_y$$

Here, the sign determines how we interpret cross price elasticity of demand for a product:

- If XPE >0, then the two goods x and y are substitutes meaning that they are in competitive demand: if one becomes more expensive then consumers will switch to the other.
- If XPE <0, then the two goods x and y are complements meaning that they are jointly demanded: if one becomes more expensive and thus people buy it less, they will also buy less of the other one.
- If XPE = 0, then the two goods x and y are unrelated. It follows that the further away from zero XPE is, the *stronger* the relationship between the goods; conversely, the closer (absolutely) to zero XPE is, the weaker the relationship between the two goods.
- Figure 2.13a illustrates the case of substitutes in which cross price elasticity of demand is positive. If the price of coffee increases from P1 to P2 then we expect that the quantity demanded per period of tea will increase from Q1 to Q2 as some will switch away from the now more expensive coffee to tea drinking. Note that this is not a demand curve as on the one axis we have the price per unit of one good and on the other the quantity demanded per period of another.

Cross price elasticity of demand continued

- Figure 2.13b illustrates the case of complements in which cross price elasticity of demand is negative. If the price of coffee increases from P1 to P2 then we expect that the quantity of sugar demanded per period will decrease from Q1 to Q2 as some will quit or decrease coffee consumption leading to less sugar demanded per period. Again, this is not a demand curve as on the one axis we have the price per unit of one good and on the other the quantity demanded per period of another.
- If instead of a positively or negatively sloped line we had a vertical line it would illustrate the case of two totally unrelated products where XPE is zero. If the price of cheesecake rises we expect the demand for iPhones to remain unaffected.

Figure 2.13 Substitutes (CPE >0) and complements (CPE <0)

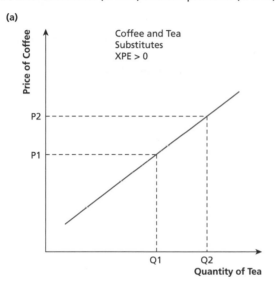

(a)

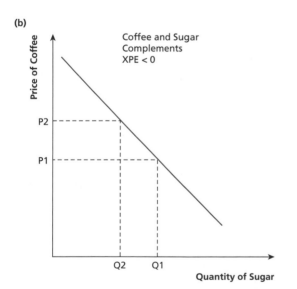

(b)

Alternatively cross price elasticity can be illustrated through the set of diagrams below:

- In Fig.2.14 the price of coffee is shown on the left to rise from P1 to P2 per unit, leading consumers to switch to tea, a substitute. Demand for tea is shown to shift to the right from D to D'.

Figure 2.14 Case of substitutes

Cross price elasticity of demand continued

Figure 2.15 Case of complements

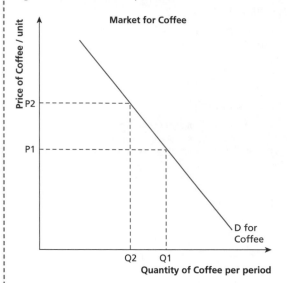

Market for Coffee

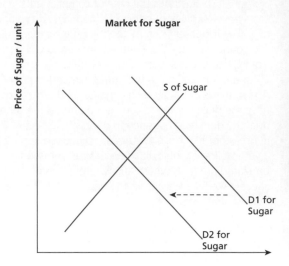

Market for Sugar

Coffee and Tea
Complements
XPE < 0

- In Fig. 2.15 the price of coffee is shown on the left to rise from P1 to P2 per unit, leading consumers to cut down on sugar, a complement. Demand for sugar is shown to shift to the left from D1 to D2.

Uses of cross price elasticity of demand

- Cross price elasticity of demand is used by policymakers to delineate markets. It helps to know the size of cross price elasticities to decide whether muffins and eggs should be considered belonging in the same market as Kellogg's cereal.
- Firms can use cross price elasticity to guide their pricing policy changes.

Price elasticity of supply

Definition: The responsiveness of quantity supplied when the price of the good changes.

Symbol: PES

Measure: The percentage change in quantity supplied divided by the percentage change in price:

PES = $\%\Delta Q_S/\%\Delta P$, thus PES = $(\Delta Q_S/Q_1)/(\Delta P/P_1)$
= $(\Delta Q_S/\Delta P)*(P_1/Q_1)$

The sign of PES is positive since supply curves typically have a positive slope (firms offer more per period at a higher price).

Ranges of price elasticity of supply

- Supply is **price elastic** (for small changes around the initial price) if the percentage change in quantity supplied is larger than the percentage change in price (PES >1) (Fig. 2.16). Alternatively we can say that if a change in price leads to a *proportionately* greater change in quantity supplied then supply for the product is price elastic.

Figure 2.16 Price-elastic supply curve

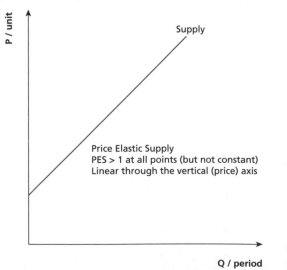

Price Elastic Supply
PES > 1 at all points (but not constant)
Linear through the vertical (price) axis

Price elasticity of supply continued

All linear supply functions that cut the P axis are price elastic:

- Supply is **price inelastic** (for small changes around the initial price) if the percentage change in quantity supplied is smaller than the percentage change in price ($0 <$ PES < 1) (Fig. 2.17). Alternatively we can say that if a change in price leads to a *proportionately* smaller change in quantity supplied then supply for the product is price inelastic.

Figure 2.17 Price-inelastic supply curve

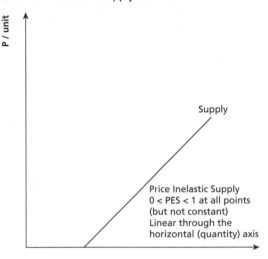

All linear supply functions that cut the Q axis are price inelastic:

- Supply is **unit elastic** if the percentage change in quantity supplied is equal to the percentage change in price (PES = 1) (Fig. 2.18).

Figure 2.18 Unitary elastic supply curve

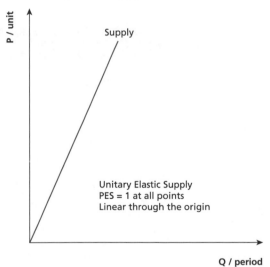

All linear supply functions that go through the origin are unitary elastic:

- Supply is **perfectly elastic** if a small change in price leads to an infinitely large change in quantity supplied (PES $\rightarrow \infty$) (Fig. 2.19). This means that the firm is willing to offer as much as the market demands at the current price. A supply curve of infinite price elasticity is a line parallel to the quantity axis.

Figure 2.19 Infinitely (perfectly) elastic supply curve

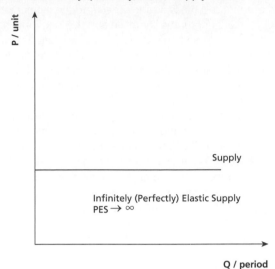

- Supply is **perfectly inelastic** if a small change in price leads to no change in the quantity supplied (PES = 0) (Fig. 2.20). Price changes have no effect on the amount offered per period. A supply curve of zero price elasticity is a vertical line parallel to the price axis.

Figure 2.20 Perfectly price-inelastic supply curve

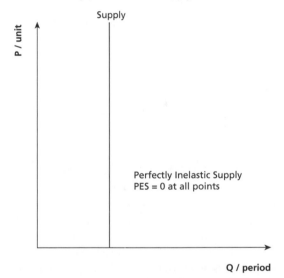

Tips

Remember that (price) elasticity (of supply) and slope are *not* the same thing. What matters is whether the supply curve cuts the vertical axis, the origin or the horizontal axis. If asked to draw the (short-run) supply curve for a farm product (e.g. wheat or coffee), draw it as a vertical line (PES = 0) as production of such products is characterized by long time lags. If asked to describe market conditions for a hotel or say, a tennis court, draw the supply curve vertical as there is limited, if any, ability to change 'quantity' offered (seats, rooms, etc.) per period following a change in demand conditions.

Determinants of price elasticity of supply

- **The time period**
  In economics, time is distinguished into the momentary (or market period), the short run and the long run. The distinction is based on the extent to which adjustments can be made. In the momentary (or market) period no adjustments are possible. In the short run some, but not all, adjustments are possible. In the long run all adjustments are possible.

  Concerning more the theory of production the above definitions become more specific. The momentary (or market) period is when all factors of production are considered fixed, the firm is operating in the short run when some, but not all, factors of production are considered fixed while in the long run all factors of production are considered variable (no fixed factors exist). It follows that in the momentary run, supply is perfectly inelastic (vertical). If demand for the product increases quantity supplied remains unchanged. The increased demand will be expressed only as a higher price. Supply is not at all responsive. In the short run, the increased demand will be partially expressed as an increase in quantity supplied and partially as an increase in price while in the long run, when all factors are variable (and thus the firm can even increase its scale of operations (its size), output could expand even more. Thus in the long run, supply is typically expected to be more price elastic than in the short run.

- **Extent of excess capacity.** The further below full capacity a firm is operating the greater the price elasticity of supply is expected to be.
- Whether the firm employs mostly **skilled or unskilled labour.** Expanding output in a production process that predominantly relies on highly skilled labour may be more difficult than if mostly unskilled workers were required.
- Whether **long or short time lags** characterize the production process. The longer the time lags involved, the longer it takes for supply to adjust to new demand conditions. Agricultural products are characterized by long time lags so supply is often considered perfectly inelastic in the short run.
- **The speed by which costs rise** as output expands. Firms will be encouraged to expand output by more per period the lower the additional (marginal) cost of doing so.

Importance of price elasticity of supply

- Price elasticity of supply determines the extent to which an increase in demand will affect the price and/or quantity of the good in a market. The more price-inelastic supply is, the greater the increase in price given an increase in demand; the more elastic supply is, the greater the impact of an increase in demand on quantity.

Price controls

Price controls refer to cases where for some reason the government considers the market-determined (equilibrium) price unsatisfactory and as a result intervenes and sets the price either below or above it.

Maximum price (setting a 'price ceiling')

- An authority, usually the government, sets a maximum price (also referred to as a price ceiling) if it considers the market-determined price as 'too high'. It thus aims to protect the buyers of the product. As such it is set on 'sensitive' products that mostly lower income households buy. A maximum price is a price set below the market price as it makes no sense to set it above.
- In Fig. 2.21 at the price Pmax firms will be willing to offer Q1 units per period whereas consumers will be willing and able to purchase Q2 units per period. A shortage thus results equal geometrically to Q1Q2 units per period (or HF).
- Since a shortage exists some consumers will end up not enjoying the good even though they are both willing and able to pay the price. This means that the price mechanism fails to perform its rationing function, i.e. fails to allocate the good to whoever is willing and able to pay for it. Therefore an alternative rationing mechanism is required.

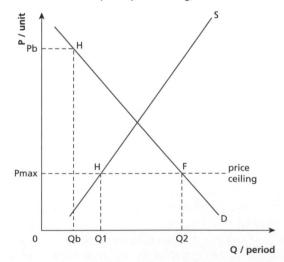

Figure 2.21 Maximum price (price ceiling)

Maximum price (setting a 'price ceiling') continued

- Allocation on a 'first come, first served' basis. This is likely to lead to queues (lines of people) developing (as people will rush to buy before supplies are exhausted) or firms adopting waiting lists.
- Sellers' preferences may decide who gets the good. The product may thus be allocated on the basis of who the customer is. Is he a regular? Is he attractive? Is she 'important'? The market is no longer impersonal (a major advantage) but becomes 'personal', so discrimination may result.
- The product could be allocated on a random basis (for example, by ballot).
- Coupons could be used to ration the good. This alternative has been used in times of war.
- A major problem with maximum prices is the likely emergence of black (parallel) markets where customers, unable to buy enough in legal markets, may well be prepared to pay a much higher price. In Fig. 2.21 there are consumers willing to pay Pb to acquire unit Qb. The willingness to pay, measured by the vertical distance from the horizontal axis to the demand curve, is greater than the maximum price, for all available units up to unit Q1.
- In the long run additional costs may emerge. The quality of certain products may worsen as producers may be tempted to use cheaper inputs. Also, if other non-price-controlled products can be produced using the same inputs then supply may shrink further, making shortages more severe.

Policies to reduce the resulting shortages

- To minimize these problems governments may attempt to reduce the shortages by encouraging supply (i.e. attempting to shift supply to the right), for example by drawing on stocks, by direct government production or by granting *subsidies* or tax relief to firms. Alternatively, they may attempt to reduce demand by encouraging the production of more and cheaper substitutes.

Tips

Remember, that even though seemingly counterintuitive, a maximum price must be drawn below the equilibrium level. To avoid confusion as to whether a maximum price should be drawn above or below the market-determined price think of the alternative term 'price ceiling': the government builds a 'ceiling' to prevent the price from rising towards the equilibrium level. Also, the shortage created is *not* an area but the distance between the quantity demanded and the quantity supplied at the set price. Linear demand and supply curves are preferable to use. Lastly, 'rent controls' are analysed in the same way with rent per unit on the vertical, apartment units per period on the horizontal, the short-run supply of apartment units drawn perfectly inelastic and the long-run supply of apartments more price elastic.

Minimum price (setting a 'price floor')

- An authority, usually the government, sets a minimum price (referred to also as a price floor) (Fig. 2.22) if it considers the market-determined price as 'too low'. A minimum price is set above the market-determined price and it aims at protecting producers (most often farmers). In order for a price floor to be effective it must be set above the equilibrium price.
- Setting a minimum price is also known as **price support**.
- In Fig. 2.22 at the price Pmin firms are willing to offer Q2 units per period whereas buyers are willing and able to buy only Q1 units per period. Assuming competitive markets, a surplus results equal to Q1Q2 units per period (or HF).
- The government is forced to buy this surplus. If it doesn't then the market price will fall below the equilibrium price as sellers will want to rid themselves of the extra units not bought at Pmin! This surplus must be bought at the promised price Pmin.

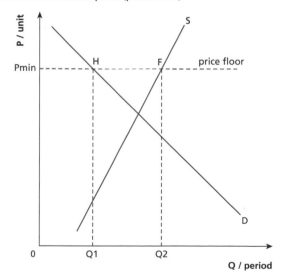

Figure 2.22 Minimum price (price floor)

Minimum price (setting a 'price floor') continued

- The government thus spends area (Q1Q2HF) which is the price it pays Pmin times the quantity it must buy, Q1Q2.
- Consumers (buyers) are worse off as they enjoy less of the product at a higher per unit price. Producers are better off as their revenues are higher. Government expenditures rise (or government spending in other areas has to decrease). If spending rises then taxpayers eventually bear the burden of this policy, as they pay for it in the form of increased taxes. An incentive to overproduce is created, resulting in resource misallocation. Too much land, for example, will be allocated in the production of this farm product.

Tips

The resulting surplus is not an area but a distance (a line segment) at the set price. Draw the supply curve rather steep so that the resulting surplus is not 'unrealistically' large. Preferably use linear demand and supply curves. Remember, that even though seemingly counterintuitive, a minimum price must be drawn above the equilibrium level: the government builds a 'floor' so that the price does not drop below the desired level. The same analytical framework can be employed to describe the effects of minimum wage legislation; the vertical measure in this case is the money wage rate (W) per worker; the horizontal depicts the number of workers (L) and the surplus created represents unemployment.

Indirect taxation and subsidies

Actions by government

Governments also affect resource allocation by imposing indirect taxes and by granting subsidies.

- **Indirect** (or excise) **taxes** can either be imposed on a per unit basis (known as 'specific' taxes; for example, €0.80 per pack of cigarettes) or as a percentage of the price (known as 'ad valorem' tax; for example a 19% value added tax). Indirect taxes are imposed to discourage consumption of demerit goods and more generally on goods that create negative externalities. They are also imposed to raise revenues for the government. Note that tariffs are taxes imposed on imported goods and services to discourage their consumption. Diagrammatically, since an indirect tax increases production costs it decreases supply, shifting the supply curve to the left. The vertical distance between the two supply curves is the per unit tax (see Fig. 2.23, below).

- **Subsidies** are payments by the government to firms, typically on a per unit of output basis, which aim at lowering production costs and thus the market price, while raising output and consumption as well as firm revenues. Subsidies are granted to support certain groups of producers (farmers) or to encourage the production and the consumption of certain goods that create positive externalities (malaria vaccines). They are also a form of protectionism as they confer to domestic producers of a product a competitive edge that leads to fewer imports or even to exports. Diagrammatically, since a subsidy decreases production costs it increases supply, shifting the supply curve to the right. The vertical distance between the two supply curves is the per unit subsidy (see Fig. 2.25, page 28).

Indirect taxation

HL

- In Fig. 2.23 a market is illustrated with a demand curve D and a supply curve S. Demand and supply conditions determine an initial equilibrium at point E with market price equal to Po per unit and an equilibrium quantity of Qo units per period.
- The unit tax may be considered as an additional cost of production. It's *as if* production costs rose by the amount of the tax so the supply curve shifts vertically upward by the amount of the tax AB to Stax. The vertical distance AB in Fig. 2.23 is thus equal to the per unit tax. (Note that in competitive markets the supply curve *is* the marginal cost curve. So an indirect tax effectively increases the marginal cost of producing each unit, shifting the MC curve up at each level of output.)

Figure 2.23 Effects of a specific indirect tax

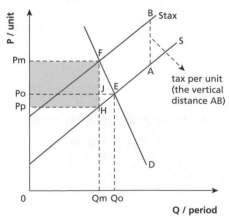

Indirect taxation continued

HL

Effects of an indirect tax

- In Fig. 2.23 the market price rises from Po to Pm per unit.
- The equilibrium quantity decreases from Qo to Qm per period. Output and consumption of the good thus shrink.
- Producers earn only Pp (= HQm) per unit as they have to pay the tax. Their new average revenue is thus less than the original, pre-tax price and average revenue Po.

- The government collects tax revenues equal to the shaded area (PpHFPm). This area is found by multiplying the tax per unit (FH) by the number of units sold (PpH) (which is equal to Qm).
- Resources are misallocated (unless the good is a demerit good or a good which creates negative externalities) as less than the socially optimal amount of the good is now produced and consumed.
- Welfare loss is equal to area FHE.

Tax incidence or tax burden

HL

- Tax incidence refers to who pays what proportion of a tax.
- Inspecting Fig. 2.23 reveals that the market price did not increase by the full amount of the indirect tax imposed. The size of the tax is FH (the vertical distance between the pre-tax and the post-tax supply curves) while market price increased only by FJ.
- It follows that the incidence of this tax is on both consumers and producers. Consumers and producers share the tax. Tax incidence on consumers is FJ (= PoPm) whereas tax incidence on producers is JH (=PoPp).
- Tax incidence depends on the price elasticity of demand *and* the price elasticity of supply. The following holds:

$$\frac{\text{\% of tax incidence on consumers}}{\text{\% of tax incidence on producers}} = \text{PES/PED}$$

Bearing in mind that the two percentages on the left must add up to 100%, the interpretation of the above is straightforward.

- Given price elasticity of supply, then the more price-elastic demand is, the greater the tax incidence on producers. This is sensible as demand will be more price-elastic the greater the number and closeness of available substitutes to consumers. Consumers will have alternatives to resort to following a tax on some good.
- In the extreme case where there are no substitutes available and demand is perfectly price-inelastic (PED = 0) and vertical then tax incidence on producers must be 0% (the denominator on the left-hand side of the equation) so it is 100% on consumers. Consumers are burdened by the full amount of the tax. The same holds if supply is perfectly elastic (PES tends to ∞) as the fraction on the left

will have to tend to infinity so the denominator must tend to zero. It follows that the incidence on producers will be 0% and so it will be 100% for consumers. Note that if PES = PED then consumers and producers share equally (50% each) a tax.

In summary:

- Equilibrium quantity will decrease less, the less elastic are demand and supply. It follows that tax revenue for the government will be greater.
- Market price will rise more and hence the consumers' share of the tax will be larger, the less elastic is demand and the more elastic is supply.
- Market price will rise less and hence the producers' share will be larger, the more elastic is demand and the less elastic is supply.

Remember:

- It is argued that a tax is typically fully paid by the consumers. How can that be the case if the law of demand has almost universal applicability? The answer is that such cases are a result of firms very often being able to supply increased quantities per period at the same price because of constant returns to scale: their average and marginal costs do not change as they expand output.
- Do consumer expenditures increase or decrease following an indirect tax? The answer is that it depends on the price elasticity of demand. Focusing on Fig. 2.23 it should be clear that the original and the final equilibrium points E and F are on the demand curve. Thus, whether area 0QmFPm is bigger or smaller than area 0QoEPo depends on PED.

Analysis of a percentage tax

- What if the tax is a percentage tax? Such a tax is analysed in the same way as a per unit tax except that the shift of supply is not parallel but the 'wedge' (= vertical distance) widens at higher prices. The effects are identical to those of a specific tax.

Figure 2.24 Effects of a percentage indirect tax (VAT)

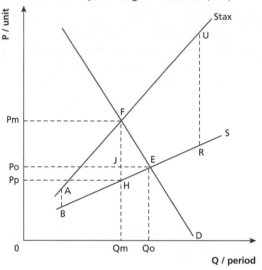

- In Fig. 2.24 a percentage tax is illustrated. Initially market demand and market supply are at D and S respectively with Po the initial market price and Qo the initial quantity bought and sold per period. Let a percentage tax (e.g. a 19% VAT) be imposed.
- The dollar (or yuan) amount of the tax at each possible price is no longer constant. This is why the vertical distance UR is greater that the vertical distance AB. The new supply curve Stax is no longer parallel to the original supply curve S. The 'wedge' at each output level, which is the amount of the tax, becomes bigger and bigger.

Tips

To draw a specific indirect tax diagram always use a ruler and start off by drawing two parallel supply curves. Label them properly and then draw the demand curve. From the intersection of the 'new' supply (Stax) and the demand curve (point F in Figs 2.23 and 2.24) drop a line to find the new equilibrium quantity (Qm). Realizing that the new price Pm is equal to line FQm you must subtract the tax (the vertical distance) to find the new net of tax price (average revenue) the producer earns per unit of output (HQm = 0Pp).

Subsidies

- A subsidy is defined as a per unit payment to firms by the government aiming at lowering their costs and thus the market price and increasing production, consumption and firm revenues. Its analysis is symmetrical to that of an indirect tax as now the government is paying (and not getting paid) a per unit amount of money to firms. Production costs are lower by the amount of the subsidy so supply shifts vertically downward by that amount (the marginal cost of producing each unit of output is now lower).
- In Fig. 2.25 the initial demand and supply conditions represented by curves D and S led to an equilibrium price of Po per unit and an equilibrium quantity Qo per period.
- The new supply following the granting of the subsidy is at Ssubsidy. The vertical distance AB is the per unit subsidy and represents the decrease in costs each firm now enjoys. The new equilibrium is at point F where market price is lower at Pm and equilibrium quantity bigger at Qm.
- Now you need to be extra careful in the next step. The new market price is Pm which is equal to line FQm. The producer though earns from each unit not just what the consumer pays but also the subsidy granted by the state. The producer thus earns QmH where FH is the subsidy per unit.
- The government spends in total area (FHPpPm) which is the product of the per unit subsidy FH times the quantity produced and consumed 0Qm (= FPm).

Figure 2.25 Effects of a per unit subsidy

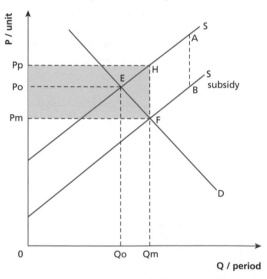

- Both the producer and the consumer of a product benefit from a subsidy. How the subsidy is split between the two parties again depends on the price elasticity of demand and the price elasticity of supply. The same relationship holds as in the case of an indirect tax (see page 27), only now the ratio on the left is the ratio of the percentage benefit from the subsidy consumers enjoy over the percentage benefit from the subsidy producers enjoy.

Subsidies continued

- Thus, for example, given PES, the producers benefit more, the more price-elastic demand for the good is.
- Subsidies are often granted to farmers to increase their income as well as to protect them from imports (imported farm products automatically become relatively more expensive). The lower price of domestic farm products may not only block imports but may lead to the creation of an artificial comparative advantage and thus penetrate foreign markets.
- Subsidies may also be granted to encourage production and consumption of goods with positive consumption or production externalities and of course in the case of merit goods and services such as health and education.

Tip

To draw a subsidy diagram always use a ruler and start off by drawing two parallel supply curves. Label them properly and then draw the demand curve. From the intersection of the 'new' supply and the demand curve (point F above) go vertically up to the initial supply curve (i.e. draw line HF) to find the new average revenue for the producers (0Pp = HQm). Failure to do so leads to most errors in this diagram.

Agriculture and agricultural policy

Why do governments intervene?

Governments often intervene in agricultural markets. This is because:

- Over the long run there are factors that lead to the decline in the relative price of such products and thus of the share of national income enjoyed by the farmer.
- In the short run (from year to year) prices of such products fluctuate a lot and thus farmers face high uncertainty over the level of their expected income (prices and incomes exhibit short-run volatility). Figure 2.26 illustrates these points.
- Over a period of n years prices from period to period fluctuate but over the long run the trend is typically downward as the trend line FH shows.

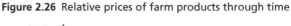

Figure 2.26 Relative prices of farm products through time

There is a long-run downward trend in relative prices because:

- Supply of agricultural products has dramatically increased due to the mechanization of production, the use of fertilizers, the advances in biotechnology, disease control, etc. which have raised land productivity. However, demand for such products has not kept pace because of its low income elasticity. As per capita income levels increase demand for food and agricultural products may increase but by proportionately much less. Coffee prices are an example. Over a period of many years world supply of coffee has increased from say S to Sn but demand though has increased only from D to Dn leading to a lower world price for coffee, Pn, as illustrated in Fig. 2.27.

But

- Lately, there has been a significant upward trend in world food prices. On the supply side, global warming is blamed for shrinking crop yields and record droughts, adversely affecting many food producers such as Australia. On the other hand, world demand for grains has been rising fast because of the growing number of people in

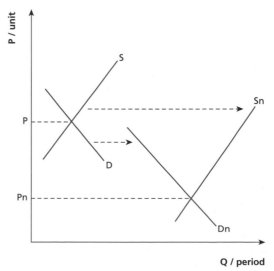

Figure 2.27 The long-run downward trend of relative farm product prices

Why do governments intervene? continued

emerging countries, such as China, who have reached levels of income that permit them to consume more meat. To produce more meat, more grains are needed to feed cattle. At these still relatively low levels of income, demand for food products may be rather income elastic for some time to come. Demand is also rising because more grain (mostly corn) is being diverted away from human consumption into the production of biofuels. Whether this trend can be considered short run or long run remains to be seen.

There is a short-run downward trend because:

- Short-run supply for agricultural products is typically perfectly inelastic (vertical) due to the associated long production time lags. Supply is also subject to shocks (shifts left or right to S1 or S2) typically as a result of the effect of weather and other random factors.
- On the other hand, demand for agricultural goods is relatively price inelastic since spending on such products is a small proportion of consumer spending (at least in high-income economies) and also since, on the whole, these goods have few substitutes.
- The shifts of supply thus lead to the sharp price fluctuations shown in Fig. 2.28.

- Note that these two characteristics also affect export revenues of developing countries since many predominantly export primary commodities (farm and non-farm products): their export revenues fluctuate from year to year and in the long run their terms of trade worsen.

Figure 2.28 The short-run fluctuations of farm product prices

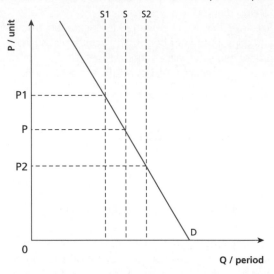

Government policies

- Governments often intervene in agricultural markets aiming at protecting producers against these characteristics. There are various forms of government intervention. One of them is granting subsidies or setting minimum prices (examined earlier). **Buffer stocks** are employed in an attempt to stabilize the price.
- Buffer stocks are also a subset of so-called **commodity agreements** that countries producing primary products have employed in order to stabilize their export earnings. **Commodities** are primary products (agricultural or non-agricultural) used as inputs in manufacturing and traded in world markets. Coffee, cocoa, cotton, jute, tin and copper are examples of primary products. Commodity agreements also include the operation of export quotas which are agreements which producing countries try to enforce to limit the amount of, say, coffee or copper that reaches world markets.

The operation of a buffer stock

- The operation of a buffer stock is illustrated in Fig. 2.29. It is assumed that the goal is to stabilize, say, coffee prices at P*.
- If output is at Q* there is no need for any action as market demand and supply conditions are such that the target price will be achieved. If output is at Q1 then the buffer stock authorities need to take action as otherwise the price will drop to P1 as a result of the excess supply FH at P*. Authorities will have to buy and stock the

Q*Q1 (= FH) units of coffee at P* (buffer stocks can thus be used only with food products that can be stored). Revenues of producers are given by area (0Q1HP*).
- If next period output is at Q2 units then price would rise above P*, as excess demand equal to JF units results at price P*. Authorities will sell from stocks Q2Q* units (= JF) of coffee at P*, maintaining the price at P*. Revenues of producers are area (0Q2JP*).

Figure 2.29 The operation of a buffer stock

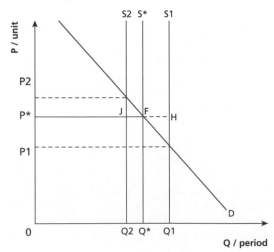

Government policies continued

Problems and effects

- The price may stabilize but incomes do not: they vary directly with the level of output.
- An incentive to overproduce results as the government in essence guarantees that it will buy whatever amount is produced and not bought by consumers.
- It is costly since storage costs and financing costs exist which could be recouped if good and bad harvests alternate and the price has been set at a true long-run average.
- Commodity agreements usually collapse (historically they all have collapsed) because of financing problems that result.

Tip

First draw just a demand curve and choose the target price. Next draw the supply curve for which no intervention by the buffer stock manager is needed (draw the supply curves vertical, a sensible choice especially if your example is an agricultural commodity such as coffee). Lastly draw two more supply curves, one to the right of the initial supply curve and one to the left of it.

Theory of production

Short-run analysis

- The short run is defined as that period during which at least one factor of production is considered fixed.
- If we assume two factors of production, capital (K) and labour (L), it is typically capital (K) that is assumed constant in the short run.
- Total product (output) can change by varying the level of labour *given* the level of capital.
- In the short run the behaviour of output is determined by the **law of diminishing marginal returns**.
- The behaviour and shape of short-run costs is a direct consequence of the behaviour of output and of the law of diminishing marginal returns.

A few points to remember

- It is a short-run law. It assumes the existence of at least one fixed factor of production (usually capital).
- Technology is assumed constant.
- The variable factor, usually labour, is assumed homogeneous.
- Thus, any differences in returns (output) as more labour is employed are not because of differences in workers' abilities but a result of the continuously changing capital to labour ratio. That's why the law is also known as the law of variable proportions.
- If capital and labour were perfectly substitutable factors in the production process then the law would not hold.
- The marginal product (of labour) is defined as the change in output because of a change in labour so it is the slope of the total product curve.

The law of diminishing marginal returns

- As more and more units of a variable factor (labour) are added to a fixed factor (capital), there is a point beyond which **total product** will continue to rise, but at a diminishing rate, or equivalently, that **marginal product** will start to decline.
- Visualize a pizzeria equipped with ovens, tables, etc. With zero workers, output per period will be zero. If one worker is employed then some level of output will be produced per period, say x units. This worker will have to do everything: taking orders, preparing the pizzas, serving the food and getting paid from all tables.
- If now two workers are employed then it should be realized that if the second worker simply 'copies' the first

worker then 2x units will be produced. But since there is so much capital compared to labour there is a lot of room for **specialization** to take place. The two workers may agree that one will be in charge of the whole kitchen, the other of all the serving. Output will as a result more than double.

- Output will thus be initially increasing at an *increasing rate* up until some unit of labour, say L1 in Fig. 2.30a. You should notice that the tangent at point b is steeper than at point a. Since marginal product is the slope of total product and this slope is increasing, it follows that the MP curve in Fig. 2.30b is rising up until L1.

The law of diminishing marginal returns continued

Figure 2.30 Production in the short run: (a) TP and (b) MP curves

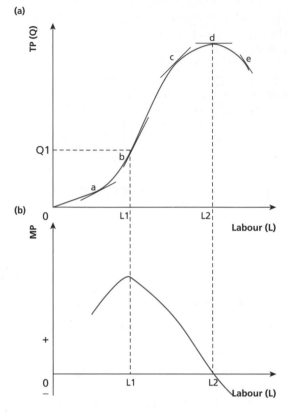

- **Average product of labour** is defined as the total product (i.e. output) over the number of workers employed (AP = Q/L).
- It is thus output per worker employed, also referred to as the **productivity of labour**.
- Focusing on Fig. 2.31, AP at any point on the TP curve is equal to the slope of a straight line drawn from the origin to that point on the TP curve. For example, AP at L' is equal to output (L'H) divided by the number of workers employed (0L'). This ratio is the slope of the straight line 0H.
- It follows that to determine the behaviour of average product one needs to examine the behaviour of the slope of the straight line from the origin to successive points on the total product curve.
- The slope of this line is the steepest at L' so AP has a maximum at that level of workers.
- In Fig. 2.31b the average product of labour increases up to L' and then decreases.

Figure 2.31 Production in the short run: (a) TP and (b) AP curves

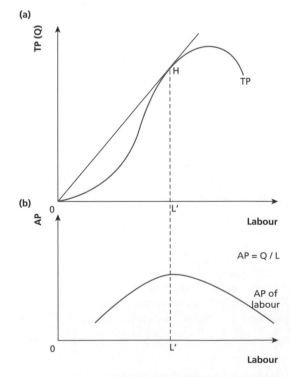

- At this point though, adding workers will *still* help *increase* total product (the TP curve in Fig. 2.30a is *still* going up) *but now it will rise at a slower rate* (it becomes flatter and flatter). Each extra worker contributes to the production of pizzas *but not as much as the previous one*. The benefits of more and more specialization are slowly exhausted. The *total product curve still rises but at a decreasing rate. Marginal product is thus positive but decreasing from L1 to L2.*
- You should note that the slope at point c is flatter than at point b and that at worker L2 the slope of TP is zero (point d) so marginal product is zero in Fig. 2.30b.
- After worker L2, labour is too much for the amount of capital available (the size and equipment of the pizzeria) so total product will start declining. Workers are so many that they get in each other's way. The contribution of each extra worker (her marginal product) is *negative* after L2 workers are employed.
- The law holds between L1 units of labour and L2 units of labour: After worker L1 total product continues to rise but at a decreasing rate, in other words marginal product is decreasing. No firm will ever employ more than L2 workers as there is too much labour compared to capital nor will it ever employ fewer than L1 workers as there would be too much capital compared to labour. Distance L1L2 is known as the economic region of production.

How to draw average and marginal product curves in one diagram

- Both the MP and the AP curves are shaped like an inverse U. But care must be taken when one draws both curves in one diagram as the relationship between marginal and average product is very specific. In general the following holds:

  If MP > AP then AP will rise.

  If MP < AP then AP will drop.

  If MP = AP then AP will be at a maximum.

- The basic idea behind these rules that govern the behaviour of marginal and average product is simple and it holds for any marginal and average magnitude.

- Think of a student taking a series of tests in her economics course. If in her sixth test (her marginal test) she earns a higher grade than her average grade to that point (in other words, if her M > A) then her average will rise. If she earns a lower grade than her average grade to that point (in other words, if her M < A) then her average grade will fall. And if she earns in her sixth test exactly the same grade as her average to that point, then her average will not change.

- Returning to our AP and MP curves, it must be that when the average product is rising then MP must exceed AP while when the average product is falling then MP must be less than AP. At the maximum of the AP curve marginal and average must be equal.

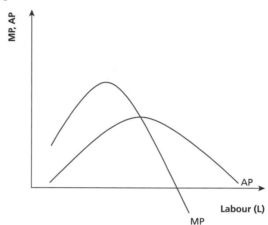

Figure 2.32 Marginal and average product curves in one diagram

Cost theory

Short-run costs

As mentioned earlier, the short run is a period of time during which at least one factor of production is fixed. As a result firms in the short run face both **fixed** and **variable costs**.

- **Fixed costs** are costs that do not vary when the level of production varies. They exist (and they have to be paid) even if output is zero. Examples typically include **rent**, interest on loans, insurance costs, fixed contract costs, etc.

- Figure 2.33a illustrates fixed costs as a line parallel to the quantity axis.

- Figure 2.33b illustrates average fixed costs. Since average fixed costs are defined as fixed costs divided by output it follows that the average fixed costs continuously decrease as output rises, but never become zero. Note that the areas beneath the AFC curve are all equal to the fixed cost the firm faces.

- **Variable costs** include costs that vary with the level of output, e.g. raw materials, components, labour. **Average variable costs** are thus defined as average costs over the level of output. The **average total cost** of producing some level of output is then the sum of average variable and average fixed costs of producing that level of output: ATC = AFC + AVC.

- **Marginal cost** is defined as the additional cost of producing an extra unit of output. It is thus the change in costs (total or variable) resulting from a change in the level of output: $MC = \Delta C/\Delta Q$. It is the slope of the total cost (or of the variable cost) curve at each level of output.

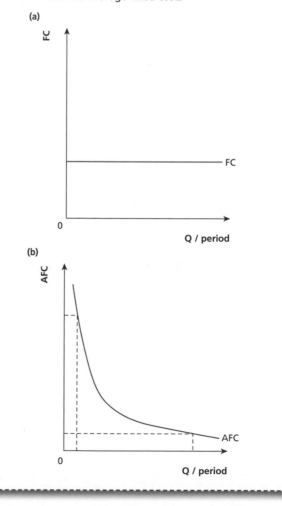

Figure 2.33 Fixed and average fixed costs

The shape of variable, marginal and average cost curves in the short run

- The shape of cost curves in the short run is a reflection of the law of diminishing marginal returns. Output (TP) in the short run initially rises at an increasing rate up until that unit of labour at which diminishing marginal returns set in.
- Thus, as more is produced, variable costs rise but initially they rise at a decreasing rate. Producing more and more output is 'easy' since with double the units of labour, the firm can produce more than double the output. If it wished to produce just double the output it would need less than double labour: variable costs rise but they do not double.
- Variable costs in Fig. 2.34.a will rise at a decreasing rate up until that unit of output Q1 at which diminishing marginal returns set in production. Beyond that level of output Q1 variable costs will rise at an increasing rate. Marginal costs will be decreasing in Fig. 2.34b until output level Q1.
- Since initially variable costs rise at a *decreasing rate* and after output Q1 they increase at an *increasing rate* it follows that MC (the slope of VC) initially will decrease and then at Q1 will start to increase leading to a 'Nike-swoosh'-like shape.
- MC falls when in production MP rises and MC rises when in production MP decreases (i.e. when diminishing marginal returns start in production).

Figure 2.34 Variable and marginal costs

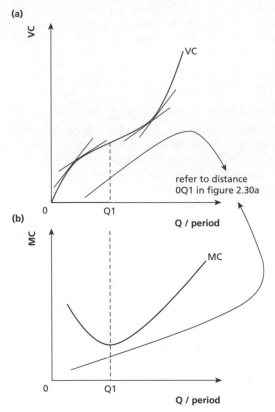

- refer to distance 0Q1 in figure 2.30a

Total, variable and fixed costs in one diagram

- Now that the shape of the variable cost curve has been explained it is possible to include in one diagram the total costs curve, the variable costs curve and the fixed costs curve.
- In Fig. 2.35 the total cost curve is shaped just like the variable cost curve except that it has been shifted up by the amount of the fixed costs.
- Thus, the vertical distance between the total cost curve and the variable cost curve is the same. Distances ab, fh, jk and uv are all equal to the fixed cost distance 0c.

Figure 2.35 Total, variable and fixed costs

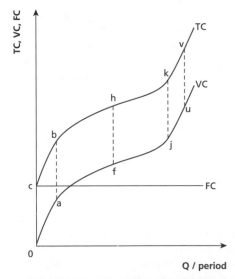

Average costs

- Average total cost is the sum of average variable cost and average fixed cost. Thus the average total cost curve lies above the average variable cost curve. Their vertical distance is equal to average fixed costs.
- Since average fixed costs continuously decrease as output increases (see Fig. 2.33b) it follows that this vertical distance (ab in Fig. 2.36) becomes smaller and smaller but the two U-shaped curves never touch.
- Both the average total and the average variable cost curves are U-shaped because of the law of diminishing marginal returns and the behaviour and shape of the average product curve (see Fig. 2.31b).
- The average variable cost curve is the mirror image of the average product curve.

Figure 2.36 The average total and the average variable cost curves

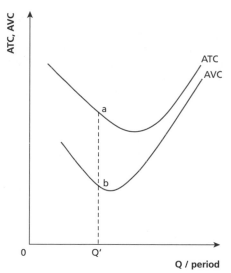

How to draw marginal and average cost curves in the same diagram

- The rules that have to be followed are exactly the same as those explained in Fig. 2.32.
- Average costs curves (ATC and AVC) are U-shaped and MC is like the 'Nike-swoosh'. It follows that if average costs are falling then marginal must be less than average while if average costs are rising then marginal must exceed average. Lastly, marginal cost on its way up must cut an average cost curve at its minimum point.

  If MC < AC then AC will drop.

  If MC > AC then AC will rise.

  If MC = AC then AP will be at a minimum.

- Figure 2.37a illustrates the general point in a simple setup with MC and an AC curve whereas Fig. 2.37b illustrates the same point using ATC and AVC curves. In both cases, note that the MC curve cuts the average cost curves at their respective minima.

Figure 2.37 Marginal and average cost in the same diagram

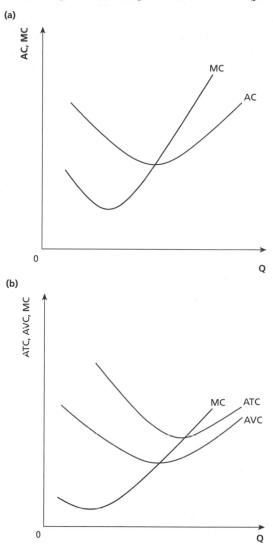

Tips

If you want to draw an ATC and an AVC curve on the same diagram, first draw the ATC curve. Note the minimum of your ATC curve. Then draw the AVC *below* it, making sure that its minimum *is to the left* of the ATC minimum and also that *they get closer and closer* (but do not touch) as you move to the right.

Production and costs in the long run

Remember, the long run is defined as that time period during which all adjustments are possible. It follows that in the long run a firm considers all factors of production variable. It can thus change its scale of production. It can grow or it can shrink in size.

In the long run there are three *possible* effects on output from an increase in the level of use of *all* factors.

- **Increasing returns to scale:** the percentage increase in output is greater than the percentage increase in all inputs. For example, doubling all factors of production more than doubles the level of output Q. Stated differently, an increase in all inputs by 1% will lead to a greater than 1% increase in output. As a result, average (unit) costs of production decrease. The firm enjoys **economies of scale**.
- **Constant returns to scale:** the percentage increase in output is equal to the percentage increase in all inputs. For example, doubling all factors of production doubles the level of output Q. Stated differently, an increase in all inputs by 1% will lead to a 1% increase in output. As a result, average (unit) costs of production remain constant.
- **Decreasing returns to scale:** the percentage increase in output is less than the percentage increase in all inputs. For example, doubling all factors of production less than doubles the level of output Q. Stated differently, an increase in all inputs by 1% leads to a smaller than 1% increase in output. As a result, average (unit) costs of production rise. The firm suffers from **diseconomies of scale**.
- Figure 2.38 illustrates economies and diseconomies of scale corresponding to increasing and decreasing returns to scale respectively. Constant returns to scale (and thus constant long-run average costs) are ignored to simplify the analysis.
- Initially, the long-run average cost curve (LAC) slopes downward. Average costs decrease as the size of a firm and output increases. The downward section of an LAC curve illustrates economies of scale (EOS).
- After some point, the long-run average cost curve (LAC) slopes upward. Average costs rise as the size of a firm and output increases. The upward-sloping section of an LAC curve illustrates diseconomies of scale (DOS).
- Note at each level of output (Q) the corresponding specific firm size (and thus a specific short-run average cost curve, SAC) with which the firm can achieve the lowest possible average costs.

Figure 2.38 The long-run average cost curve: economies and diseconomies of scale

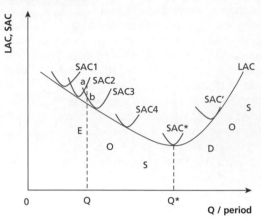

- For example, curve SAC2 is the short-run average total cost curve when a firm employs, say, K2 capital (imagine a firm with a size '2' factory). The SAC3 curve is the average total cost curve when a firm employs K3 capital which is greater than K2 (imagine a firm *having grown to a factory size '3' which is larger than the factory size '2'*). If this firm in Fig. 2.38 now would like to produce 'Q' units it *could* do so with either a 'size 2' factory or with a larger 'size 3' factory. But it pays to grow in size as it could produce these Q units of output at an average cost of Qb rather than Qa.
- It follows that the long-run average variable cost curve (LAC) describes the minimum average cost of producing each output level (Q) *when the firm is able to adjust all inputs optimally*, i.e. when the firm is able to adjust its scale of operation.

Tip

Draw the U-shaped LAC curve rather shallow, making sure that on its decreasing region the SAC curves are tangent to it *on the left* of their lowest points while on its rising section the SAC curves are tangent to it on the right of their minima. Also note that the size corresponding to short-run average cost curve SAC* is the optimal scale as it is with this scale (size) that the firm can achieve minimum long-run average costs.

Economies of scale

Economies of scale (EOS) are defined as cost savings due to increased scale of production. They can be distinguished into *internal* EOS and *external* EOS. Internal EOS are cost savings due to actions of the firm itself. External EOS are cost savings originating from developments *outside* the firm, for example because the industry in which it operates grows.

Sources of economies of scale

Internal economies of scale can result from technical, marketing, management, financial or risk-related reasons. More specifically:

Technical EOS arise because:

- A larger firm may be able to adopt technologies of production not available for smaller firms. Capital equipment is often indivisible (e.g. the assembly line).
- Larger firms offer more possibilities for specialization.
- As a result of the 'container principle' (or the 'law of dimensions'). Cost savings may arise because volumes rise faster than surfaces. For example, a storage tank that can store double the volume of something costs less than double to manufacture. This applies to blast furnaces, pipes, trucks and of course shipping transportation.

Marketing EOS arise because:

- On the input side, a larger firm buys inputs in bulk and thus may secure better prices from suppliers.
- On the output side, distribution costs are usually lower for larger firms.

Financial EOS arise because:

- A large firm often can borrow from banks at lower interest rates.

Management EOS arise because:

- Larger firms can employ specialists in each department (a large supermarket hires financial experts to manage its cash flow on a daily basis; a large department store hires specialist buyers, etc.)

Risk-related EOS arise because:

- A larger firm is often more diversified, selling not one but many products, in not one but many markets (or even in many countries). Risks, and the associated costs, are thus better spread and minimized.

External economies of scale

Sometimes, as an industry grows, unit costs of the firms in it may decrease. Typically this is a result of similar firms locating together in one area (also referred to as agglomeration economies). Why? Because:

- A specialized labour force may develop (technical schools, catering to their needs, may also be established in the area).
- Complementary firms may also be established.
- Better transportation and telecommunications networks may develop.
- Marketing of by-products may be possible.

Diseconomies of scale

These are defined as increases in average costs due to increased scale of production. They can originate within a firm (*internal* DOS) or outside the firm (*external* DOS).

Internal diseconomies of scale

After a point, size may become a problem. When firms grow beyond a certain size then unit costs may start increasing. Possible reasons include:

- Management problems of coordination, control and communication associated with huge size.

- Motivation may decrease.
- Interdependencies within a huge firm may lead to problems if there are hold-ups or bottlenecks in any particular part of the firm.

External diseconomies of scale

- After a point, congestion costs in an area may develop.
- As an industry grows, factor prices (for materials, for specialized labour, etc.) may also start increasing as a result of the higher factor demand.

Goals of firms

Maximizing profits

The working assumption in economics is that firms aim at maximizing economic profits. This is not though the only available behavioral assumption. Firms may have other goals.

- It may be that they aim at maximizing revenues or long-run profits or long-run revenue and market share.
- There are also 'satisficing' theories. The term was introduced by Herbert Simon ('satisfy and suffice'): because of informational limitations firms cannot

maximize profits or revenues but they only strive to achieve *at least some* predefined level (of profits or revenues).

- Also, *managerial theories of the firm* (Baumol, Williamson and others) suggest that managers may seek to maximize their own 'utility' which may include salary, security, power and/or prestige.

The meaning of economic profits (π)

- Economic profits are defined as the difference between total revenues and total economic costs of production.

  $\pi(q) = TR(q) - TC(q)$

- The key to understanding the term **economic profits** is to realize that *from an economist's point of view* the term **economic costs** refers to the value of *all* resources that are sacrificed during the production process. This is because in economics the driving force is the fundamental economic problem of scarcity. It implies that economic costs include not only the so-called **explicit** costs of a firm (the explicit payments it makes for the use of factors known also as 'out-of-pocket' costs) but also **implicit** costs. These refer to the value of firm-owned resources for which the firm is not forced to make any payment but, from the economist's point of view, represent sacrificed scarce resources.
- Implicit costs also include the minimum reward that the factor 'entrepreneurship' requires to remain in that line of business. This is known as **normal profit** and is an element of economic costs.
- The idea is that, to secure in a business activity the *scarce* factor 'entrepreneurship', some minimum reward is necessary *for the risk that is undertaken*. This minimum is equal to what could be earned by entrepreneurship in the next best alternative available. If this minimum reward does not materialize, then the firm will close down so that the financial capital tied up in it will be freed and moved into the next best alternative project that commands the same level of risk.

- Remember, for a firm to secure the scarce factor 'labour', wages have to be paid which, of course, are an element of cost. In the same way, to secure the scarce factor 'entrepreneurship', a minimum reward would also be required which, symmetrically, should also be included in costs.
- It follows that if total revenues are equal to economic costs *thus defined*, then economic profits are zero but the firm is making money. *It is making the minimum required to remain in this business*. We say that it is making **normal profits**. **Zero economic profits** thus imply normal profits so there is no reason for the entrepreneur to exit and move on to the next best business opportunity with the same risk.
- If total revenues exceed total economic costs thus defined then the firm is making more than the minimum it requires to remain in this business (i.e. more than normal profits). It is making **supernormal profits**.

Tips

Bear in mind that **accounting profits** are narrower in scope than economic profits as they refer to the difference between total revenues collected and **accounting costs**. The latter include only explicit costs. Also, the level of output at which total revenues equal total production costs is known as the **breakeven level** of output. The term is used both in the accounting sense and in the broader economic sense.

Role of economic profits in a market economy

- Profits are the reward for entrepreneurship. They differ from wages in that profits are not contracted, as wages are, but are a residual and may thus even be negative (losses).
- Supernormal profits attract resources into an industry whereas losses free up resources, permitting their use in other industries. *Relative price changes coupled with supernormal profits and losses drive resource allocation in a market economy.*
- Striving to achieve profits results in less waste and thus in greater (technical) efficiency.
- Supernormal profits provide the incentive and funding for firms to finance expansion (investment).

- Supernormal profits can be used to finance research and development programmes and may thus lead to product and process innovations (to dynamic efficiency).

Condition for profit maximization

- It can be shown that if a firm wishes to maximize profits it must choose an output level q at which **MR = MC and the MC curve is rising**.
- Many erroneously think that this means that profits are zero, forgetting that the term *marginal* refers to one more unit, the extra unit.
- To realize why profits are maximum when MR = MC one must consider the *alternatives*. The alternatives are two. Marginal revenues could be either greater or less than marginal cost.

The meaning of economic profits (π) continued

Case 1: MR > MC

- Assume that at the chosen level of output q, marginal revenue is greater than marginal cost (MR > MC). Reading this *carefully* means that the *extra* revenue collected from selling *one more* unit of output exceeds the *extra* cost of producing that extra unit.
- But, if that is the case, then, *whatever* the level of profits, the firm would be able to increase these by producing that extra unit. It follows that if MR > MC then profits *cannot* be at a maximum as they can be increased.
- Note that even if the firm was incurring losses at that chosen q, it would be able to decrease these losses by producing that extra unit, so the chosen q could not have been the right (the best, the optimum) choice.

Case 2: MR < MC

- If the firm had chosen an output rate q at which MR < MC, then, by producing one unit *less* it would not collect the associated revenues but it would not incur the greater associated cost. It follows, that whatever was the level of profit, it would *increase* profit by producing one less unit.

Thus, profits *cannot* be at a maximum if MR > MC (case 1) or if MC > MR (case 2).

- If MR > MC then the profit-maximizing firm should *increase* its output rate to achieve its goal whereas if MC > MR it should *decrease* its output rate to achieve its goal.

A firm should thus neither increase nor decrease its output rate if MR = MC.

Why should MC be rising?

- To understand why at the chosen level of output q at which marginal revenue is equal to marginal cost it must *also* be that the marginal cost curve is rising, consider the alternative (that MC was declining) and assume that the

firm decided to produce one more unit of output. Profits would further increase as the extra revenue would exceed the extra cost incurred. It follows that at the chosen output q not only must MR equal MC but also the MC curve must be rising.

Market structures

Effects of market structure

It turns out that resource allocation and efficiency considerations are greatly affected by market structure. The structure of a market (whether there are many, few or one firm) is important as it determines the conduct of firms (whether they have pricing power) and consequently their performance, i.e. whether efficiency is achieved in resource allocation. This model will be contrasted later with the theory of contestable markets in which structure is not relevant.

Types of market structure

Four market structures are traditionally distinguished:

- Perfect competition
- Monopoly
- Monopolistic competition
- Oligopoly.

Market structures are distinguished on the basis of the number of firms in the market (very many, few, one), the type of the product (**homogeneous** or **differentiated**) and whether entry barriers exist or not.

Perfect competition

Characteristics

- Very many small firms.
- Homogeneous product, meaning that the product is considered by consumers *identical* across sellers. Examples of such products are few and mostly found in the primary sector (farm products, metals).
- No entry barriers exist (i.e. perfect mobility of factors of production).
- Perfect information available to all market participants.

Is the perfectly competitive model realistic?

Very few markets in the real world will share these characteristics. Why?

- First of all, scale economies, especially in the manufacturing sector, are very common. Very often larger firms can produce at a lower unit cost than smaller firms can. Firms thus have an incentive to grow either internally (through investment in physical capital) or through mergers and acquisitions. This explains why large firms are typically found in most industries.
- Firms also have the incentive to differentiate their product (by improving quality, changing characteristics, etc.) in order to acquire some degree of monopoly power. Monopoly power is defined as the ability to raise price above marginal cost. The Lerner index of monopoly power is given by the ratio (P − MC)/P. A firm that manages to produce and sell even a slightly differentiated product will face a negatively sloped demand curve for its product and thus have the ability to increase price without losing all customers.

- Firms also try to create entry barriers so that they can maintain any supernormal profits in the long run. In addition, **exit barriers** in the form of 'sunk costs' also are common. Sunk costs are costs that a firm cannot recover upon exiting an industry.
- Information in the real world is not free. Uncertainty and risks surround all business and consumption decisions. Search costs exist and may be significant.
- Lastly, perfect mobility seldom characterizes factors of production. Labour, for example, often suffers from occupational and geographical immobility.

Why then is perfect competition still useful to study?

- Despite these limitations, perfect competition retains its usefulness. It is simple and it is capable of successfully predicting change. Most importantly, its efficiency properties are considered desirable and it thus serves as a model against which real-world markets can be compared and perhaps, if necessary, 'corrected'.

Short-run equilibrium in perfect competition

- Assume a perfectly competitive market illustrated in Fig. 2.39b. Market forces determine the market price at P. Each firm in a perfectly competitive market is a 'price taker' meaning that the market-determined price P is a given for each firm. Since there are so many other firms offering an identical product to perfectly informed consumers it cannot increase the price above the market-determined level as no one would purchase even a single unit from it.
- It also has no incentive to lower the price below the market-determined level as it is, by assumption, so small compared to the market that it can sell all it wants at the going market price. Picture a sandy beach with each grain of sand being a firm. Even if it doubles its size and becomes as big as two grains of sand it would make no difference. This implies that a perfectly competitive firm can sell more at the same price. So it is as if it is facing a perfectly elastic demand for its product at the going market price P.
- Since it can sell all it wants at P per unit it means that the extra revenue from selling an extra unit is P and that, on average, it earns P per unit. Price is thus equal to marginal revenue for a perfectly competitive firm and is, of course, equal to average revenues:

  P = MR = AR, in perfect competition

- This perfectly competitive firm (think of a farmer named Joey) has only to decide how much output to offer in the market per period given the prevailing market price P. Since we assume that Joey is a profit maximizer, we know the answer. He will choose that level of output for which:

  MR = MC and the MC curve is rising

- The MC curve in Fig. 2.39a intersects the MR curve at point H which is right above output q*. It follows that Joey will choose to sell q* units per period at P per unit.

Figure 2.39 Perfect competition: short-run analysis in (a) the typical firm (b) the market

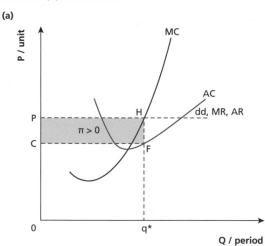

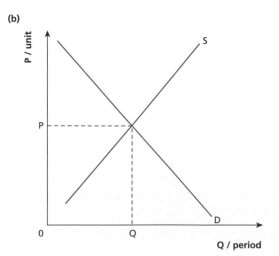

Short-run equilibrium in perfect competition continued

- The average cost of producing each of the q* units is given by the average cost curve. Going up from q* toward the AC curve we find point F and from there we turn left and find that it costs Joey C on average to produce each of the q units.
- Total revenues collected are equal to the number of units sold times the price per unit or q* times P. This is the area of rectangle (0q*HP).
- Total costs are equal to the number produced times how much it costs on average to produce each or (0q*) times (q*F). This is the area of rectangle (0q*FC).
- Economic profits are the difference between total revenues collected and total costs of production, so geometrically on Fig. 2.39a they are equal to the pink area (CFHP).
- Economic profits for Joey, the typical firm, are positive. This means that firms in this market are making more than the minimum they require to compensate for the resources employed and the risk taken (defined as normal profits). Joey is making supernormal profits.

Tips

A typical mistake students make is when they 'shade' the profit area. Make sure you correctly identify on your diagram the average cost associated with the chosen level of output. Also, line FC on Fig. 2.39a cannot be tangent to your U-shaped average curve in the short run as MC is shaped like the 'Nike swoosh'.

Short-run equilibrium in perfect competition: case of economic losses

- It is not necessary for the typical perfectly competitive firm to be making supernormal or normal profits in the short run. It could be making losses. Figure 2.40 illustrates this case.
- In Fig. 2.40b market demand is such that the equilibrium price is determined at P. The firm in Fig. 2.40a selects its optimal level of output at the intersection of MR and MC at q*. Average costs are equal to q*F while average revenue (price) is only q*H. This firm is making losses equal to area (HFCP).

Figure 2.40 Perfect competition: short-run analysis: case of losses in (a) the typical firm (b) the market

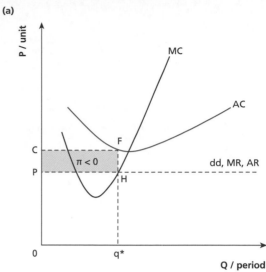

(a)

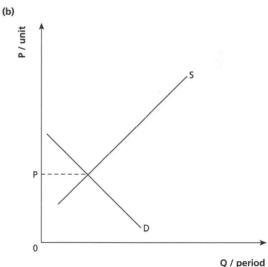

(b)

Long-run equilibrium in perfect competition

- Resources are attracted into an industry in which firms earn supernormal profits as this implies that these firms earn more than in the next best alternative use. On the other hand, economic losses will induce exit of firms from the industry as the resources they employ could earn more in their next best alternative. It follows that if economic profits in an industry are zero neither entry nor exit will be observed as firms in such an industry make just as much money as they would in their next best alternative. Why enter or exit such an industry?

- Assume, as illustrated in Fig. 2.41, a perfectly competitive industry in which the typical firm is making supernormal profits. As mentioned on page 38, this will induce entry of new firms into the industry. As new firms enter, market supply increases, shifting the market supply curve to the right and pushing the market price lower. This process (the entry of firms) will stop when there is no incentive for more firms to enter, i.e. when economic profits are driven to zero. Figure 2.41 illustrates exactly this situation. The market price in Fig. 2.41b has been driven to P. The typical firm in Fig. 2.41a produces q* units. At this level of output total revenues and total costs are equal to area (0q*FP).

Short-run equilibrium in perfect competition continued

Figure 2.41 Perfect competition: long-run equilibrium in (a) the typical firm (b) the market

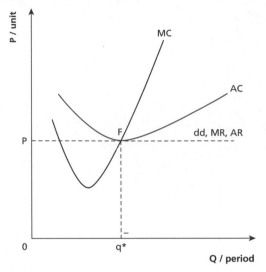

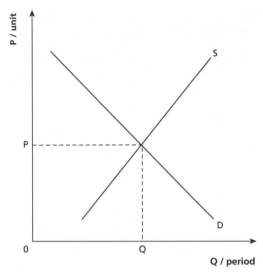

- Long-run equilibrium thus requires that at the chosen output rate q the typical firm is maximizing profits *and* that these economic profits are zero (normal) so no entry or exit is induced:

MR = MC (and MC is rising)

$\pi(q)$ = zero

- Note here the role of profits and losses in allocating and reallocating scarce resources in a market economy. Profits attract scarce resources as new firms enter the industry (assuming no entry barriers) while losses force firms to exit, freeing up scarce resources. Bankruptcy thus performs a most important role in a market economy as it makes scarce resources available again for use in other, more productive areas. Of course, whether freed-up resources may or may not be channelled into more productive uses also depends upon their mobility. In addition the affected parties (workers and owners of capital) may face significant adjustment costs.

- In the case of short-run losses, illustrated in Fig. 2.40, firms will exit, decreasing and shifting to the left the market supply and thus pushing up market price and thus average revenue. The process (the exit of firms) stops when average revenue becomes equal to average cost, in other words when the typical firm is making zero economic profits, i.e. as much as it would earn in the next best alternative (normal). There is no reason for more firms to exit. Figure 2.41 illustrates exactly this situation.

Tips

To illustrate long-run equilibrium in perfect competition, start by drawing a U-shaped average cost curve for the firm and then draw, *using always a ruler*, a horizontal tangent at its minimum. This line will be the demand (and MR and AR curves) this firm faces and thus determines the price. Make sure the MC curve is drawn in such a way that it cuts the AC curve it its minimum. At the intersection of the MR and the MC curves drop a line to determine the equilibrium output of the firm. When the right-hand market diagram is then drawn make sure the market demand and supply curves intersect at the price you determined on the left-hand diagram. You could of course start the other way around by first determining the market equilibrium price and extending it all the way to the left-hand diagram.

The shutdown rule

Long run:

- It should be clear that in the long run a loss-making firm will shut down and exit the market. In the long run all possible adjustments have been made and the firm has no fixed factors and thus faces no fixed (and thus unavoidable) costs.

Short run:

- In the short run though some factors of production are considered fixed. This implies that the firm faces fixed costs, costs that are unavoidable in that they have to be paid even if the firm produces zero units of output.

- Figure 2.42 illustrates a perfectly competitive firm operating in the short run. This shutdown diagram requires that both the ATC and the AVC curves are present. The market price is determined at P which this firm must take and determine the optimal, profit-maximizing level of output. Marginal revenue and marginal costs are equal exactly above output level q1.

- This firm is making losses. Average revenue (price) is equal to q1J while average (total) costs are equal to q1F so per unit losses are equal to distance JF. Multiplying this by PJ (equal to output 0q1) gives the loss area (JFCP), the red rectangle.

- Should this loss-making firm shut down? If it shuts down it will still face and have to pay its fixed costs (for example, monthly payments for an outstanding bank loan). If these unavoidable fixed costs are bigger than the losses faced by producing, then it should remain in business as it will be losing less.

- Note that the vertical distance at each output level between the average total and the average variable cost curves is equal to the average fixed costs. For example at output level q2 the corresponding average fixed costs are distance ab, the difference between average total costs q2a and average variable costs q2b.

- Geometrical comparison between fixed costs and the losses incurred at output q1 is facilitated if we calculate the fixed cost area using the average fixed costs at the chosen output level q1. Multiplying output C'H (= 0q1) by FH (the AFC at q1) is area (HFCC'), the firm's fixed costs, the thick black outline rectangle.

- It follows that in the short run this firm should remain in business. It will lose less money by producing than if it shuts down. By producing it not only covers its variable costs but also part of the unavoidable fixed costs.

Figure 2.42 Shutdown rule for a perfectly competitive firm: short-run analysis

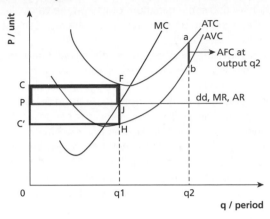

- So, any loss-making firm in the short run should shut down only if average revenue (the price) does not cover average variable cost. At any price below the minimum AVC the firm should shut down.

Shut down in the short run if P (=AR) < minimum AVC i.e. if TR < VC

Tip

This is a tricky diagram to draw and needs some practice. Start off by drawing the U-shaped ATC and AVC curves, ensuring that their vertical distance (the average fixed costs) becomes smaller and smaller as output increases. Make sure the MC curve (the 'Nike-swoosh' curve) cuts through them on its way up. Choose a price level between the minima of ATC and AVC and denote the line MR and AR. Find the intersection of the MC and MR curves and bring a line down to the Q axis to find the profit-maximizing output rate. Make sure that point F is not at the same level as minimum ATC. The vertical distance FH is the AFC so multiplied by CF (= 0q1) will give area (HFCC'), the fixed costs and losses incurred if the firm decides to shut down. To find the ATC when q1 units are produced you go up from q1 until point F is reached. Loss per unit, if the loss-making firm continues to produce, is FJ.

The supply curve of the perfectly competitive firm

- In the short run the supply curve of a perfectly competitive firm is that portion of its marginal cost curve that lies above the minimum of its average variable cost. In Fig. 2.43, the supply curve is thus the red segment of the MC curve. Why?
- Remember that a supply curve shows how many units a firm will be willing to offer per period at each price, ceteris paribus. Referring to Fig. 2.43, if the market price was at P1 then the profit-maximizing perfectly competitive firm will offer q1 units per period as its MR curve intersects the MC curve at point f. Similarly, if the market price was at P2 then the profit-maximizing perfectly competitive firm will offer q2 units per period as its new MR curve intersects the MC curve at point h. Lastly, if the market price was at P3 then the profit-maximizing perfectly competitive firm will offer q3 units per period as its new MR curve intersects the MC curve at point j.
- Points f, h and j thus show how many units this firm will offer at different prices. It follows that the MC curve is the firm's supply curve.

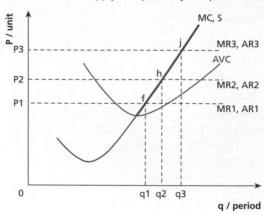

Figure 2.43 Short-run supply of a perfectly competitive firm

However, in the short run it will be only that segment above the minimum AVC as at any lower price it was established that the firm will not offer any units but will shut down. In the long run, it will be that section of the MC curve that lies above the ATC curve as it will not offer any units and shut down if price is less than ATC.

Efficiency issues and perfect competition

Given that the fundamental problem of any economy is scarcity, it is imperative to consider efficiency issues. Several types of efficiency are distinguished in economics.

- **Allocative efficiency** exists if 'just the right amount' of a good is produced *from society's point of view*. Allocative efficiency is achieved if all units of a good that are valued by consumers more than the cost to produce each are indeed produced up until that unit for which price is equal to marginal cost. If, for the last unit produced, P = MC then allocative efficiency is achieved.
- **Technical (or productive) efficiency** exists if production takes place with minimal resource waste, i.e with minimum average costs.

If markets are perfectly competitive then both allocative and productive efficiency are achieved.

Allocative efficiency in perfect competition

- In Fig. 2.44b all units that are worth more to consumers than what it costs to produce them are produced. This is a full version of Fig. 2.5 with all the necessary background knowledge present. Unit Q1 is worth Q1a and the marginal cost of producing it is Q1b. It should be produced and in a perfectly competitive market it will be produced. All units worth producing from society's point of view are indeed produced. For the last unit Q* produced in a perfectly competitive market, P = MC.
- Focusing on Fig. 2.44b it can be seen that social welfare, defined as the sum of consumer and producer surplus, is maximized. Consumer surplus is equal to area (FP*E) and producer surplus is area (HEP*). Their sum, area (HEF) is maximum since allocative efficiency is achieved. If any other quantity was produced, social welfare would be less.

Efficiency issues and perfect competition continued

Figure 2.44 Efficiency in perfect competition (a) the firm (b) the market

(a)

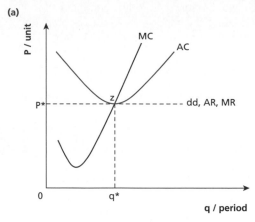

(b)

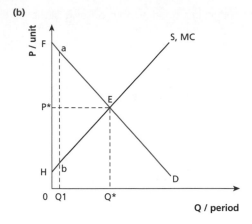

Technical (or productive) efficiency in perfect competition

- In the long run, firms in perfectly competitive markets are technically efficient as they are forced to produce with minimum average costs. In Fig. 2.44a long-run equilibrium output q* is achieved with minimum average costs q*z. Minimal resource waste is thus achieved. A firm incurring higher than q*z unit costs would be forced to exit the industry as it would be making losses.
- It follows that perfectly competitive markets not only lead to the optimal product mix but also scarce resources are not wasted.

Evaluation of perfectly competitive markets

- There is no guarantee that the goods produced will be distributed to the members of society in the fairest proportions. There may be considerable inequality of income.
- Remember that market demand is defined as the willingness *but also the ability* to buy a good at each price. Ability reflects the level of income each member of society faces. Poor households may not be 'counted' in the market demand for a 'basic' product if they do not have enough 'euros' to cast their 'votes'. There is thus no guarantee that perfect competition leads to a *truly* socially optimum combination of goods produced.
- Perfectly competitive firms do not have an incentive to innovate. Not only may they not be able to afford spending on research and development but they also know that their innovation (a new product or a better process) will be copied by the other firms. Such investment spending would be a waste of money.

- Perfectly competitive industries produce undifferentiated products. This lack of variety might be seen as a disadvantage to the consumer.
- Price in competitive markets changes given *any* change in demand or cost (supply) conditions. These fluctuations increase uncertainty and may deter long-term investment in an industry. In contrast, the price stability often found in oligopolistic markets may seem desirable for investment planning considerations.
- The perfectly competitive model is not compatible with increasing returns to scale, i.e. with economies of scale. If economies of scale were present then this would mean that there would be a cost advantage in bigger size so the industry would end up with few large firms. The absence of scale economies in perfect competition may imply that price after all is higher than it would have been if there were few large firms involved.

Monopoly

Characteristics

- One firm producing a good without close substitutes; the industry coincides with the firm.
- Unique product (as there is by definition only one firm in the market).
- Barriers to entry.

The concept of monopoly is relative since it crucially depends on how narrowly or broadly the product and the market are defined. Note also the importance of the geographical factor, i.e. location in relation to transportation costs.

Some interesting points concerning the monopoly firm

- A monopolist can choose either the level of output or the price but not both, since the monopoly firm is still constrained by a negatively sloped demand curve.
- A monopoly firm does not necessarily make huge profits. It may even make losses; remember that profits are a function of the relative position of the demand (the AR) curve and the average cost curve.
- A monopoly firm (more generally, any firm facing a negatively sloped demand curve) does *not* have a supply curve: the marginal cost curve is *not* a supply curve for such firms; each output rate corresponds to more than one possible price as an infinite number of MR curves may go through any point on the MC curve.
- It can be shown that if the demand curve (the AR curve) is linear, the marginal revenue curve is also linear, has the same vertical intercept and *double* the slope.
- A monopoly firm can set the price (it is a price-setter and not a price-taker); the degree of monopoly power is given by the difference between the price charged and marginal cost expressed as a proportion of price.
- A profit-maximizing monopoly firm will never choose a rate of output Q that corresponds to the price-inelastic segment of the demand curve it faces. It will always locate below the elastic segment. This is because for profit maximization MR must equal MC but since marginal cost is necessarily a positive number it follows that MR must also be a positive number at the profit-maximizing output. Marginal revenue is positive (i.e. lies above the Q axis) only for that set of output rates that correspond to the elastic region of the demand curve.
- The profit-maximizing output level is necessarily *less* than the revenue-maximizing level of output (where MR = 0) and thus the corresponding price charged is higher. In other words, revenue maximization leads to more units being produced at a lower price.

Equilibrium (short-run and long-run) of a monopoly firm

- A monopoly, being the only firm in the market, faces the negatively sloped market demand curve. If it is a profit-maximizing firm it will choose that rate of output at which MR = MC and MC is rising. In Fig. 2.35 this is the case at output Q*. Having determined the profit-maximizing output it will determine the price at which this quantity will be absorbed by consumers. This information is given by the demand curve. It will thus set the price at P*. It cannot set it any higher because at any price above P* fewer than the profit-maximizing level of output Q* will be bought.
- Focusing on Fig. 2.45, at Q* units of output per period, profits are equal to area (GFP*C). The difference between the average revenue Q*F and the average cost Q*G is the profit per unit which, if multiplied by the number of units CG (equal to Q*), gives us the profit area (GFP*C).
- This firm is making supernormal profits but since, by assumption, barriers exist, no new firms will enter the industry. If demand conditions, cost conditions and the entry barriers persist then this equilibrium (P*, Q*) will not change so it is also a long-run equilibrium condition.
- Note that if the monopolist aims at maximizing *revenues* instead of profits then it will choose that level of output at which MR = 0 (refer to Fig. 2.11a). In Fig. 2.45 this is the case at Qr.

Figure 2.45 Monopoly: short-run and long-run equilibrium

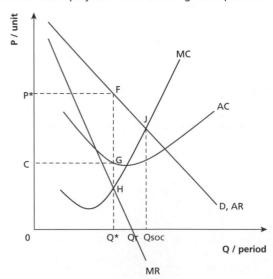

Efficiency considerations and monopoly

Allocative efficiency is not achieved under monopoly. Why?

- At the level of output Q* chosen by the monopoly firms, price exceeds marginal cost. Society would value more units to be produced. Society would like to enjoy all units up until unit Qsoc in Fig 2.45, which is valued as much as it would cost society to produce (distance JQsoc). Units Q*Qsoc are not produced and thus society does not enjoy welfare equal to area (HJF). Area (HJF) is the resulting welfare loss referred to as deadweight loss as it is net value that is lost.
- This is a case where market forces lead to inefficient allocation of scarce resources. It is a market failure.
- Productive inefficiency also results under monopoly. Why? The monopoly firm is not forced to produce with minimum average costs. At Q* average costs are Q*G which are higher than minimum.
- Lastly, Harvey Leibenstein coined the term **X-inefficiency** for a different type of inefficiency that some very protected monopoly positions may lead to. 'X-inefficiency' refers to the *internal slackness* that characterizes some monopolies. This is the case when, on a diagram, the AC curve is not as low as it could be, given the available technology.

Is there a case in favour of monopoly and, more generally, in favour of large firms with monopoly power?

- The answer is yes. Assume a perfectly competitive industry with a market supply at S (also the MC curve) and market demand at D as in Fig. 2.46. Equilibrium price will be at Pc and equilibrium quantity at Qc. We have shown that this outcome is efficient. Assume now that somehow this perfectly competitive industry is monopolized but that the production technology remains unchanged. Thus, the marginal cost curve for the monopoly firm remains at MC. The monopolist will choose Q* units and sell at a price P*. We have also established that this outcome is inefficient. The monopolist restricts output and raises price. Welfare is reduced.
- However, this result rests on the rather unlikely assumption that a larger monopoly firm employs the same technology that the small perfectly competitive firms ('Joey') employ. It is very probable that the monopoly firm will enjoy economies of scale.

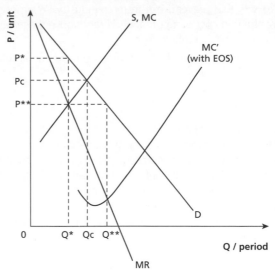

Figure 2.46 Monopoly and perfect competition

- If that is the case then the monopoly will have a new marginal cost curve that could be as low as MC'. MC' reflects the idea of scale economies. If this is the case then the monopoly *may* end up producing even more (Q**) than the perfectly competitive industry at an even lower price P**.
- Perhaps, even more importantly, a large firm with monopoly power may lead to a faster rate of technological advancement. Innovations, defined as new products or new processes, may result at a faster rate in such markets. Why? Because, assuming the monopoly firm is not *entrenched*, meaning that it is not protected by state-created barriers such as licences, then in order to maintain its position it may be forced to innovate. In addition, the supernormal profits it enjoys act as bait that lures other firms to innovate in an attempt to displace the monopolist. Perfectly competitive firms would not have the incentive to innovate because free entry would eliminate the possibility of a profitable return. These ideas are often referred to as **dynamic efficiency** and are associated with the Austrian economist Joseph A. Schumpeter.

Barriers to entry

Barriers are defined as anything that deters entry into an industry or that prevents exit from an industry. A barrier raises the unit cost of a potential entrant above the level enjoyed by the incumbent firm.

Barriers can be classified into natural, state created and firm created.

Natural barriers

- **Natural monopoly**
  Often, production technology is such that very significant economies of scale are present. As a result, given market size, only few or even only one firm can profitably coexist. When only one firm can profitably exist in a market it is the case of natural monopoly. Figure 2.47 illustrates the point. In this diagram significant economies of scale are present as the LAC curve slopes downward throughout the length of the demand curve that defines the relevant market. Assume that initially there is only one firm in this market and that the profit-maximizing output is at Q while the price at which these Q units will be absorbed is P. This firm is profitable and it enjoys profits equal to ab per unit. If now this market is equally shared by two firms, each producing and selling Q/2 units, then the total amount entering the market will still be Q units and

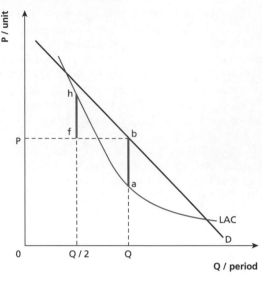

Figure 2.47 Natural monopoly

the price will remain at P. Each firm now is making a loss equal to hf per unit. It is much too expensive to produce Q/2 units, as Fig. 2.47 illustrates.

- **Exclusive ownership** of some vital input could also lead to a monopoly position.

State created

- **Patents** are granted by governments and are rights to produce exclusively for a fixed period of time. Patents aim at protecting the incentive to spend on research and development.
- **Licences** are exclusive permits that one or few firms have. TV and radio broadcasting firms require a licence.
- **Tariffs** limit competition from foreign firms and create monopoly power.

Firm created

Firms have every incentive to try to erect barriers in order to enjoy monopoly power and long-run supernormal profits.

- **Advertising and brand name** image creation: The stronger the brand name in a market the more difficult it is for a newcomer to enter.
- **Product differentiation**: Firms try to differentiate their product or produce many varieties of it to make entry more difficult.
- Incumbent firms may deliberately maintain **excess productive capacity**. Potential entrants know that the incumbent firm can thus easily increase output, depressing price to unprofitable levels.

Monopolistic competition

Characteristics

- Very many small firms (each firm has a very small share of the market).
- Differentiated product (differentiation can be along quality, durability, design or product service and can be real or imaginary).
- No barriers.
- It is the second characteristic that confers such firms with a very small degree of monopoly power. Since the product is not homogeneous then each firm faces a negatively sloped demand for the product it sells. If it increases price it will not lose all of its customers.
- Typical examples of monopolistically competitive industries include hairdressers, restaurants and DVD rental stores.
- Note that often, especially in manufacturing, the existence of many brands for consumers does not necessarily imply monopolistically competitive markets. For example, in the detergent industry there may be very many brands to choose from but behind these brands there are only two or three firms.

Monopolistic competition continued

Short-run and long-run equilibrium in monopolistic competition

- The illustration of short-run equilibrium in monopolistic competition is identical to the monopoly diagram (Fig. 2.45). A monopolistically competitive firm may enjoy supernormal profits in the short run. Supernormal profits in this case will induce entry as no barriers are assumed in this model. If hair salons in a market are enjoying supernormal profits, other such firms will be attracted. Sooner or later other hair salons will open up and lure away customers.

- As entry takes place, the demand that the typical incumbent firm faces will 'shrink and tilt'. Demand will 'shrink' because more firms imply a smaller market share for each. At each price the quantity demanded per period will decrease. Demand will 'tilt' and become flatter because the resulting bigger choice available to consumers means that demand will become more price elastic. Remember that price elasticity increases when consumers face more and closer substitutes.

Figure 2.48 Monopolistic competition: long-run equilibrium

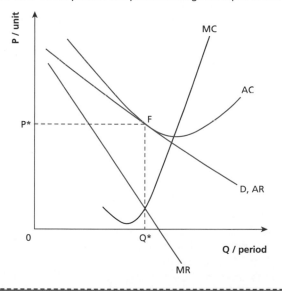

- Entry will continue until there is no longer an incentive for it to take place. This will be the case when supernormal profits are competed away and the typical hair salon is making normal profits, i.e. zero economic profits. Long-run equilibrium will be achieved when the typical firm in such a market is maximizing profits and these profits are zero, i.e. normal. Figure 2.48 illustrates long-run equilibrium as at Q* the firm equates MR and MC and thus maximizes profits (Q* is the optimal output rate) but AR and AC are equal to Q*F so economic profits are zero.

Evaluation of monopolistic competition

- Allocative inefficiency results. Price exceeds marginal cost at the equilibrium level of output for each firm.
- Technical inefficiency and excess capacity also result. Each firm produces less output than the one corresponding to minimum average costs. Restaurants typically have many empty tables and one does not have to wait in line to rent a DVD.
- The greater variety of products available is considered an advantage for consumers. Firms though are forced to advertise and to resort to other methods of non-price competition. The higher than minimum unit costs in such markets can be interpreted as the 'cost' of variety.

Tips

Figure 2.48 is very tricky to draw. First draw a U-shaped AC curve. Then draw a linear demand curve at a tangent to the AC curve. Automatically, the profit-maximizing output rate is determined below the tangency point as at all other levels of output AC > AR and the firm is making a loss. Next draw the MR curve as its position is strictly determined at double the slope of the demand curve. Draw the MC ('Nike-swoosh') curve last, making sure that on its way up it cuts the MR right above the profit-maximizing level of output Q* and that it also cuts the minimum of the U-shaped AC curve.

Oligopoly

Characteristics

- Few interdependent firms.
- Homogeneous (oil, steel or cement) or differentiated product (almost any industrial product, e.g. cars, detergents, appliances, aircraft, banking, insurance).
- Significant entry barriers.

Illustrating interdependence

- The defining characteristic of oligopoly is interdependence. Firms are considered interdependent if the outcome of any action of one firm depends on the reaction of the rival firms. For example, the success of an advertising campaign of firm A depends on whether rival firm B decreases its price at the same time or not. Interdependence can be illustrated in a diagram. In Fig. 2.49 a market with two firms, A and B, is assumed (a duopoly).
- Assume that firm A is currently selling Qo units at price Po. Increasing the price to P1 may lead either to a relatively sharp decrease in its sales or to a relatively mild one. It depends upon how rival firm B will react. If firm B decides to follow the price increase then firm A will see quantity demanded decrease only to Q1f (f: follow) as both firms will be more expensive in the market. If though rival firm B does not follow the price increase then A's sales will shrink to Q1nf (nf: not follow) as many of its customers will switch to firm B.
- Symmetrically, by decreasing the price to P2 sales may expand significantly to Q2nf if the rival does not follow, while they may increase but not as substantially if the rival firm does follow and also decreases its price.
- Note that interdependence is much broader than the case described here as rivalry between firms may extend in many other dimensions, e.g. the decision to invest or to advertise.

Figure 2.49 Interdependence in a duopoly

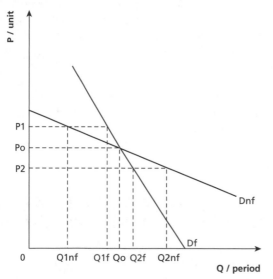

To compete or to collude?

- The dilemma characterizing interdependent oligopolistic firms is whether to compete or to collude.
- Through competition they may increase their own market share and their profits at the expense of rivals.
- Collusion, on the other hand, decreases uncertainty and firms may maximize joint profits as if they were a monopoly.

Collusion

- **Collusive oligopoly** exists when two or more firm agree to fix prices or to engage in other anticompetitive behaviour. Agreement can be either formal or informal.
- If the agreement is formal we have the case of a **cartel**. Cartels are generally illegal. In most countries firms cannot sign legally enforceable contracts. Firms that have made formal agreements try to make sure that their agreements remain secret. OPEC is a case of a formal agreement between oil-exporting countries in which deliberations and decisions are publicized as it operates above national laws.
- If the agreement is informal then we have the case of 'tacit' collusion. To illustrate the collusive behaviour where firms behave as a monopoly firm, one can employ the monopoly diagram (Fig. 2.45). The equilibrium output is the joint profit-maximizing output and the profits must somehow be shared.

How likely is it for a collusive agreement to collapse?

Collusive structures are unstable because of the inherent incentive to cheat. Each member would prefer others to abide by the output restricting agreement while it doesn't and exceeds it. Such agreements are more likely to collapse,

- the greater the number of member firms;
- the smaller the proportion of total industry output members of the agreement control;
- if the good is differentiated and many varieties exist;
- if production costs differ;
- if market demand is shrinking.

Conversely, when the market is dominated by very few large firms, producing a rather homogeneous product with similar production costs and demand is rising, then any agreement will be more likely to last.

Non-collusive oligopoly

- The term refers to the case where oligopolistic firms have no agreement concerning their behaviour and tactics. Still, repeated interaction leads oligopolistic firms to avoid changing output even if cost conditions change.
- The kinked demand curve model (Fig. 2.50) illustrates this point. It was introduced by P. Sweezy in 1939 and it aimed at explaining the observed price stickiness in oligopolistic markets even when cost conditions changed. It is typically considered a model of non-collusive oligopoly.

The kinked demand curve model

- The behavioral assumption in the kinked demand curve model is simple: given the current price, if a firm increases price then rival firms will not follow while, if a firm decreases price, then rival firms will follow and cut prices too. Thus a kink will form in the demand curve the individual firm faces at the current price.

Figure 2.50 The kinked demand

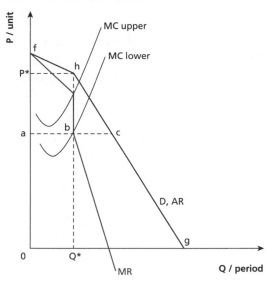

- In Fig. 2.50, the kink is at point h corresponding to the initial price P* and the initial quantity Q*. Segment fh of the demand curve is relatively more price elastic than segment hg as a consequence of the behavioral assumption. Note that demand below the kink does not have to be price inelastic but only less price elastic than it is above it, as the existence of a positive segment for MR illustrates above.
- The kink leads to a *discontinuity* in the marginal revenue curve which has to be double the slope *of each section* of the kinked demand.
- Since the firm is assumed to be a profit maximizer it follows that marginal cost must have intersected the marginal revenue curve right above the chosen output Q*.
- This could be the case either with the MC_{upper} curve or with the MC_{lower} curve. By inference, any change in costs within this range will also lead to Q* units chosen and thus to the same price P*. Price is sticky at P* in a non-collusive oligopoly even if cost conditions change.

- The model is useful as it illustrates the observed stickiness in prices in oligopolies in a simple way.
- It has been criticized though on theoretical grounds as it fails to explain how the original price P* is formed and also because the range of possible strategies and responses in such setups is much more complicated.

Tip

Start drawing this diagram by first choosing the kink somewhere in the upper left corner of the graph space; then draw the demand curve making sure that the section reflecting the result of a price decrease is not too steep. Next draw first the MR section corresponding to the relatively elastic segment of the demand curve, maintaining the double-the-slope rule. The MR which corresponds to the lower right segment hg of the demand curve should start at such a point b (see Fig. 2.50) that ab = bc and also maintain the double-the-slope rule.

Non-price competition

Oligopolistic firms avoid competing through price cuts. Such a strategy could lead to a competitive downward spiral in prices (a price war) which could leave all firms worse off.

Non-price competition can take several forms, such as:

- heavy advertising and brand-name creation (e.g. Pepsi and Coca Cola);
- gifts and coupons (e.g. newspapers and magazines);
- continuous product differentiation (cars, cell phones, DVD players, TV sets, TV stations, etc.);
- excessive product proliferation to cover all imaginable market niches (e.g. ice cream, breakfast cereal);
- extended guarantees (typically in electrical appliances, computer hardware devices);
- aftersales service (customer plans of car makers);
- volume discounts (often in products such as shampoo and conditioners).

If a price war occurs in the real world, some participants (typically those with 'deep pockets') look forward to weaker firms being forced to go out of business or be acquired.

Price discrimination

- **Price discrimination (PD)** is a pricing policy that certain firms adopt to further increase their profits. Formally, price discrimination exists when a firm sells the same product at two or more different prices in two or more markets provided that the price differences do not reflect cost differences.
- Examples include airline tickets, train and bus fares, theatre and cinema tickets, phone services, lawyer/doctor/consultant fees.
- In international trade, dumping is also considered a form of international price discrimination as it involves selling abroad at a lower price than in the protected domestic market.

Conditions permitting a firm to price discriminate

- The firm must enjoy some degree of monopoly power. It must face a negatively sloped demand curve. Thus a perfectly competitive firm cannot practise price discrimination.
- No resale of the good (referred to as 'seepage') from the cheaper to the pricier market should be possible. The two markets must be somehow separable, otherwise 'arbitrage' (buying low and selling high) will guarantee that eventually one price will dominate in both markets.
- Price elasticities of demand between markets must differ. Some consumers must be prepared to pay more, either because fewer substitutes are available to them or because they enjoy a higher level of income.

First-degree price discrimination (or perfect price discrimination)

- A highly theoretical case where the seller is assumed to be fully aware of the consumer's willingness to pay and charges her the maximum price she is willing to pay *for each* unit consumed.
- In the simplified diagram, Fig. 2.51, the first unit Q1 is sold at the maximum price possible, P1. The next unit, Q2, is also sold at the maximum price it can fetch, P2, and so on.

Figure 2.51 Price discrimination: first degree (perfect PD)

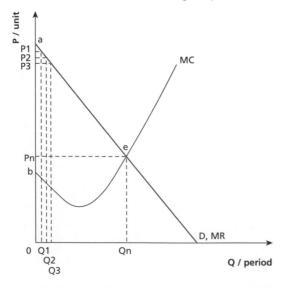

- In perfect PD the entire consumer surplus is appropriated by the producer who enjoys a surplus equal to area (bea).
- Also, allocative efficiency is achieved as all units for which price exceeds marginal cost are produced and sold up until that unit (Qn in the diagram) for which price is equal to marginal cost.
- The closest real-world approximation of this highly theoretical construct may be open-air markets where 'haggling' is common.

Second-degree price discrimination (or block price discrimination)

- In second-degree PD 'blocks' of output are sold at different prices to the same consumer. For example, many parking garages in city centres price the first hour at, say €10.00, the next 2 hours are at €6.00 per hour and any additional hours are at €2.00 per hour. This way they extract a greater portion of the consumer surplus compared to charging a single price per hour.
- In the simplified diagram, Fig. 2.52, the profit-maximizing firm initially is assumed to charge a single price P, selling Q units per period and making maximum profits equal to some π. It now decides to adopt second-degree price discrimination and charges a price P′ for the first Q′ units while it charges a price P for units Q′Q.
- Total costs have remained the same as it is still producing Q units (0Q′ + Q′Q = 0Q) but its revenues are higher by area (PhfP′). It follows that it has managed to increase profits above the level π achieved with a single price.

Figure 2.52 Price discrimination: second degree (block PD)

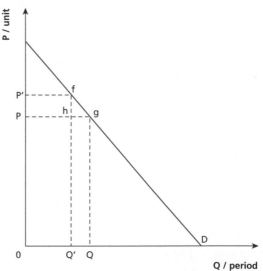

Tip

Use this diagram to show that price discrimination can increase firm profits above the single-price profit-maximizing level.

Price discrimination continued

HL

Third-degree price discrimination

- This is the commonest type where markets are segmented across some characteristic that takes advantage of differing price elasticities and that does not permit resale. For example, airline tickets bought a day in advance cost more than if they were purchased a month in advance of a flight. Since the name is on the ticket the company tries to take advantage of the fact that if one decides to travel a few days before a flight either she has important business to conduct or she is wealthy and the ticket expense is a small proportion of her income.
- Either way, the higher price is charged in the market characterized by the more price-inelastic demand.
- In the simplified diagram, Fig. 2.53, the two markets are drawn side by side. Da, on the right-hand side, reflects the demand conditions prevailing in market 'a' assumed to be more price inelastic (e.g. business travellers). Db, on the left-hand side, reflects the more price-elastic conditions prevailing in market 'b' (for example, tourist travellers). Marginal costs are assumed, for simplicity, to be constant at h.
- The firm will choose the profit-maximizing output in each market by equating MC with MR. In market 'a' this occurs at output Qa resulting in price Pa. In market 'b' with the more price-elastic demand the profit-maximizing output is at Qb and the price is lower, as expected, at Pb. The higher price is charged in the market characterized by the more inelastic demand conditions.

Figure 2.53 Price discrimination: third degree

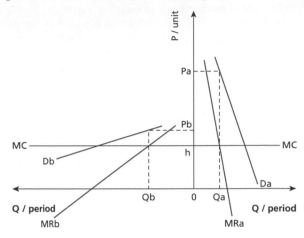

Tip

When drawing the two demand curves make sure their slopes differ substantially so that the resulting prices differ significantly.

Consumers and price discrimination

HL

In general, a price-discriminating firm appropriates part (or in the extreme case of first-degree PD, all) of the consumer surplus. Since the price-discriminating firm is able to charge closer to what consumers are at the most willing to pay, it follows that this policy in general runs against the interests of consumers.

Yet, there may be situations where certain groups do benefit:

- The group that pays the lower price, if it is lower than the price charged in the single-price case.

- This pricing policy may permit a firm to sell a greater volume of output and as a result enjoy economies of scale. If these cost savings are passed along in the form of overall lower prices then consumers benefit.
- If offering the good was unprofitable at any single price, then price discrimination may make the provision of a good profitable to a group of consumers that otherwise would have to do without it.

Theory of contestable markets

- In contrast to the orthodox theory of market structures, the theory of contestable markets does not focus on the number and size of the firms present in a market. Instead it focuses on entry and, especially, exit conditions.
- The idea of market contestability rests on the absence of **sunk costs** defined as entry costs that are not recoverable upon exit. Examples of sunk costs include product development costs (which are high in the pharmaceutical or the car industries), advertising costs, specialized machinery, etc.
- If there are no sunk costs involved then a contestable market is subject to 'hit-and-run'. Firms can enter, reap the profits for as long as possible and then exit without incurring any exit costs.
- This possibility forces incumbent firms to set a price that reflects their costs of production. Without barriers to entry and sunk costs, it is potential competition that will ensure 'competitive' performance even in highly concentrated markets with few large firms present. Firms will be forced to earn zero economic profits and price will be close to marginal cost, ensuring in equilibrium a socially efficient outcome.
- In Fig. 2.54 a profit-maximizing monopolist will choose to offer Q units at a price P making supernormal profits equal to area (P*hfP). If now this market was perfectly contestable then this monopoly firm would be forced to set the price at P* selling Q* units, as at that level of output the resulting economic profits are normal and no 'hit and run' entry will be induced. Output is at the socially efficient level as at Q* price is equal to marginal cost.
- Perfect contestability does not exist in the real world as perfect competition does not exist either. What matters is

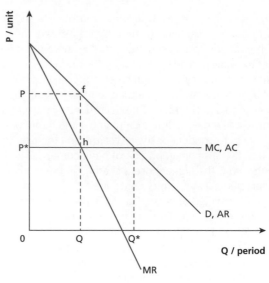

Figure 2.54 Contestable markets

thus the degree of contestability. Contestability increases, the lower the size of sunk costs, the lower the size of barriers to entry and the higher the size of supernormal profits.
- The main policy implication of contestable market theory is that if only few firms exist in a market it *should not necessarily* imply inefficiency. Thus markets with few large firms do not necessarily need government intervention and the scale economies often associated may even be an additional reason to make them desirable.
- Contestability theory has forced policymakers to focus more on potential competition and reduce their emphasis on firm size and market concentration.

All in one

Figure 2.55 illustrates a monopoly or imperfectly competitive firm, i.e. any firm facing a negatively sloped demand curve for its good or service. In this diagram all major diagrammatical points are illustrated.

At the output level:

Q1: maximization of profits is achieved, as MR = MC (point a) and MC is rising

Q2: technical (productive) efficiency is achieved, as MC = AC (point h) and thus AC is minimum

Q3: allocative efficiency is achieved, as P(=AR) = MC (point f)

Q4: maximization of revenues is achieved, as MR = 0

Q5: normal (zero economic) profits are achieved, as P(=AR)= AC; a firm in a concentrated perfectly contestable market would be forced to price at that level.

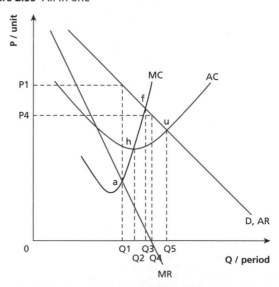

Figure 2.55 All in one

Market failures

Free markets: successes and failures

- The fundamental economic problem that all societies face is scarcity: limited resources versus unlimited wants. This necessitates choices, i.e. decisions about which goods will be produced and in what quantities. How will scarce resources be allocated?
- In a market economy, the answer is given by the market (the price) mechanism. The interaction of demand and supply, with consumers aiming to maximize utility and firms trying to maximize profits, determines 'the way the blades of a pair of scissors act', how much of each good will be produced and consumed. Relative price changes coordinate economic activity *as if an invisible hand exists*. Relative price changes provide the signals and the incentives for producers and consumers to change their behaviour.

If markets are free and competitive then we have shown that the outcome is socially efficient. But, in the real world:

- markets are often not competitive as firms may possess significant monopoly power;
- the costs and benefits of economic transactions are often paid or enjoyed by third parties outside the market;
- true preferences are not revealed.

The above three points refer to three important types of **market failure**: the existence of monopoly power, the existence of **externalities** and the case of **public goods**. A market failure exists if market forces fail to reach efficient outcomes. In such a case either too much or not enough is produced or consumed so scarce resources are not allocated in the socially optimal way.

- One should note though that the underlying income distribution of the population may be very unfair. And since the market demand for any good reflects not just willingness to consume it but also ability to do so, households with severe income constraints, living, say, below the absolute poverty line, will not 'exist' in the market expression of the demand for perhaps even the most basic products such as food. Paraphrasing Samuelson's famous expression, these households do not have any dollars to vote with. It follows that the resulting output mix may reflect allocative efficiency but may still be socially undesirable.

Monopoly power as a source of market failure

This market failure has been established earlier in the presentation of monopoly and oligopoly. Firms with monopoly power are able to restrict output below the competitive ideal and charge a higher price, leading to a welfare loss.

Possible solutions to monopoly power

- The government should ensure that competitive conditions prevail in markets. It should ensure that no mergers or acquisitions materialize that excessively increase the monopoly power of any firm.
- It should monitor firm practices that seem anti-competitive; it could tax or fine firms found guilty of such practices; it should even break up such firms into smaller independent pieces.
- However, there may be very significant dynamic benefits arising from the existence of such large monopoly firms in the form of faster rates of innovation and technological change and economies of scale.

- In addition, contestability theory strongly suggests that even highly concentrated industries may be capable of approximate competitive outcomes. The regulator should thus make sure that such scale economies are not sacrificed nor the potential rate of innovation compromised.
- A most effective way to reduce domestic monopoly power is through liberalizing international trade. Free trade automatically increases competition, leading to increased efficiency and lower prices.

Externalities as a source of market failure

- An externality is present if an economic activity (production or consumption) creates benefits or imposes costs on third parties for which the latter do not pay or do not get compensated respectively. Equivalently, an externality exists whenever there is a divergence between private and social costs of production or between private and social benefits of consumption.
- An externality leads to market failure as if it is present then either more (**overprovision**) or less (**underprovision**) than the socially optimal amount is produced or consumed. Market forces alone fail to lead to an efficient resource allocation.
- Externalities may arise in the production process in which case they are known as **production externalities** or in the consumption process in which case they are known as **consumption externalities**. They may impose costs on third parties in which case they are considered as **negative externalities,** or create benefits in which case they are considered **positive externalities**.

Externalities as a source of market failure continued

Necessary terms

- **Marginal private costs (MPC)**
  The costs of production that the firm takes into consideration in its decision-making process. They include wages, raw materials, etc. It follows that the MPC curve is the supply curve of a (competitive) firm.
- **Marginal social costs (MSC)**
  The costs of production that are borne by society. These reflect the value of *all* resources that are sacrificed in the specific production process. They thus include not just the labour and other resources that are sacrificed and which comprise the costs that are taken into consideration by the firm, but also any *external costs* that are not taken into consideration in the form of, say, pollution. In this case the marginal social costs of production exceed the marginal private costs and should be drawn above the MPC (the supply) curve. This would be the case of a negative production externality. If though a *production* process creates benefits for a third party (say, another firm) then the MSC curve lies below the MPC (supply) curve as there is an **external production benefit** involved in the process.
- **Marginal private benefits (MPB)**
  The benefits the individual enjoys from the consumption of an extra unit. Private benefits determine the willingness to pay and thus the demand curve is always based on and reflects the marginal private benefits curve.
- **Marginal social benefits (MSB)**
  The benefits that society enjoys from each extra unit consumed. They thus include the private benefit enjoyed by the individual but in addition any benefits others may enjoy as a result. The social benefits include the private benefits enjoyed plus any external benefits. It follows that the MSB curve lies above the MPB (and demand) curve. If though the consumption activity of individuals imposes a cost on others then the MSB curve will lie below the MPB (and demand) curve as there is an external cost of consumption generated by the process.

Analysis of a negative production externality

- Figure 2.56 illustrates a steel market in which firms are polluting the environment. The market outcome is found at the intersection of the market demand curve D and the market supply curve S. The market will lead to Q units of steel at a price of P per unit.
- Production externalities arise on the production side so we focus on the market supply in the diagram. The supply curve reflects the private costs that firms take into consideration so it is also the MPC curve. The pollution costs are the external costs which firms are assumed to ignore. Social costs of production (what society sacrifices) are thus bigger than the private costs of production and the MSC curve lies above the MPC curve for all levels of steel output. It follows that MSC = MPC + external costs.
- The demand curve reflects the benefits enjoyed by consumers at each level of output so it is also the MPB curve. Since in this example there are no consumption externalities involved, the social benefits are not higher

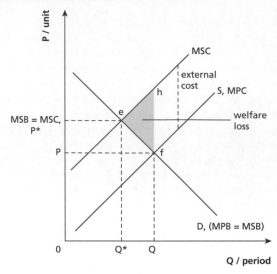

Figure 2.56 Negative production externality

or lower than the private benefits so the demand curve reflects both private and social benefits.

- Society would want only Q* units of steel produced and consumed. At unit Q* the MSC is just equal to the MSB.
- For all units beyond unit Q* the marginal social cost exceeds the marginal social benefit. The last unit Q that is produced in a free market is worth to society only Qf (= 0P), since this is how much consumers are willing at the most to pay for it, but society sacrifices for its production more, namely Qh. The production of unit Q by market forces leads to a welfare loss equal to fh. Since for all units Q*Q the MSC exceeds MSB, the welfare loss is equal to the pink area (efh) reflecting the market inefficiency.
- The market fails because it leads to overproduction (Q*Q) of the good. Ignoring the external pollution costs leads to too much steel at too low a price for society.

Tip

To find the welfare loss triangle take any unit of output between Q and Q* and compare the marginal social cost to the marginal social benefit. Their difference is the welfare loss for that unit. Doing the same for all units QQ* will give you the resulting welfare loss.

Analysis of a positive consumption externality

- Figure 2.57 illustrates the market for hybrid cars. Owners of such cars create benefits to society as they help decrease pollution in a city. Alternatively, you can think of the market for flu vaccinations. If an individual gets vaccinated it is not her alone who benefits as the probability that others suffer from the flu somewhat decreases. In both cases the market outcome is found at the intersection of the market demand curve D and the market supply curve S. The market will lead to Q units of hybrid cars or vaccines at a price of P per unit.

Externalities as a source of market failure continued

Figure 2.57 Market for hybrid cars

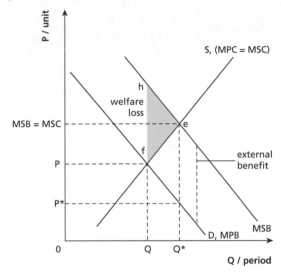

- Consumption externalities arise on the consumption side so we focus on market demand in the diagram. The demand curve reflects the private benefits that the individual enjoys and takes into consideration in making buying decisions, so it is also the MPB curve. The external benefits from driving a hybrid car or from getting vaccinated are ignored by the individual. Thus, the social benefits of consumption are bigger than the private benefits of consumption and the MSB curve lies above the MPB curve for all levels of output. It follows that MSB = MPB + external benefits.
- Since the production of the cars or the vaccinations does not create any externality it follows that the supply curve reflects both private and social costs.
- The market fails as at the last unit produced and consumed Q the MSB (= Qh) exceeds the MSC of production (= Qf). The socially optimal amount produced and consumed per period is more at Q*.

- All units between Q and Q* should have been produced from society's point of view as for each the social benefit enjoyed is bigger than the cost of production (MSC). Thus, the market fails as it leads to underconsumption of vaccines and hybrid cars and the resulting welfare loss is equal to the pink area (efh).
- Note that for the last unit society would like consumed (Q*) the marginal social benefits equal the marginal social costs. But since individuals do not consider the external benefits their consumption creates and base their decisions on their demand curve the market price must somehow be set lower at P* for the socially optimal amount of vaccines and hybrid cars to be consumed. This could be achieved through a subsidy.

Tips

If the external benefits from the consumption of the good or service are very significant in size then we have the case of a **merit good**. Vaccinations and health care services as well as education are typical examples of merit goods. They are also a case of market failure. Analysis of merit goods is identical to the one above. Note that other definitions of merit goods stress:
- The fact that individuals are often not fully aware of the true benefits derived from the consumption of a good so that the government has to step in and ensure that people do indeed consume these goods in adequate amounts. Thus in many countries children have to attend some schooling, they have to be vaccinated, etc.
- The fact that low-income individuals often cannot afford to consume such goods so the government has to ensure that all, rich and poor alike, consume sufficient amounts of these goods.

Analysis of a negative consumption externality

- Figure 2.58 illustrates the market for cigarettes. Smoking is presumably enjoyable to the smoker but it creates costs to society as a whole. There are external costs in the form of the ill effects of passive smoking as well as the probable health-related care costs that smokers often impose on society as their habit may result in less health-related resources available to others.
- Since this is an externality generated in the consumption of the good we focus in the diagram on market demand. The demand curve reflects the private benefits that the individual enjoys and takes into consideration in making buying decisions so it is also the MPB curve.
- The external costs of consuming the good, i.e. of smoking, are ignored by the individual. Thus, the social benefits from smoking are less than the private benefits of consumption and the MSB curve lies below the MPB curve for all levels of output. It follows that MSB = MPB – external costs of consumption.

Figure 2.58 Market for cigarettes

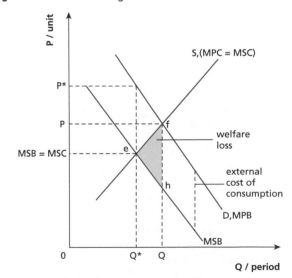

Externalities as a source of market failure continued

- Since the production of cigarettes does not create any externality it follows that the supply curve reflects both private and social costs of producing cigarettes.
- The market fails as at the last unit Q produced and consumed the MSB (= Qh) is less that the MSC of production (= Qf) in Fig. 2.58.
- The socially optimal amount of cigarettes produced and consumed per period is less at Q*. All units between Q* and Q should have not been produced from society's point of view as for each the social benefits enjoyed are less than the social cost of production (MSC). Thus, the market fails as it leads to overconsumption of cigarettes and the resulting welfare loss is equal to the pink area (efh).
- Note that for the last unit society would like consumed (Q*) the marginal social benefits equal the marginal social costs. But since individuals do not consider the external costs that their consumption of cigarettes creates and base their decisions on their demand curve, the market price must somehow be set higher at P* for the socially optimal amount of cigarettes to be consumed. This could be achieved through a tax.

Tip

If the external costs from the consumption of some good or service are very significant, as is the case with smoking and drinking alcoholic beverages, then we have the case of a **demerit good**. Demerit goods are also a case of market failure. Analysis of demerit goods is identical to the one above.

Alternative diagrammatic approaches: the decision to drive one's car

- One can analyse the effects of a negative externality of consumption differently. Figure 2.59 illustrates the individual's decision to drive. How much should one drive their car from society's point of view?
- The individual will drive more and more kilometres per period as long as the extra benefits enjoyed from driving exceed the extra costs he incurs from driving.
- These extra benefits he enjoys from more and more driving become smaller and smaller and this is shown through the negatively sloped marginal benefits of driving curve MB which can be thought of as a demand for driving schedule. As no one else benefits from his driving it follows that MPB = MSB.
- The extra private costs (MPC) from driving include gasoline costs as well as the value of time and any discomfort the driving per period of time causes. They are assumed for simplicity constant at c pounds for each extra kilometre driven.
- Driving one's car imposes costs on others in the form of increased pollution and congestion. These are external costs and for simplicity are assumed constant and equal to cc'. Thus the MSC curve which includes both private and external costs of driving is constant at c'.

It follows that the individual will choose to drive too much, specifically Q kilometres per week, whereas society would have wanted him to drive less at Q* kilometres per week. There is thus reason for the government to intervene.

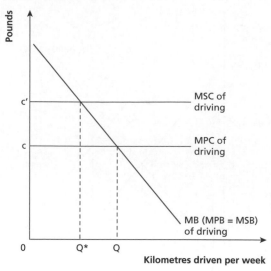

Figure 2.59 The decision to drive

Alternative diagrammatic approaches: the decision to educate a child

- Imagine a poor Chinese farmer facing the decision whether or not to send his daughter to the nearby primary school. He will weigh the benefits he expects to enjoy from sending his daughter off to school against the costs he will incur from doing so.
- If he is not capable of realizing the true future benefits his child may enjoy in life from schooling, he may consider the private benefits derived very low, as MPB in Fig. 2.60 shows.
- On the other hand, the costs he incurs (private costs) from each extra year of schooling include the lost labour and income (as his child could have helped him on his farm) plus any transport and other costs. In Fig. 2.60 the MPC are for simplicity assumed constant and equal to c.
- He will thus decide *not* send her off to school. But the social benefits from educating a child far exceed the private benefits. There are significant external benefits arising from primary education. The MSB curve thus lies above the MPB curve. From society's point of view the child should attend Q* years of schooling. There is thus reason for the government to intervene.

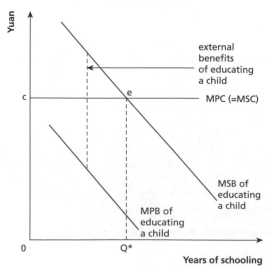

Figure 2.60 The decision to educate a child

Solutions to externalities

It is usually too costly for the affected parties to negotiate and arrive at a mutually beneficial solution. As a result government usually intervenes and tries to correct the externality either using the market mechanism or circumventing it through 'command and control' policies.

Market-based solutions

Externalities are market failures where either too much or not enough of a good is produced and consumed. The reason is that prices for some reason may not exist or may fail to reflect the true benefits or the true costs of an activity. It follows that one type of solution could try making sure that a price exists and that it is the correct one.

- **Assigning and enforcing property rights over assets**. Assets may include a pasture that otherwise would be overgrazed, the rights to a clean lake that otherwise would be polluted or the right to drive one's vehicle downtown. In this way the owner will need to consider the costs and benefits of his actions. If property rights exist then prices can be set and the benefits and costs of an activity can be estimated. For example, if a government sets a price for the right to drive downtown then a driver will have to include this price to his private costs of driving in Fig. 2.59. All too often it is impossible to assign private property rights, as in the case of the atmosphere or the sea.
- **Imposing taxes** equal to any external costs of production or any external cost of consumption. Green taxes on polluting firms and taxes on cigarettes fall within this category.
- **Granting subsidies** when the full benefits of an activity are not captured by the individual or the firm creating them. This is the case in many health-care related products. The price is effectively lowered so consumption increases to the socially desirable level.
- **Tradeable pollution permits**. These are licences to pollute a specific amount that the government allocates to polluting firms that are tradable in the open market. An incentive system is thus created as cleaner firms which find it cheaper to lower their level of pollution will have an incentive to sell unused permits to older and dirtier firms that find it costly to reduce pollution levels. Pollution permits are scarce and a market is created for the right to pollute. After all trading is completed, a new allocation of permits will emerge with the following properties:
  - the target level of total pollution is achieved;
  - the loss of output is smaller than if the government had assigned for all firms the same maximum level of emissions.

Potential problems of such a market-based solution include:

- the initial allocation of permits may be difficult for the government to determine;
- monitoring compliance is expensive.

Command-and-control solutions

Often it is not possible or not effective to rely on changing market signals. Governments thus resort to direct regulation. Governments can directly regulate output, prices, location, operating hours of production as well as who has the right to drink or smoke and where. In many cases direct regulation may be the only realistic and cost-effective solution but it may also lead to costly and inefficient outcomes.

Advertising (or banning of), moral suasion, education

This is a different set of solutions whereby the government attempts to change the preferences and practices of consumers and of firms by increasing their awareness of the external costs or benefits of certain activities they undertake. By making schoolchildren aware of the benefits of recycling today the government aims at creating citizens making better choices later.

Public goods as a case of market failure

A good is considered a public good if consumption is non-excludable and non-rival.

- Consumption is **non-excludable** if once the good is available to even one consumer it automatically becomes available to all, so no one can be excluded from consuming it. Consequently, individuals have the incentive to conceal their true preferences and behave as '**free riders**' (people who cling to the bus and get a free ride without paying the fare) because they know that they can enjoy the good without having to pay for it once it becomes available for others.
- Consumption is **non-rival** if consumption of the good by one does not decrease the amount available for all others; this implies that the *marginal cost of an extra user* is nil.

Examples

- Few examples of pure public goods exist. A lighthouse, national defence and traffic lights are typical examples. If a lighthouse becomes available in some island no fisherman can be excluded from its benefits while if it is 'used' by one the amount of services available to the rest are the same (the marginal cost of one more fishing boat using the services is zero).
- 'Law and order' and 'price stability' are somewhat different examples but they satisfy both criteria and their implications are interesting. Law and order can even be extended to imply a functional institutional framework, which is especially important for a developing economy and only a government can provide it.
- A last example is TV and radio broadcasting. Both criteria are satisfied. If *Friends* is broadcast for one household, no household with a TV set (a separate private good) can be excluded and if I enjoy the show you can enjoy it as much. These services though are often privately provided as the broadcasting firm does not sell the shows but advertising time, which is both excludable and rival.

- Public goods are a case of market failure because consumers have the incentive to conceal their true preferences, hoping to benefit as free riders. As a result, private profit-oriented firms will (normally) not have the incentive to produce and offer such goods and services through the market. The market fails. Compulsory taxation and provision (but not necessarily production) by the government is the typical solution.

Tips

Whether a good is considered a public good or not depends on whether it satisfies the two criteria above. A common mistake is for students to believe that any good that a government or the state produces is a public good.

Further, the problem of pollution exceeds national borders. Global warming is obviously a global problem. Pollution is in this sense a 'public bad': if it exists for one, it exists for all and, if one suffers the rest will suffer the same. It is an international problem requiring international cooperation. Unfortunately, no supra-national body exists that can impose solutions on sovereign nations. Treaties are a movement in that direction (Kyoto treaty, the Bali Summit) but even if a nation signs, it may still choose not to abide by it. Worse, some countries are not willing to sign such treaties. An interesting solution proposed by Nobel laureate Joseph Stiglitz is to consider the firms of such nations (as the US) as recipients of state subsidies. Not paying the full costs of production is equivalent to receiving a state subsidy. Since subsidies within the WTO trade system are illegal, other nations would have the right to impose trade sanctions on these nations, forcing them to cooperate and reduce emissions.

IB Questions: Sections 1 and 2

SL Long Essays

1a Explain the signalling and incentive function of prices in a market economy. (10 marks)

1b Evaluate the proposition that government intervention in the market for tobacco is justified. (15 marks)

2a Explain why underprovision of merit goods in a market economy is considered to be a market failure. (10 marks)

2b Evaluate the possible measures that a government might use to correct such a market failure.

3a The basic economic problem is one of scarcity of productive resources. Explain how resources are allocated between competing uses in a market economy. (10 marks)

3b Discuss the view that there is strong justification for government intervention in the market for health care. (15 marks)

4a Evaluate the importance of price in allocating scarce resources. (10 marks)

4b Evaluate the possible consequences of implementing maximum and minimum price controls. (15 marks)

5a Explain how a buffer stock may be used to stabilize agricultural prices. (10 marks)

5b Discuss the view that intervention in agricultural markets causes more problems than it solves. (15 marks)

6a What are positive externalities and how do they arise? Illustrate your answer with examples. (10 marks)

6b Evaluate the options available to governments to overcome the failure of markets to take account of positive externalities. Refer to real-world examples in your answer. (15 marks)

7a What factors determine the price and income elasticities of demand for a product? (10 marks)

7b Why might firms and governments be interested to know the price and income elasticities of demand for various products? (15 marks)

HL Long Essays

1a Explain how barriers to entry may affect market structure. (10 marks)

1b Evaluate the view that monopoly is an undesirable market structure. (15 marks)

2a Explain the necessary conditions for price discrimination to take place. (10 marks)

2b Discuss the advantages and disadvantages of price discrimination for consumers and producers. (15 marks)

3a Carefully distinguish between merit, demerit and public goods. (10 marks)

3b Evaluate the view that governments should always intervene in markets for such goods as cigarettes and alcohol. (15 marks)

4a Explain the differences between monopolistic competition and oligopoly. (10 marks)

4b Discuss the differences between collusive and non-collusive oligopoly. (15 marks)

5a Explain how profit is determined in perfect competition. (10 marks)

5b 'Whatever the type of market structure, profit maximization will always be the only goal of firms.' Discuss. (15 marks)

6a Outline the ways in which monopoly power might arise. (10 marks)

6b Evaluate the extent to which governments should seek to control the growth of monopoly power. (15 marks)

7a What role do prices play in the allocation of resources in a market economy? (10 marks)

7b Evaluate the options available to governments to overcome the failure of markets in the production and consumption of demerit goods. (15 marks)

8a Why are environmental problems considered to be an example of market failure? (10 marks)

8b To what extent can government intervention correct this government failure? (15 marks)

9a Carefully explain what it is that price, income and cross price elasticities of demand are meant to measure. (10 marks)

9b Discuss the practical importance of price elasticity of demand for firms and for the government. (15 marks)

10a What does an economist mean by efficiency in the operation of a firm? (10 marks)

10b Discuss whether the achievement of efficiency is possible and desirable. (15 marks)

HL Short Essays

1 The choice between military products and the provision of health care illustrates the problem of 'opportunity cost'. Explain the nature of the problem using a production possibilities curve.

2 'Normally it would be expected that more would be determined at lower prices as opposed to at higher prices, all other things being equal, but this may not always be the case.' Explain this statement.

3 'As price falls, quantity supplied falls. As supply increases, price falls.' Use supply and demand analysis to explain why these two statements do not contradict each other.

4 Using demand and supply analysis explain how resources are allocated in a market economy.

5 How might the price elasticity of demand affect the shape of a firm's total revenue curve?

6 Explain why the price elasticities of both demand and supply of primary commodities tend to be relatively low in the short run.

7 Define cross price elasticity of demand and using diagrams explain what determines whether cross elasticity is positive or negative.

8 In many countries the price of houses has risen steadily over recent years while more and more people have

IB Questions: Sections 1 and 2 continued

been buying houses. Use supply and demand analysis to explain why this has happened.

9   The price of tickets in a major tennis tournament is fixed by the organizing body. At the set price, many more people wish to attend the tournament than there are seats available. Draw a diagram to illustrate this situation and use your diagram to examine the likely consequences.

10   A government imposes an indirect tax on the supply of a good with zero price elasticity of demand. Using a diagram, explain why consumers, not producers, could end up paying this tax.

11   Use a diagram to explain how producers and consumers might benefit from a government subsidy to an industry.

12   Explain why economists distinguish between the short run and the long run when examining how the costs of a firm behave as output increases.

13   Explain the difference between 'diseconomies of scale' in the short run and 'diminishing marginal returns' in the short run.

14   Explain why firms in a perfectly competitive market would be able to make only normal profits in the long run.

15   Under what circumstances might consumers benefit from monopoly?

16   A perfectly competitive industry is turned into a monopoly. Predict the possible effect on efficiency.

17   A monopoly firm decides to maximize profits rather than revenue. Using a diagram explain how price and quantity will change.

18   How might a firm be able to stay in business in the short run even if it is not covering all of its costs?

19   Explain the term 'cartel' and why they are considered unstable.

20   Explain why an oligopolistic firm may not wish to alter its prices.

21   A survey among 200 passengers in an aircraft reveals that people might have paid 50 different prices. Why has this happened?

22   In what ways might a company operating within an oligopolistic market structure attempt to increase its share in the market?

23   Explain how indirect taxation could be an appropriate response to the problem of negative externalities.

24   Use a diagram to explain why the underprovision of merit goods is considered to be an example of market failure.

25   What are the distinguishing features of a pure public good?

Macroeconomics

Macroeconomics examines issues relating to an economy as a whole, such as unemployment, inflation, growth and the balance of payments. The focus of macroeconomics is thus on *aggregate* economic variables.

Macroeconomic goals

Generally, governments and policymakers aim at achieving the following:

- satisfactory and *sustainable* real (non-inflationary) growth;
- price stability (which implies low or no inflation);
- high levels of employment (and low unemployment);
- long-run equilibrium in the balance of payments and the exchange rate (or, that the foreign sector should not impose a constraint on achieving domestic policy objectives);
- equitable (fair) distribution of income.

Measuring overall economic activity

Gross domestic product

Gross domestic product (GDP) is perhaps the single most important macroeconomic variable and it is defined as the value of all *final* goods and services produced *within* an economy over a certain period of time, usually a year or a quarter (by factors of production residing in the country).

Bear in mind that:

- Only final goods and services are included. Intermediate goods (goods used in the production of other goods) are not included. Only the 'value-added' (defined as the difference between the total revenues a firm collects from the sale of a good and the cost of raw materials, services and components the firm purchased to produce the

good) contributed by each firm is included. If *all* produced goods and services were included, double counting would result and thus overestimation of the true value of output.
- Used goods transactions (e.g. the sale of a used car) are not included since GDP measures current production.
- Financial transactions (such as the buying and selling of shares, etc.) are not included since they represent only transfer of ownership (of the financial asset) and they do not reflect a contribution to current production.
- Transfer payments (such as pensions and unemployment benefits) are not included since they do not reflect a contribution to current output.

Nominal GDP vs. real GDP

- Note that even though we are truly interested in an *output* measure, we are forced to sum *values* (prices times quantities) which makes our GDP measure dependent not only on output changes (in which we are interested) but also on price changes (which typically do not interest us).
- Thus comparison of GDP figures in successive years becomes a problem since, assuming that an increase in GDP is recorded, we cannot know whether the bigger figure is due to an increase in output of goods and services produced or whether it is due to an increase in prices (an increase in the general or average price level, i.e. due to inflation). In other words, we cannot know to what extent the increase in the nominal (money) GDP figure recorded is 'real' and to what extent it is 'inflationary'.
- For example, if GDP measured at current prices increased from one year to the next by 5.5%, it cannot be known what proportion of this increase is due to an output increase and what proportion is due to inflation. It could be, for example, that output increased by, say, 4% (i.e. real GDP increased by 4%) and that the remaining 1.5% was due to price level increases, i.e. inflation, or that output increased only by 0.5% and prices by 5.0%.

Thus:

- **Nominal GDP** (or money GDP, or GDP at current prices) is a measure of output of a certain period *valued at the prices prevailing in that same period.*
- **Real GDP** (or GDP at constant prices) is a measure of output of a certain period valued at the prices prevailing at some 'reference' period (known as the 'base' period or, base year). It is a measure of output *after having isolated (or adjusted for) the effect of inflation.* It is thus measured in terms of goods. *Real* GDP figures reflect the *volume* of production, not the *value.*
- To arrive at the real GDP figure for a certain year we divide nominal GDP of that year by a price index for that year (usually the retail or consumer price index) and multiply the result by 100:

Real GDP = (nominal GDP/price index) * 100

- Many other economic variables are also often adjusted for inflation. One of the most important for our purposes is the money (or nominal) wage rate, the payment to workers. The **real wage** is the wage rate adjusted for inflation and it is found by dividing it by the average level of prices. It thus measures what workers can actually buy with the money they earn. If a worker gets a 5% increase

Gross domestic product continued

in her money wage but prices of goods and services have also increased by 5% then her real wage has remained constant as she can buy on average exactly the same as before.

Measurement of GDP

There are three conceptually equivalent ways of arriving at the GDP figure for a country:

- the **output method**, where we add all domestically produced final goods and services;
- the **expenditure method**, where we add all expenditures made on domestically produced final goods and services;
- the **income method**, where we add all incomes generated in the domestic production process.

Conceptually the three methods are equivalent and, with some minor adjustments, the figures arrived at through each method are equal. The value of all output produced did not become thin air but ended up in 'pockets' in the form of wages, profits, interest or rent, i.e. as income to the factors of production involved. This income is then spent on this output. Each method is useful because of the breakdown it permits. The output method, for example, will give us the share of total output accounted for by each of the three sectors of an economy as well as the output of different industries. The expenditure method permits us to monitor the level of investment spending through time or the proportion of government expenditures in total economic activity. The income method provides information about the proportion of total income earned by labour in contrast to owners of capital.

Two minor accounting complications

Domestic output or income vs. national output or income

- Gross domestic product refers to output produced within the boundaries of a country independently of the nationality of the factors of production involved. Gross national product refers to the value of final output produced by domestically owned factors of production independently of where production actually takes place. For example, UK GNP figures will include the income earned by British multinational corporations abroad but will not include the income earned by foreign multinational corporations in the UK.
- To convert GDP to GNP:

GNP = GDP + Net Factor Income from Abroad

where Net Factor Income from Abroad = (income earned abroad – income paid abroad)

Gross vs. net

- Some portion of investment spending is aimed at replacing obsolete capital equipment (known as depreciation, or capital consumption). The stock of capital of an economy actually increases only by the difference between (gross) investment spending and depreciation.

Net Investment = Gross Investment – Capital Consumption

and

NNP = GNP – Depreciation

Problems in GDP measurement

- GDP measurement is fraught with problems.
- Official GDP figures in many countries understate the true level of economic activity because of the existence of a large parallel (or black, shadow) economy. Individuals in many countries underreport their incomes *to avoid taxation*. A heavy tax burden, especially high marginal (i.e. top) tax rates may be responsible for this tax-evading behaviour. Some productive activity may also be illegal per se (drugs, prostitution, etc.).

- Furthermore, 'do it yourself' activities are not included. If Joey repairs his car himself instead of taking it to the mechanic the value of the service he produces will not show up in official statistics.
- This becomes an important issue in the case of many developing countries because **subsistence farming** (defined as farming to feed one's family) is not included in GDP measurements, thus tending to underestimate per capita income levels.
- Lastly, data collection in many countries is poor and unreliable.

A timeline of macroeconomics

- The distinction between macroeconomics and microeconomics did not always exist. As a matter of fact, it is relatively new and started to be widely known only after World War II as a result of the publication in 1936 of the *General Theory of Employment, Interest and Money* written by John Maynard Keynes who transformed the theoretical landscape of economics.
- Figure 3.1 serves as a very broad guide to the evolution of ideas in macroeconomics and policymaking.

Figure 3.1 Timeline

| < 1870 | 1929 | 1936 | 1970 | 1980 | 1997 | 2008 > |

Pre-1929: The Classical School of thought: 'laissez-faire, laissez-passer'. Market forces guarantee that an economy will rest at, or close to full employment. There is thus no need for the government to intervene. **(non-activists)**

Keynes's 'General Theory' is published in 1936. There is no guarantee that a market economy will rest at 'full employment'. Thus, there is an active role for the government. Through fiscal policy the government can stabilize the economy and achieve full employment. **Keynesian interventionist** ideas reign after WWII until the mid 1970s. **(activists)**

In the 1970s, **Monetarism** emerges at the **University of Chicago** with Nobel Prize laureate **Milton Friedman** being the most widely-known advocate of monetarist ideas. Monetarists slowly deconstructed the Keynesian edifice, initially doubting the effectiveness of fiscal policy and later suggesting that even monetary policy should be avoided. Markets 'rule'.

In the 1980s the **Rational Expectations School (New Classical)** of thought through the work of **Lucas, Sargent** and others emerges; the **Supply Side** is emphasized. The role of the government is further questioned and reliance on market forces is further emphasized.

The **General Theory** was written in response to the **Great Depression** which started in 1929 and marked the greatest and longest contraction of output and employment in the 20th century.

The **East Asian crisis** in 1997-8 cast doubts on extreme pro-market policies and on the **'Washington Consensus'**. Many speak of the necessity to *manage* globalization. Inequalities within and between countries are rising.

The concept of equilibrium in economics

- Essentially, the concept means the same as in the sciences: a system is considered to be in equilibrium if there are no inherent (endogenous) forces inducing change.
- In our case, an economy (or economic activity, i.e. national income, GDP) is considered to be in equilibrium if there is no tendency for it to change (i.e. for the level of total output to rise or fall).
- In equilibrium, aggregate demand (AD; see below) is equal to aggregate supply (AS; see page 67) or, as explained on page 69, injections (J) must equal withdrawals (W).

Introducing aggregate demand and aggregate supply

Aggregate demand

- The term **aggregate demand** (AD) refers to total spending on domestic goods and services.
- Spending can originate either from the **private sector** (households and firms) or from the **public sector**.
- Private sector spending includes consumption expenditures (C) that households make and investment expenditures (I) that firms make.
- The public sector expenditures are usually termed government expenditures (G) in which both consumption and capital public spending are included.
- Spending on domestic goods can also originate from abroad. These are the exports (X) of an economy. Since some of domestic spending is on foreign goods, imports (M) are subtracted to arrive at aggregate demand.

AD = C + I + G + (X − M)

- The aggregate demand curve (Fig. 3.2) is downward sloping but not for the same reasons that the demand for a single good is downward sloping, as on the vertical axis we have the average price of all goods and not of one good. In macroeconomics aggregate demand is negatively sloped because, as the average price level increases, planned spending decreases because people feel poorer and domestic products become less competitive abroad.

Figure 3.2 The aggregate demand curve

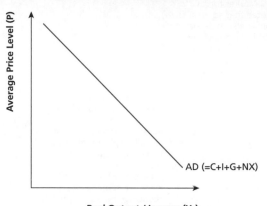

Tips

Draw the AD either as a straight line or slightly curved. It is easier though to draw it with a ruler. Make sure you fully label the axes. The vertical is not 'price' but the 'average price level' as it is aggregate demand and not demand for one good or a service. The horizontal is often denoted as 'Q'. This should be avoided as it again may lead to confusion. 'GDP' should also be avoided as GDP refers to the actual output produced and not to planned output. 'Real output/income' and Yr are often considered an appropriate choice. Remember that output and income are conceptually identical terms.

Aggregate supply

- **Aggregate supply** is defined as the planned level of output per period at different price levels.
- The shape of aggregate supply is controversial in macroeconomics.
- It is instructive to initially distinguish between the long run (when all adjustments have been made) and the short run (when only some adjustments are possible).
- In the long run, aggregate supply of an economy is constrained by the amount of its resources and by its technology. As a result, long-run aggregate supply (LRAS) is considered fixed (vertical) at the 'full employment' level of output where all resources are employed.
- Typically, in the short run though, AS can rise since firms will be willing to offer more if prices rise but money wages increase at a slower rate.
- The slope of the AS determines to what extent a rise (i.e. a shift to the right) of AD will be expressed as a rise in real output and thus employment and to what extent it will be expressed as a rise in prices (i.e. inflation). See Fig. 3.3.

Figure 3.3 The short-run aggregate supply: the typical case

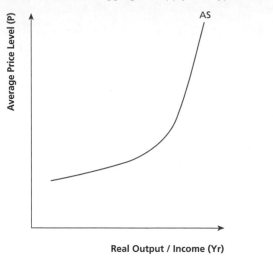

Variations in aggregate supply

The extreme Keynesian aggregate supply curve

- For an economy that is operating significantly below the full employment level of output, the extreme Keynesian aggregate supply is assumed perfectly elastic at the prevailing average price level.
- 'Operating significantly below full employment' means that there are very many workers eager to work but unable to find a job as well as many machines and factories available that are not being used.
- Thus, any increase in aggregate demand will be expressed as a rise in real output without any increase in the average price level. The expansion of output can take place without firms having to offer higher wage rates to attract more workers and face higher costs.
- Once the economy reached the full employment level of output Yfe as in Fig. 3.4 then AS would become vertical.
- Any further increase in aggregate demand cannot lead to an expansion of output as there are no more factors available to employ. The increase in aggregate demand will only lead to a higher price level.

Figure 3.4 The aggregate supply curve: extreme Keynesian case

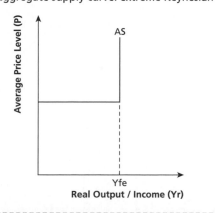

The intermediate Keynesian aggregate supply curve

- It is more plausible to consider that, as aggregate demand increases, some industries will reach capacity levels of output before others. An economy after all consists of many different industries each employing many different types of factors of production. Engineers, for example, may be in shorter supply than bricklayers.
- This implies that, following an increase in AD, output in the economy can continue to increase but prices will also be increasing giving rise to an 'intermediate' upward sloping section HF on the aggregate supply curve as in Fig. 3.5.
- As the economy is getting closer and closer to the full employment level of output Yfe the aggregate supply curve becomes steeper and steeper. At the full employment level of output it becomes vertical.

Figure 3.5 The intermediate Keynesian aggregate supply curve

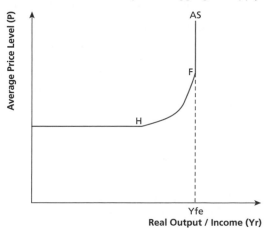

Variations in aggregate supply continued

The classical (and extreme monetarist) aggregate supply curve

- The Classical School as well as the extreme Monetarists viewed the economy as producing whatever its resources and technology would permit.
- Aggregate supply would thus be vertical, as in Fig. 3.6, at the full employment level of output and any change in aggregate demand would only affect the price level and no real variable.

Figure 3.6 The aggregate supply curve: the classical and extreme monetarist case

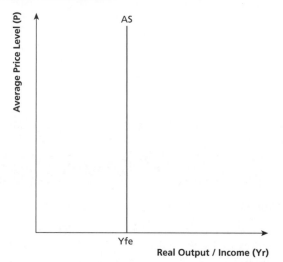

The long-run aggregate supply curve

- In the long run, defined as the period when all adjustments are possible and money wages are flexible, the aggregate supply curve is vertical at the full employment (capacity) level of output as shown in Fig. 3.7. It can be thought of as roughly the equivalent of the production possibilities frontier.

Figure 3.7 The long-run aggregate supply curve

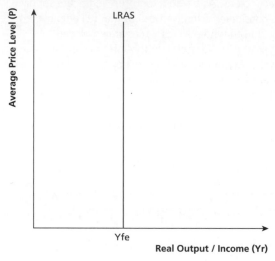

Which AS do I use?

- The answer is 'it depends'! Typically one should employ an upward sloping AS as in Fig. 3.3 or in section HF of Fig. 3.5. It shows that an increase in aggregate demand will lead to an increase in the average price level (inflation) as well as to an increase in real output and thus employment. It also shows that the effect on the average price level of a rise in AD is more pronounced the steeper the AS becomes or, in other words, the closer to capacity (to full employment) an economy is operating.

- On the other hand, if one wishes to illustrate an economy in long-run equilibrium when all adjustments are made, then a vertical AS at the full employment level of output is in order (Fig. 3.7).
- Lastly, the extreme Keynesian (Fig. 3.4; horizontal up until Yfe) and the extreme Monetarist (Fig. 3.6; as well as Classical and New Classical) cases could be employed only if one wishes to show the differences in these schools of economic thought.

Injections and withdrawals in the circular flow model

- The **circular flow model** is a simplified representation of how the basic decision-making units of an economy (households, firms, the government and, in an 'open' economy, the foreign sector) interact. It describes the flows between these units.
- At the most basic version, where there are only households and firms, it is understood that households own the factors of production which they offer to firms. In exchange, firms offer payments for these factors in the form of wages, rents, interest and profits, the sum of which is defined as income. Firms combine these factors to produce goods and services which they offer to households in return for payments that constitute consumption expenditures on domestically produced goods.

- Also, part of income may be saved (a 'withdrawal' from this system) while firms will also spend on capital goods (= investment spending). This latter expenditure is an 'injection' to the system.
- For equilibrium to exist, injections (investment spending) must equal withdrawals (savings).
- If the government and a foreign sector are added then injections also include government spending on domestically produced goods and services as well as expenditures that foreigners make on our goods (= exports), while withdrawals also include expenditures that domestic entities make on foreign goods (= imports) as well as taxes the government collects.

The trade or business cycle

- The ups and downs (phases) through time of the level of overall economic activity (in other words of real GDP) are referred to as the **trade cycle** (or **business cycle**). More formally, the business cycle is defined as the short-run fluctuations of real GDP around its long-run trend.
- Periods of expansion ('booms') are followed by periods of contraction (**recession**, busts). The downturn's major characteristic is increasing levels of unemployment. If on the other hand expansion is 'too rapid' it *may* give rise to inflationary pressures. Ideally, steady, sustainable, non-inflationary long-term growth would be desirable.
- The economy depicted in Fig. 3.8 is a growing economy. Growth exists when total output rises through time; a sustained increase in real GDP. It follows that this economy is growing between time period t2 and t3 but also over the long run as the 'trend line' is upward sloping. The trend line reflects the average annual long-run growth of the economy.
- Between time t1 and t2 the economy is in recession. Real GDP is decreasing (technically, for at least two consecutive quarters) and thus the economy is registering negative growth rates. At t1 it was at a peak (as well as at t3). At t2 it is at a trough and it is about to enter recovery.
- Note that if the growth rate is decreasing (from, say, 2.1% to 0.8%) real GDP continues to increase but at a slower and slower rate. Various expressions are used to describe this phase, e.g. 'the economy is losing steam' or 'it is peaking out' 'approaching recession'. An economy about to enter recession is, in Fig. 3.8, somewhere just to the right of a peak.

- Lastly, the idea of potential GDP (when all resources are fully employed) can be illustrated either as a peak-to-peak line or as a separate line located slightly above all peaks in the trade (business) cycle diagram.

Figure 3.8 The trade (or business) cycle

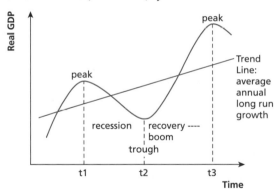

Tip

Make sure that after you finish drawing the trade cycle there is only *one* level of real GDP corresponding to *each* time period t. A common error is to draw it in such a way that at each point 't' on the horizontal axis there are more than one corresponding levels of real GDP.

The components of aggregate demand

Consumption expenditures

- **Consumption expenditures** (C) are made by households on goods and services. In many advanced economies consumption expenditures are the largest component (about 60% or more) of aggregate demand. In other economies this proportion is significantly lower.

Several factors may affect spending by households and lead to a shift in AD. The most important factors include:

- **Consumer confidence**
  Households feeling secure and confident about their future will tend to spend more. A stable and growing economy with low inflation and unemployment will boost consumer confidence and thus favorably affect household spending, shifting AD to the right. On the other hand, uncertainty over future job prospects and insecurity about one's future income adversely affect present consumption. Spending on durable goods, such as cars and appliances, as well as on housing, are greatly affected by consumer moods.

- **Interest rates** (the price of borrowing money over a period of time)
  Lower interest rates (i.e. easy **monetary policy**) will tend to increase consumption expenditures, and consequently the overall level of aggregate demand, shifting the AD curve to the right. This may happen because:

  - Consumer durable goods (cars, appliances, furniture, etc.) are usually purchased on credit. Lower interest rates mean that borrowing to finance these purchases is now cheaper for households.

- The single largest expenditure of a typical household is the purchase of its house. Households borrow from banks to finance this purchase and these specialized very long-term loans are known as mortgage loans. The interest rate charged on such loans is often 'adjustable', meaning that if market interest rates decrease, mortgage rates will also decrease and so will the monthly payments. Households with such housing loans will thus have more money available every month to spend on goods and services.

- A drop in interest rates will make saving (defined as income not spent on goods and services) less attractive so households will tend to save less and spend more.

- **The level of consumer indebtedness**
  If private (household) debt (from taking out loans, mortgages for house purchase, and/or credit card spending) has accumulated, household spending is bound to decline as they will need to pay more and more to service their debt.

- **Wealth**
  The total value of a household's assets may affect the level of its spending. If, for example, wealth increases then consumption will be positively affected. A stock market boom or rising property values tends to increase spending and lower savings.

Investment spending

- **Investment spending** (I) is defined as spending by firms on capital goods and is thus equal to the change in the stock of capital of an economy over a period. When firms spend to acquire **capital** (K) we say that they invest. Investment is important both because of its short-run influence on aggregate demand and because in the long run it affects aggregate supply and thus the rate of (actual and potential) growth of an economy. Investment spending is the most volatile component of aggregate demand.

Factors affecting investment spending

- **Interest rates**
  Investment spending requires funds, which are either borrowed from the banks or are part of past-retained firm profits. If firms borrow, they will be charged interest on the loan, while if they use their own funds, they will sacrifice the return (interest) that they would have earned from investing the funds. Consequently, a fall in the market interest rate will tend to increase investment spending in the economy as at lower interest rates more investment projects will be considered profitable.

If one plots investment spending against the market interest rate as in Fig. 3.9, the function will be negatively sloped. How responsive investment spending of firms is to a change in interest rates (i.e. how elastic) is an empirical issue.

Figure 3.9 Investment spending and interest rates

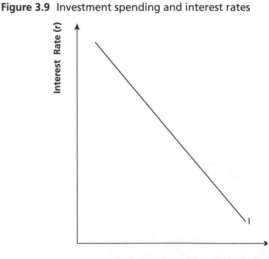

Investment spending continued

- **Business confidence**
  The greater the degree of business confidence in an economy, the more willing firms will be to invest and expand. Economic and political stability are necessary for investments to take place. J. M. Keynes considered the behaviour of entrepreneurs with respect to private investment decisions similar to that of a herd ('imitation') and, in his opinion, the observed instability of investments was due to these 'animal spirits'. Expectations can be changed radically by a host of unpredictable factors leading to wild swings in the prevailing business climate and thus to changes in the level of investment spending.
- **Public policy toward investment**
  Governments often attempt to influence investment by offering tax incentives to firms, subsidies, preferential loan terms, protection from foreign competition, etc. Note that the size itself of the public sector in an economy may influence the growth of private investment. Also bear in mind that 'institutions' affect private investments. A large bureaucracy (of 'red tape') and complicated regulations burden the operation of firms in a country and negatively affect the rate of investment. Investment levels are, ceteris paribus, higher in countries with low levels of bureaucracy and with transparent economic and business environments. Lastly, corruption adversely affects investment, especially foreign direct investment (investments by multinational corporations in foreign countries).
- **The overall macroeconomic environment**
  A 'sound' macroeconomic environment where policymakers ensure low inflation, low budget deficits, sustainable public debt and flexible labour markets usually leads to higher rates of investment spending.
- **Income and its growth**
  Rising income leads to rising consumption and thus may induce more investments as firms may be forced to increase their capacity to meet this increased demand for goods and services. This is the idea of the 'accelerator' principle discussed below.

The accelerator principle ##HL

- The accelerator is a theory aiming at explaining the level of investment in an economy.
- This theory claims that the level of investment depends on *changes* in national income (more generally, changes in output, in demand, or in sales).
- It provides an additional reason for the observed instability of investment spending and, together with the multiplier (explained later), it is a theory explaining the existence of the business (trade) cycle.
- It is considered part of Keynesian theory even though Keynes himself considered expectations (animal spirits) much more important.
- The accelerator rests on the assumption that firms wish to maintain a fixed capital to output ratio.

For example, a shoemaker needs one new machine for every 10,000 extra pairs produced. If sales rise by 20,000 then he will need to change his stock of capital by two extra machines to maintain the fixed capital to output ratio. Investment in that period would thus equal two machines.

- Generalizing for an economy, it follows that for annual investment to remain stable total sales (total output or national income) have to be rising at a constant rate. If output (or income; remember they mean the same thing as the one is the flip side of the other) continues to rise but at a slower rate (thus, if growth just slows down) investment will decrease.
- Investment is thus a very volatile component of AD.

Government spending

- **Government spending (G)** is in many economies a large part of total spending on goods and services.
- Government spending is distinguished into **current** spending on goods and services, **capital** (public investment) spending which refers to spending on roads, ports, telecommunications, schools and other infrastructure and also on **transfer payments** which basically refer to pensions and unemployment benefits.
- Note that transfer payments are not included in national income since they do not represent rewards for current productive effort.
- Governments spend to ensure that adequate amounts of public and merit goods and services are consumed such as national defence, educational services and health services. They spend to regulate markets in their attempt to guarantee product safety, environmental standards, competitive conditions, etc. They may also spend to redistribute income so that a socially acceptable minimum is guaranteed. Such spending includes state pensions, unemployment benefits, subsidies, disability benefits, etc.
- Lastly, they spend to affect aggregate demand. By increasing or decreasing government spending, aggregate demand will increase or decrease, shifting to the right or to the left. This is part of what is known as **fiscal policy**.

Government spending continued

(Net) export demand (NX, or X–M)

- Foreigners spend to buy domestically produced goods and services but since part of domestic spending is on imports it follows that aggregate demand is affected and shifts when net exports change, the difference between export revenues and import spending.

- Many factors can change the level of net exports and thus shift AD, such as the exchange rate and the extent of protectionism.

A closer examination of aggregate supply

Adverse supply shocks

- These are changes that negatively affect a country's productive capacity. They result in a shift to the left of the aggregate supply curve. A sharp and sustained increase in the price of oil is a typical such example. Oil is the principal form of energy and is used as an input by virtually all firms. Its significance though has decreased in advanced economies in recent years as a bigger proportion of GDP originates from the tertiary sector (services). A bank needs less oil to operate than a car manufacturer. Another example of an adverse supply shock is general increase in wage costs for firms as a result of powerful labour (trade) unions. A broad increase in indirect taxation or higher commodity (raw material) prices are also possible sources of such adverse supply shocks. Lastly, natural catastrophes (such as those resulting from the tsunami a few years ago or from an earthquake or a hurricane), wars, major terrorist attacks and institutional setbacks may shrink the productive capacity of an economy and shift AS to the left.

- An adverse supply shock can be illustrated either by leftward shift of an upward sloping short-run aggregate supply curve or by leftward shift of a vertical long-run aggregate supply curve as it does not make much of a difference. As a broad rule, input or factor price-related supply shocks should be preferably illustrated with a short-run upward sloping aggregate supply curve shifting left. Thus, the effect on an economy of a sharp and sustained increase of the price of oil can be better shown through Fig. 3.10.

- On the other hand, if the adverse shock is because of a natural catastrophe or an institutional setback (e.g. a new government nationalizes most industries or proves prone to corruption) this is perhaps best illustrated by shifting leftward a vertical at the full employment level of output long-run aggregate supply curve, as in Fig. 3.11.

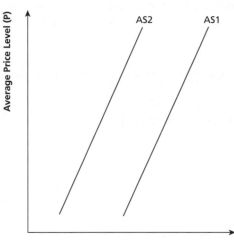

Figure 3.10 An adverse supply shock as a result of higher oil prices

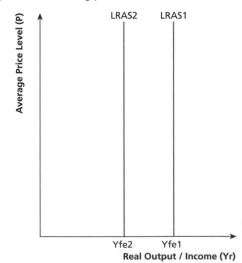

Figure 3.11 An adverse supply shock as a result of a corrupt government taking power

How could aggregate supply shift to the right?

- A rightward shift in aggregate supply is a positive development for an economy as it implies an increase in its productive capacity. Since it is conceptually equivalent to an outward shift of the production possibilities frontier of an economy, any factor responsible for shifting outward the production possibilities frontier of an economy will also shift its AS curve to the right.

- First of all, the productive capacity of an economy may increase and its aggregate supply shift to the right if human and physical capital increase. Investment as well as more and better education and health services increases labour productivity (output per worker) and thus aggregate supply. Technological advancements (e.g. the assembly line or the internet) and an improved institutional framework (including a better legal system, simplified business rules and regulations, better banking practices, credible policymaking and more generally 'good governance') both lead to a rightward shift of the aggregate supply. Lastly, more 'land' (through discovery, as in the case of oil reserves or annexation) would also do the job.

- A rightward shift of a vertical long-run AS curve should be employed but it is acceptable to use an upward sloping aggregate supply curve as well.

- Obviously governments attempt to and can influence the supply side of an economy. Few would disagree that a government can increase aggregate supply by improving health care services and education. Or, for that matter, that public investment in infrastructure would have the same effect as it creates significant external benefits to firms in the form of lower production costs. But beyond these obvious choices there is considerable disagreement, which will be discussed later in the section on supply-side policies.

- Note that rarely a shift to the right of AS can be a source of significant problems if this increase in the productive capacity of an economy is not matched by increases in spending on domestic output i.e. on AD as it may lead to deflation (examined later). Also, the discovery of a natural resource such as oil can be a mixed blessing as many countries have found out.

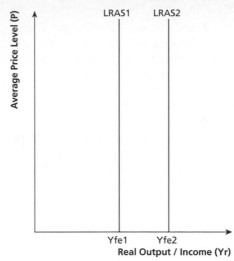

Figure 3.12 A rightward shift in aggregate supply

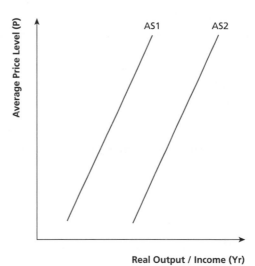

The effects of AD/AS shifts

The AD–AS framework

- The aggregate demand–aggregate supply framework is very simple but also very useful. Movements of the average price level and of real output provide information on three major policy goals. **Inflation** (and **deflation**) as well as growth can be directly illustrated on the diagram while changes in employment and unemployment can be indirectly inferred.

- It follows that *if government is in a position to affect aggregate demand* then it may be in a position to achieve the macroeconomic goals mentioned in the very beginning.

Effects of a rightward shift in aggregate demand in the extreme Keynesian case

Aggregate supply in this case is horizontal up until the full employment level of output Yfe where it becomes vertical.

Let Yfe be the full employment level of output. If aggregate demand is at AD1 then equilibrium output is at Y1 which is way below the full employment level. In the Keynesian framework, equilibrium output is 'demand-driven', meaning that it is aggregate demand which determines how much the economy will be producing and thus the level of national income. As a result:

- Equilibrium income (output) does not need to correspond to full employment of resources (see Fig. 3.13).
- A **deflationary (or recessionary) gap** equal to distance fh in Fig. 3.13 results. A deflationary (or recessionary) gap exists when equilibrium output is less than full employment output.
- If aggregate demand somehow increased to AD* then the economy will have reached full employment.
- Expansionary demand-side policies can lift an economy out of a recession without any inflation resulting.

On the other hand, if aggregate demand increases past AD* to AD2, then inflation results without any further increase in output and employment. Distance hj is known as an **inflationary gap**.

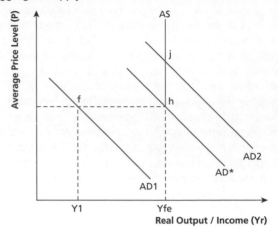

Figure 3.13 The extreme Keynesian case: perfectly elastic aggregate supply

Effects of a rightward shift in aggregate demand in the extreme Monetarist case

Aggregate supply in this case is perfectly inelastic (vertical) at the full employment level of output, reflecting the belief that an economy will always be in equilibrium at the full employment level of output.

- Aggregate demand in this case does not determine 'real' variables, such as how much output the economy will produce, or what the level of employment will be. Real output is determined by the quantity and quality of available resources and by technology.
- Aggregate demand only determines the average price level. In Fig. 3.14, if aggregate demand increases from AD1 to AD2, then real output will remain at Yfe and only inflation will result as the average price level will rise from P1 to P2.
- It follows that expansionary demand-side policies are totally ineffective in increasing real output and employment and can only prove inflationary. In the long run, the equilibrium level of real output can be increased only through policies aiming at the supply side of the economy.

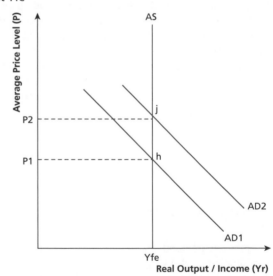

Figure 3.14 The extreme monetarist case: vertical AS curve at Yfe

Effects of a rightward shift in aggregate demand in the intermediate case

Aggregate supply in Fig. 3.15 is drawn upward sloping, reflecting the typical case. Originally, equilibrium is assumed at the intersection of AD1 and AS with Y1 being the equilibrium level or real output and P1 the average price level.

- An increase in aggregate demand from AD1 to AD2 can succeed in increasing real output from Y1 to Y2 and thus employment, but at a cost. The average price level is higher at P2 so inflation is the price paid.
- The extent to which an increase in aggregate demand will be expressed as growth of output or inflation depends on how close to capacity the economy is operating, in other words on how steep it is.
- This diagram thus reveals that demand-side policies can be used to raise output and employment but at the cost of higher inflation, or to lower inflation but at the cost of slower growth or recession.

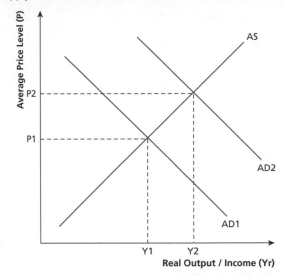

Figure 3.15 The intermediate case: upward-sloping aggregate supply curve

Effects of a rightward shift in aggregate supply

The possible effect of policy attempts to increase aggregate supply are illustrated in Fig. 3.16.

- It is assumed that aggregate demand is rising through time from AD1 to AD2. If somehow policymakers are successful in increasing aggregate supply of the economy then they will have achieved a rise in output without a rise in the average price level, i.e. non-inflationary growth.

Tip

One can employ typical upward-sloping AS curves (AS1 to AS2) to arrive at this result but it is preferable to use long-run vertical aggregate supply curves (LRAS1 to LRAS2) as this shows that the **full employment level of output** will have increased.

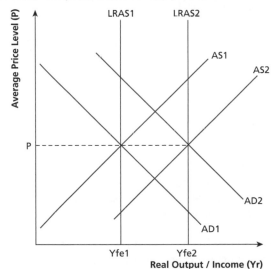

Figure 3.16 The possible role of supply-side policies

Demand-side policies

- Demand-side policies attempt to increase or decrease (or, more precisely, to slow down the increase) in aggregate demand in order to affect output (growth), employment and the average price level (later it will be shown that these same policies are also used to correct a trade imbalance and are referred to as expenditure-changing policies).

- They are distinguished into **fiscal policy** and **monetary policy**. Fiscal policy refers to the manipulation of the level of government expenditures and/or of taxes while monetary policy refers to changes in interest rates.

Fiscal policy

Expansionary (reflationary) fiscal policy

- Keynes introduced the idea that the (equilibrium) level of output was demand-driven. The level of aggregate demand determines the level of overall economic activity. There is thus no guarantee that equilibrium output and full employment output will coincide. There could very well be a deflationary gap (see Figs 3.13 and 3.33). Aggregate demand could be insufficient if, for whatever reason, the private sector (households and firms) decides to hold back on their spending. A recession could thus result. He thus introduced the idea of expansionary fiscal policy (see below).
- Expansionary (reflationary) fiscal policy aims at increasing aggregate demand to increase national income and employment and thus close a deflationary gap.
- It requires an increase in government spending and a decrease in taxation.
- Since government spending is a component of AD, a rise in G will directly increase AD, shifting it to the right.
- In other words, if private spending (C + I) is not sufficient to generate full employment then the government should increase its spending (G) by borrowing from the private sector (deficit spending, G > T).

- A decrease in **taxation (T)** will indirectly also increase AD as it will increase disposable income (defined as income minus direct taxes) that people have and induce more spending.

Contractionary (deflationary) fiscal policy

- On the other hand, an overheating economy, defined as an economy where aggregate demand is rapidly increasing creating inflationary pressures, requires contractionary fiscal policy.
- The government must decrease government expenditures and increase taxes so that AD decreases.

In summary

- **Expansionary fiscal policy**: raise G and lower T (deficit spending) to increase AD and thus income and employment.
- **Contractionary fiscal policy**: lower G and increase T to decrease AD and thus inflationary pressures.

The multiplier effect

Expansionary fiscal policy according to the Keynesian school is very powerful tool to lift an economy out of a recession as a result of the operation of the multiplier effect.

- Assume that a government wishing to close a deflationary gap decides to increase its expenditures by some amount, say, ΔG (the difference between the new level of spending and the original level of spending).
- Aggregate demand will automatically increase by ΔG and shift from AD1 to AD2 as in Fig. 3.17. But according to the multiplier effect the process will not end there. Aggregate demand will continue to increase and shift to the right all the way to AD3.
- The multiplier effect states that an increase in government expenditures (or, more generally, in any injection) will lead to a greater change in income: $\Delta Y = \kappa \Delta G$, where ΔY is the resulting change in income, ΔG is the change in government spending and κ is the multiplier.

Why will national income increase by more than the increase in government expenditures? The explanation rests on two ideas:

- One person's spending is automatically someone else's income.
- Economic activity takes place in successive rounds.

Figure 3.17 The multiplier effect

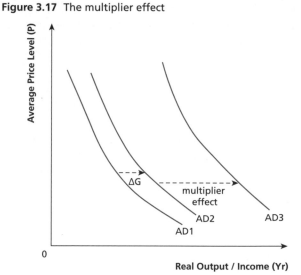

The multiplier effect continued

Example

- Assume that the government decides to increase expenditures by 10,000,000 pounds and hires some unemployed workers to dig holes and bury bottles and other unemployed workers to dig them up. National income has increased by 10,000,000 pounds, the income that these workers earned for the 'service' they produced. Spending by the government is income for the workers.
- But, economic activity will not stop there. There is a second and a third and an nth round that follow. Why? Because these workers will spend *part* of this extra income on domestic goods and services that others produce and the process will continue.
- If extra spending on domestic goods and services is constant and equal to 0.8 (80%) of any extra income then national income will rise by 50,000,000 pounds.

How does one arrive at this figure?

- Define the extra spending on domestic goods induced by extra income earned as the marginal propensity to consume (MPC_d) domestic goods. The multiplier κ is equal to:

$$1/(1 - MPC_d)$$

- In the example the MPCd is assumed to be 0.8 (as 8 million pounds are spent out of 10 million pounds of extra income) it follows that the multiplier κ is equal to 5. Given that the initial increase in government spending is 10,000,000 and that $\Delta Y = \kappa \Delta G$, the increase in income is equal to 5 times 10 million pounds, i.e. 50 million pounds.
- Since only 8 out of the 10 million were spent on domestic goods it follows that 2 million were not spent. This income not spent on domestic goods must have been spent on foreign goods (imports) or paid in taxes or simply saved.
- Import expenditures, tax payments and savings are all withdrawals in the circular flow model.
- It follows that $(1 - MPC_d)$ is the marginal propensity to withdraw (MPW) so if $\kappa = 1/(1 - MPC_d)$ it is also equal to $1/(MPW)$ or $1/(MPM + MRT + MPS)$ where MPM is the marginal propensity to spend on imports, MRT is the marginal rate of taxation and MPS is the marginal propensity to save.
- The multiplier effect is greater, the greater the proportion of any increase in income that is spent on domestic goods and services or the smaller the proportion of any increase in income that is saved, spent on imports or taxed by the government.

Tips

Note that one mechanism through which trade cycles are transmitted internationally is the export multiplier. A recession in the US economy will lead to lower US imports and thus lower European and, say, Japanese exports. Depending on the size of this decrease as well as on the openness of these economies, economic activity in Europe and Japan will be adversely affected (their AD will shrink) and this effect will be magnified through the export multiplier which is the change in national income resulting from a change in export revenues.

Also, note that the effect is not instantaneous as there is a time lag between receipt of income and subsequent spending.

Evaluating fiscal policy

Fiscal policy can be useful and has been used successfully in the past and even recently in the US. It suffers though from several disadvantages that were exposed mostly by the monetarists and which weaken its effectiveness or may even transform it to a source of macroeconomic instability. More specifically:

- Fiscal policy is characterized by long and potentially destabilizing **time lags**. These refer to the time between when an economy 'gets sick' (enters a recession) and the time the 'medicine' (the expansionary fiscal policy administered) has an impact (full employment is restored). It may thus be the case that by the time the impact of a policy switch is felt, the economy has already moved on to a new cycle phase destabilizing rather than stabilizing economic activity.
- Fiscal policy has an **expansionary bias**. The cyclical nature of economic activity would require that governments alternate between contractionary and expansionary fiscal policy. But politicians in power who are responsible for economic policy may in general be reluctant to cut government expenditures and raise taxes as this choice could drastically decrease their popularity.

- **Contractionary fiscal policy** is difficult to employ not only because of reluctant politicians but also because certain public expenditures are considered inelastic by society. Decreasing government expenditures on health, education or social security may be considered socially unacceptable; defence expenditures are also often difficult to cut. On the other hand, increasing taxation beyond a point will adversely affect incentives (see Laffer curve, page 92).
- Expansionary fiscal policy may lead to a **widening trade deficit**; if a higher level of income results then more imports will be absorbed, while if the average price level increases then exports will shrink as they become less competitive and imports will rise as they become relatively more attractive.
- (HL Only): Expansionary fiscal policy and deficit spending may end up *crowding out* private investment and thus be less effective. The resulting **budget deficit** must somehow be financed. Government borrowing from financial markets may drive interest rates up and as a result private investment will decrease (and so will consumption expenditures). If this decrease in private spending matches the increased government spending, the crowding-out is said to be complete and fiscal policy is totally ineffective.

The crowding-out effect

- Crowding-out is a monetarist criticism of Keynesian inspired expansionary fiscal policy.
- If the government increases government spending by ΔG then, as a result of the multiplier effect, AD will rise from AD1 all the way to AD2. Fiscal policy thus seems, according the Keynesian School, like a very powerful tool to reflate an economy in recession. Not so, claim the monetarists. The increased government spending and resulting greater budget deficit *needs to be financed* (e.g. how can a government spend €850m when it earns from taxes only €700m? It must somehow borrow the missing €150m). If the government borrows (by selling bonds to the non-bank private sector) then interest rates may rise (as there is going to be greater demand for loanable funds) as shown in Fig. 3.19.
- If interest rates increase from r1 to r2 then private sector investment spending may decrease (see Fig. 3.9). Consumption expenditures may also decrease. Since AD includes not only G but also C and I it may not after all increase to AD2 but only (if, at all) to AD3 as shown in Fig. 3.18. Expansionary fiscal policy is thus not as powerful as was thought.

Tip

The effects of **crowding out** also depend on the type of government expenditures financed. If capital (investment) expenditures are financed then, given that infrastructure investments may create substantial positive externalities to private firms, economic growth may even accelerate. This is an especially valid argument for developing countries where improved infrastructure is much needed and is considered complementary to market forces. Also, if the budget deficit is financed by foreigners then domestic interest rates may not increase (but other problems may result).

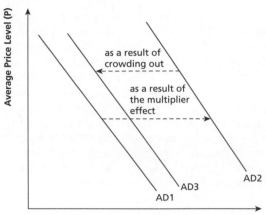

Figure 3.18 The crowding-out effect

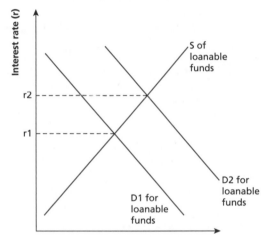

Figure 3.19 The loanable funds market and the effect of government borrowing on interest rates

Monetary policy

Expansionary (easy or loose) monetary policy

- If an economy is about to enter recession or if it already is suffering negative growth rates then policymakers (the central bank or the government) may decrease interest rates (r) in an attempt to increase aggregate demand and thus output and employment. How does it work? How are lower interest rates expected to reflate a failing economy? It is hoped that aggregate demand will increase as consumption expenditures, investment expenditures as well as net exports will tend to rise.
- Consumption expenditures of households will tend to increase, as
  - borrowing to finance the purchase of durables (cars, appliances, etc.) becomes cheaper so spending on such goods may increase;
  - reduced interest rates mean lower monthly payments on variable rate mortgage loans so households will have more available to spend in general;
  - the lower rate of return will make saving less attractive so households will tend to spend more.
- Investment spending by firms will tend to increase as borrowing costs to finance purchases of capital goods (equipment) and expansions (new factories) are lower. Also, lower interest rates imply that the opportunity cost to firms of using their own past retained profits to finance investments is also lower.
- Lastly, as a result of lower interest rates the exchange rate will tend to depreciate so exports will become more competitive abroad and imports less attractive domestically, increasing AD.

Monetary policy continued

Contractionary (tight) monetary policy

- Assume an overheating economy in which inflation is becoming a problem. Policymakers (the central bank or the government) may increase interest rates in an attempt to decrease AD. Aggregate demand is expected to decrease as higher interest rates will work in the opposite direction as the one described above. Saving will become more attractive, borrowing costs will rise for households and firms and the exchange rate will tend to appreciate, rendering exports pricier and thus less attractive to foreigners.

Evaluation of monetary policy

- Central banking is both an art and a science: the timing of an interest rate change, the statements issued by the central bank, the size of the interest rate change are all crucial for the success of any policy change. There are very many factors that determine the extent to which a policy response will or will not be successful. In general, monetary policy is extensively used throughout the world to regulate the strength of total spending on domestic goods and services. It is considered rather flexible as central banks can alter interest rates often, they can alter them gradually and they can also reverse any decision.

On the other hand, it is also characterized by several problems.

- Most importantly, spending by both households and firms does not depend only on interest rates. Consumption and investment expenditures depend on a host of other factors. The degree of consumer and business confidence is extremely important in determining the response of spending to a change in interest rates as well as is the degree of household and firm indebtedness. For example, let the central bank lower interest rates in an attempt to prevent a recession. If businesses are pessimistic and/or if households are already burdened by heavy debts there is no guarantee that they will be tempted by lower interest rates to borrow and spend more, and so the policy may fail.
- Also, if the borrowing rate is already too low (close to zero) then it cannot be lowered any further as negative interest rates do not make any sense.
- Monetary policy is also characterized by potentially destabilizing time lags, just like fiscal policy. These time lags may be shorter but they are variable, creating uncertainty as to the success of any policy change.
- Under a fixed exchange rate system monetary policy is ineffective. Interest rate changes have to be used only to ensure that the exchange rate remains fixed at the chosen level.
- Today, financial markets are largely global so most firms and even households can and do borrow from anywhere in the world. These developments weaken the effectiveness of monetary policy.

Supply-side policies

- Supply-side policies are policies that aim at increasing the aggregate supply of an economy, shifting the AS curve to the right as illustrated in Fig. 3.16, page 75.
- One may group supply-side policies into a set which includes measures that all will agree are crucial in enhancing the productive capacity of an economy and into another set that includes more controversial measures.

Commonly accepted supply-side policies

- Improving education (especially primary and secondary where the rate of return is the highest) or making education universal will improve labour productivity and increase AS.
- Better health services made available to the general population would also have the same effect.
- A government providing better infrastructure will also boost the supply side. 'Build yourself a road to get rich' is an old saying and it expresses a universal truth. Roads, harbours, airports, telecommunications, all serve to lower production costs of all firms in a country.

- Lastly, improving the institutional framework would also serve to improve productivity and the supply side of an economy. Unfortunately, there is no unique set of laws, rules and regulations that can be transplanted to any economy and prove optimal. Russia's lost decade following the attempt in the early 1990s to create a market economy contrasted with the recent Chinese experience illustrate the point.

More controversial supply-side policies

Pro-market supply-side policies

The second and more controversial set includes the measures that the so-called 'supply-siders' espouse. Supply-siders are a group of economists who are known for their extreme pro-market ideas. These measures include:

- Labour market-related policies: these include policies that try to make the labour market more flexible. They include lowering or even abolishing the minimum wage; decreasing the power of labour unions and reducing non-wage labour costs to employers (such as national insurance contributions) so that labour becomes cheaper to firms and more labour is hired; making hiring and firing of workers easier so that managers do not hesitate to hire more labour when demand rises; making pension plans transferable across occupations (so that labour mobility increases); reducing unemployment benefits so that those out of work are more motivated to find jobs, etc.
- Product market-related policies: these include policies that aim to increase the extent of competition in markets so that the economy reaps the resulting efficiency benefits. Deregulation (reducing the amount of rules and 'red tape' for firms) and privatization as well as trade liberalization are typical candidates.
- Decreasing tax rates to improve the incentive to work, to save and to invest (see Laffer curve, page 92).

Overall, the benefits expected by implementing supply-side policies are a result of increased levels of competition and the expected enhanced efficiency, fewer distortions to the price mechanism, fewer built-in disincentives and increased flexibility in labour markets.

On the other hand, pro-market supply-side policies can be criticized on the following grounds:

- Benefits usually take a long time to materialize. They are thus long-run policies incapable of dealing with short-run problems.
- Tax cuts may instead induce more leisure and less labour and investment, proving more of a gift to the better-off segments of the population.
- Privatization often has led, at least in the short run, to increased unemployment.
- Deregulation may prove unsuccessful in raising competition and lowering prices. The 1990s energy crisis in California is perhaps a good example of the dangers that deregulation of utility companies may bring, as the market may become dominated by a single private monopoly which has no incentive to keep prices down.
- The smaller safety net that results from, say, lower and stricter unemployment benefits may lead to increased income inequality and segments of the population may be marginalized.

Industrial policy

- Within this second, rather controversial, group one may also include 'industrial policies'. 'Industrial policies' are championed by policymakers who considered government intervention and guidance necessary for the productive capacity of an economy to increase. This group considers market forces inadequate to guide financial capital and investments to their most productive uses and thus government was necessary to do the job and 'pick

winners', i.e. industries and firms to support as they were thought to be the most promising for growth. Subsidized low interest loans, lower rates of taxation or tax allowances, and protection from foreign competition are some of the measures employed. Some successful as well as unsuccessful developing countries have adopted such measures. Many, if not all, advanced economies have also employed such policies in varying degrees.

Inflation

Inflation is defined as a sustained increase of the average level of prices. The **inflation rate** is the percentage by which the average price level, expressed as a price index, has risen between two periods.

A price index (a number without units of measurement) makes comparisons through time much easier. Using statistical criteria some year is chosen to be the 'base' (or reference) year and all other years are expressed as a percentage of it. The price index for the base year will be equal to 100.

Measuring inflation

- The average level of prices is measured through a price index which is a *weighted average* of the prices that the *typical consumer* faces expressed as an *index number*.
- Statisticians determine through surveys the basket of goods and services that the *typical* household buys.
- The average is a *weighted average* as goods and services are not of equal significance to the typical consumer. The weight for each good are the expenditures on it expressed as a proportion of total expenditures made.
- The cost of purchasing the basket is recorded and then expressed as an *index number*.

Problems of measurement

- The typical consumer is a fictitious person. This person is both young and old, lives both in a city and on a farm and is both well off and relatively poor. As a result it is problematical to use the inflation rate figure to determine, for example, by how much a government should increase pensions, as an older person consumes more health care and less entertainment than a younger individual.
- The weights used to construct the average price level are fixed. As a result the effect on the inflation rate of an increase in the price of some good is overestimated. Even though consumers will switch away from it and purchase other cheaper substitutes, its significance (its weight) in the construction of the average will be the same. The official inflation rate may thus overestimate true inflation. This is referred to as the 'substitution bias'.
- New products are not immediately taken into account in the construction of the average price level. It took a few years for the price of cell phone services to enter the typical basket of goods and services in many countries. This is referred to as the 'new product bias'.
- Prices from new retail outlets such as online stores (Amazon) or mega and discount stores may not be sufficiently sampled. Since these retail outlets usually have lower prices the official inflation rate may overestimate true inflation. This is referred to as the 'new retail outlet bias'.
- Improved quality of goods and services may not be properly accounted for in the construction of the average price level. A better version of a product may be 10% more expensive but may last 50% longer than the older version, rendering it effectively cheaper. Again, the official inflation rate may overestimate true inflation. This is referred to as the 'quality bias'.

Costs of inflation

- Inflation increases uncertainty in business decision-making so it makes it more difficult for firms to judge whether an investment prospect will or will not be profitable. As a result investment spending decreases and thus, in the long run, growth and employment rates may decrease.
- Exports become less competitive in foreign markets. As a result, the export sector shrinks and trade imbalances may result.
- Households on fixed money incomes (such as wage earners and pensioners) suffer a decline in their purchasing power. Income distribution may worsen.
- The efficiency of the price mechanism is lost because inflation distorts the signalling power of relative price changes. A consumer or a firm witnessing the price of good X rising cannot be sure that it is now relatively more expensive as she cannot know whether the prices of other similar goods have increased by the same percentage. This confuses the decisions of consumers and of firms.

- Inflation, in general and on average, redistributes national income from the poor to the well-off since the former have fewer choices to hedge against inflation and, in addition, they cannot borrow. The wealthy can borrow from the banking system and proceed to invest in assets whose value is expected to rise faster than inflation.
- If actual inflation proves higher than expected inflation, then borrowers gain at the expense of lenders. The money they will be paying back will be worth less than expected.

But mild inflation reduces the real wage costs of firms and may thus help their competitiveness.

Tip

Have in mind that the costs of inflation may easily be rewritten as benefits of price stability.

Deflation

Deflation refers to a process of continuous decreases in the average price level. If the inflation rate is negative then the economy is suffering from deflation. In January 2006 consumer prices changed by –0.8% in Japan. This means that the average consumer price level had decreased by 0.8% compared to January 2005. Japan was suffering from deflation.

Tip

Disinflation refers to a decrease of inflation. Prices continue to rise but at a slower rate. If, for example, inflation has decreased from 8.7% to 5.5% annually then prices continue to increase but at a slower rate.

Costs of deflation

- Consumers delay purchases since they come to expect further price decreases. Aggregate demand decreases even more, pushing even lower the average price level.
- Firms are forced to cut prices to win over customers, squeezing their profit margins and forcing them to cut down on costs. Wages fall and layoffs follow so AD shifts further to the left.
- The real value of outstanding debt increases. Indebted consumers become hesitant to make purchases and indebted firms hesitate to make investments so AD decreases even more and so does the average price level.
- Since the real value of outstanding debt increases, some households and some firms cannot service their loans.

Banks accumulate 'bad' loans (loans that are not repaid) and thus the risk of a banking crisis with repercussions on the real economy increases.

- Since nominal interest rates cannot decrease below zero the central bank cannot use easy monetary policy to reflate the economy. Expansionary fiscal policy may also prove ineffective as households may prefer to save and postpone spending.

But exports become more competitive abroad and AD may increase as a result of a rise in net exports.

Causes of inflation and deflation

Through the AD/AS diagram it is clear that any factor that increases aggregate demand will lead to an increasing price level, i.e. inflation, as well as any factor causing an adverse shift of aggregate supply. The former is known as demand-pull inflation and the latter as cost-push inflation, even though once an inflationary process begins it is difficult in practice to distinguish between the two.

Demand-pull inflation

In the case of demand-pull inflation the extent of the inflationary effect resulting from the increase in aggregate demand depends on how steep the AS curve is, in other words how close to full employment the economy is operating. The closer to the full employment level of output (the steeper AS is), the greater the effect on the average price level of an increase in aggregate demand.

Figure 3.20 illustrates demand-pull inflation as the average price level is shown to increase from P1 to P2 following a shift to the right of aggregate demand from AD1 to AD2.

Figure 3.20 Demand-pull inflation

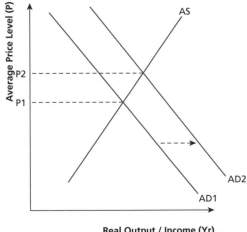

Causes of inflation and deflation continued

Causes of demand-pull inflation

- Rapid increase in consumption and investment expenditures caused by excessively optimistic and confident consumers and firms.
- A surge in exports. Exports may increase as a result of an undervalued or depreciating currency especially if the price elasticity of supply of exports is low (i.e. if bottlenecks exist in the production of exports). Faster growth abroad may also suddenly increase foreign demand for our products.
- Profligate government spending is a typical cause of demand-pull inflationary pressures. Also, poorly designed tax cuts may feed demand and inflationary pressures instead of increasing the incentive to work or to invest.
- Inflationary expectations themselves are a common cause of continuing inflation. If prices are expected to continue climbing then all firms and workers with pricing power will increase their prices and wages to keep up.
- Perhaps the single most important cause of inflation is 'excessive monetary growth'. The easiest way to understand this is by quoting Milton Friedman's famous saying that inflation exists when 'too much money is chasing after too few goods' and thus that inflation is a purely monetary phenomenon.

Tip

Bear in mind that increases in AD will affect not only the average price level but also real output. Mild inflation may thus accompany a rise in real output and employment.

Cost-push inflation

Figure 3.21 illustrates cost-push inflation as the average price level is shown to increase from P1 to P2 following a shift to the left of aggregate supply (an adverse supply shock) from AS1 to AS2.

Figure 3.21 Cost-push inflation

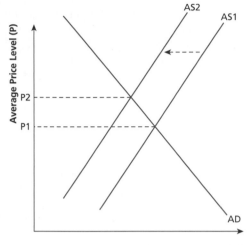

Causes of cost-push inflation

- A rise in the price of oil (energy costs) is perhaps the most common cause of cost-push inflation. Oil is still the predominant form of energy for firms so a sustained and sharp increase in the price of oil will increase production costs across the board and thus prices.
- Powerful labour unions, as they may be in a position to achieve for their members wage increases higher than any productivity gains.
- A devaluation (or a sharp depreciation) of the currency since it makes import prices higher. Not only will the average price level immediately rise and lead workers to demand higher wages but domestic production costs will also increase if firms import a lot of raw materials and intermediate products.
- Rising commodity prices (as these are products used as inputs in manufacturing) because of rising world demand. The explosive growth in China has increased manufacturing and construction costs in many other countries.
- An increase in indirect taxation. This would be a one-off increase in the average price level so it would hardly qualify as a cause of inflation (a *sustained* increase in prices) unless it leads to demands for higher wages and an inflationary spiral begins.
- A productivity slow-down. Production costs would rise but such a development would typically require some unfavorable institutional change.

Tip

The shift toward services in many advanced economies has decreased their dependence on oil, so increasing oil prices do not prove as inflationary as in the past.

Causes of inflation and deflation continued

Causes of deflation

Figure 3.22 illustrates a case of deflation since the average price level is shown to decrease from P1 to P2 as a result of decreasing aggregate demand from AD1 to AD2.

Deflation can be caused by:

- A decrease in aggregate demand, often the result of a domestic crisis, like a banking crisis or the collapse of a major industry but possibly a result of an external crisis that led to a sudden contraction of the export sector.
- Aggregate demand rising more slowly than expected. Extremely optimistic firms may have overinvested in new capacity leading to a large shift to the right of aggregate supply. If aggregate demand fails to rise as fast as originally anticipated, a decreasing average price level may result.

Figure 3.22 Deflation

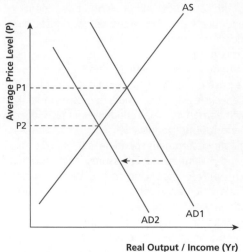

Policies to deal with inflation and deflation

Policies to deal with demand-pull inflation

- In the case of demand-pull inflation, typically, tight monetary policy is adopted (increasing the interest rate) often accompanied by fiscal 'restraint' (meaning lowering government spending and raising taxes; lowering budget deficits). To show how tighter monetary policy (and fiscal restraint) will hopefully help lower inflation use Fig. 3.23.
- Given AD1 and AS, the average price level is at P1. As a result of demand-pull inflation aggregate demand would increase to AD2 and the price level to P2. If the central bank increases interest rates (tight monetary policy) some households may cut down their spending on durables and some firms may lower their investment spending so aggregate demand will not increase as fast all the way to AD2 but will increase only up to AD*. Prices will rise but not as much. Inflation will be lower.
- Note though that whereas real output would rise to Y2 it will now as a result of the contractionary policy employed rise only up to Y*. Output increased but not as fast so economic growth slowed down.

Figure 3.23 Dealing with demand-pull inflation

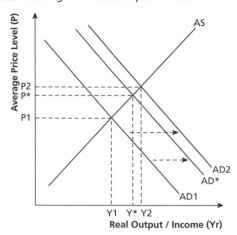

Policies to deal with cost-push inflation

- The policy response is less obvious in the case of cost-push inflation. It may seem that supply-side policies are in order but supply-side policies are difficult to adopt and implement and take a long time to have any effects. Of course, appropriate supply-side policies are always helpful to contain inflation since by shifting AS to the right any increase in AD will be absorbed without the average price level rising. Non-inflationary growth will be achieved (refer to Fig. 3.16).
- Thus, even if inflation is 'cost-push', it is contractionary demand management policies that are employed by policymakers. The typical immediate response to any inflationary pressures emerging in an economy is for policymakers to tighten monetary policy, i.e. to increase interest rates and make borrowing more costly.
- Figure 3.24 illustrates the situation. Initially real output is at Y1 and the average price level at P1. Assume an adverse supply shock shifting AS from AS1 to AS2 (arrow a) and leading to a higher price level P2. Cost-push inflation is even more costly than demand-pull inflation as real output has also decreased from Y1 to Y2 and unemployment rises.

Figure 3.24 Dealing with cost-push inflation

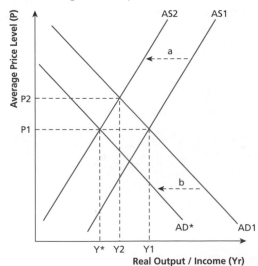

Policies to deal with inflation and deflation continued

- Let policymakers tighten monetary policy by increasing interest rates in an attempt to maintain the average price level at P1. If the policy is successful and the increased borrowing costs decrease spending by households and firms, then AD will shift to AD* (arrow b) maintaining prices stable at P*. Note though that the negative effect on economic activity (on real output) will be more severe as it will further decrease to Y* and unemployment will increase more. Usually this is considered a short-run cost worth suffering as price stability helps accelerate growth and employment generation in the long run.

> ### Tip
>
> Increased exposure to international competition also exerts a dampening effect on inflation. Not only are domestic firms forced to become more efficient and lower their prices but also they may benefit from cheaper sources of supply.

Dealing with deflation

- Deflation has proven to be a most difficult problem to deal with. Japan, a major advanced economy, suffered the consequences of deflation for many years. Deflation creates a vicious circle of decreasing prices leading to decreasing aggregate demand leading to decreasing prices that is extremely difficult to break. Monetary policy is ineffective and fiscal policy is weakened. Somehow policymakers have to convince the public that inflation should be expected. Governments have resorted to printing dated vouchers to force recipients to spend them and not save them. Deflation is often corrected through the increase in aggregate demand that results from cheaper exports.

Unemployment

Who are the unemployed?

An individual is considered unemployed if she is actively searching for a job and cannot find one. The unemployment rate is the ratio of the number of unemployed over the size of the labour force (also referred to as the workforce or the working population) times 100. The labour force includes the employed and the unemployed.

Problems in measuring unemployment

- Even though there seems to be a clearcut distinction of who should and who shouldn't be considered unemployed, measuring the unemployment rate is fraught with problems. The unemployment rate may underestimate or overestimate the true level of unemployment in a country. How do governments arrive at the unemployment rate? The answer is either through surveys (survey method) or by counting the number of those registered as unemployed and receiving unemployment benefits (claimant method).
- The numbers of unemployed and the unemployment rate are estimates in that they are based on household surveys. For a surveyed individual to be considered unemployed she must be without work, available to start work and she must have actively sought gainful employment at some time, usually during the previous four weeks. Surveyed individuals may misrepresent their true status. Survey-based statistics often overestimate the true level of unemployment. In addition they may suffer from poor sample and questionnaire design and limited coverage of the population.
- On the other hand registered unemployment data count the number of individuals registered as unemployed and receiving unemployment benefits. These national statistics are dependent on whether the eligibility conditions are satisfied. Claimant unemployment statistics often underestimate true unemployment as governments have been accused of manipulating eligibility requirements to underreport the unemployment statistics.

Costs of unemployment

Private costs (costs that the individual suffers)

- The single most important cost an unemployed individual incurs is his lost income.
- Another cost is the possible loss of up-to-date skills.
- Being unemployed increases the chances of remaining unemployed. Employers prefer to hire an individual currently employed elsewhere to hiring an unemployed worker. Not only will her skills be up to date but also the employer avoids the risks created by asymmetric information (not knowing why the unemployed lost her job in the first place).
- The loss of self esteem that often results and the increased probability that the person will resort to alcohol or drugs are other possible private costs.

Social costs (costs that society suffers)

- Given that the so-called 'economic problem' is scarcity, it becomes evident that the greatest cost of unemployment is the lost output that could have been produced and never will. The economy operates inside its production possibilities frontier.

- Tax revenues collected are lower because of the lower incomes and the resulting decreased private spending.
- Government spending increases because of the unemployment benefits paid and the increased number of training and retraining programmes that government often finances.
- If unemployment is high and prolonged, society may experience higher levels of drug and alcohol abuse and hence higher incidences of crime and violence and other negative externalities.
- If unemployment is concentrated in regions and/or in age groups such problems may become even more pronounced.

However, there may be some benefits arising from unemployment. 'Free marketeers' believe that union power weakens and thus there is reduced cost inflation pressure in the economy and greater labour market flexibility. Increased geographical and occupational mobility is also mentioned as a possible positive side effect of unemployment as workers are forced to move or change occupation.

Types of unemployment and policies to lower it

Seasonal unemployment

- Construction workers are laid off in the winter. This type of unemployment is expected and there is nothing the government can do about it. Unemployment statistics though are often corrected ('seasonally adjusted') so that policymakers can determine true changes in unemployment, not those due to the changing seasons.

Frictional unemployment

- Frictional unemployment refers to people who are between jobs. This is unemployment of a short-term nature and is largely unavoidable in an economy since people will always voluntarily switch jobs searching for better ones or relocating.
- Faster and better labour market-related information will decrease but not eliminate frictional unemployment. Governments can thus minimize frictional unemployment by ensuring that job vacancies as well as the profiles of those available for work become known faster and more widely.

Cyclical (Keynesian or demand-deficient) unemployment

- This type of unemployment is directly related to the business cycle. Higher unemployment will necessarily accompany a recession because of the lower level of economic activity. A decrease in aggregate demand will force some businesses to shrink and others to close down.

- In Fig. 3.25a aggregate demand decreases for some reason from AD1 to AD2 resulting in a decrease in economic activity and a decrease in real output from Y1 to Y2. The economy has entered a recession illustrated in the trade cycle in Fig. 3.25b. The lower level of economic activity forces firms to decrease their demand for labour. Some firms

Figure 3.25 Cyclical unemployment

(a)
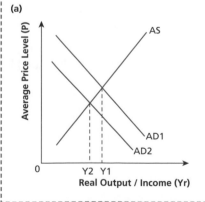

(b)
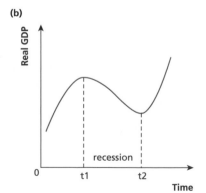

(c)
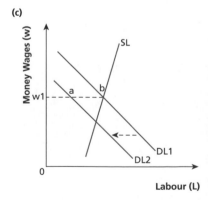

Types of unemployment and policies to lower it continued

may shrink, others may even shut down because of the recession. In Fig. 3.25c the labour market is illustrated with demand for labour decreasing from DL1 to DL2. Money (nominal) wages are assumed to remain at w1 as a result of labour unions and/or contracts ('sticky wages'). Excess supply of labour results, equal to ab, reflecting the resulting cyclical unemployment.

- Unemployment due to cyclical reasons is dealt with by expansionary demand-side policies. Effectively the government will attempt to close the deflationary gap. Interest rates are cut in the hope that households and firms will be convinced to spend more and the government may even lower taxes and increase expenditures depending on the state of their finances.

Structural unemployment

- Structural unemployment is perhaps the most serious type of unemployment since it is of a long-term nature. It represents those remaining unemployed long after recovery is under way in an economy. An economy may be booming but structural unemployment will not decrease.
- It is the result of the evolving structure of an economy because of rapid technological advancement or shifting comparative advantage. The changing structure of

an economy results in a mismatch between the skills available by the unemployed and the skills required by the labour market. New technologies render certain professions obsolete but at the same time create new job opportunities. The internet may have, for example, decreased the demand for shop workers and postmen but created new jobs for web designers and software engineers. But if the laid-off shop worker or the employee of the postal service is not trained in computers then he or she may find it difficult to get a job.

- It is also the result of labour market rigidities. Minimum wage laws and wages set through collective bargaining between industries and labour are examples of labour market-related rigidities. They both result in higher unemployment as wage rates are set above their equilibrium, market-clearing level. If pension plans in one industry are not easily transferred to another industry then occupational mobility is hampered. Consider a worker losing his job in industry A but prevented from taking a job offer in industry B because he cannot transfer his pension rights so he will be unemployed.
- Lastly, institutional disincentives are considered as causes. Laws preventing firms from firing employees as well as high unemployment benefits are examples.

Policies to lower structural unemployment

Eliminating structural unemployment is not possible but the following are considered to help decrease it:

- Training and retraining seminars permit structurally unemployed workers to find new jobs.
- Ensuring that school curricula are capable to prepare individuals who are creative and willing to learn.
- Reducing the power of trade unions.
- Eliminating minimum wage laws and collective bargaining.
- Reducing non-wage labour costs (such as national insurance contributions).
- Reducing the level of unemployment benefits and the length of time that benefits can be collected.

However:

- The reduction in structural unemployment that some of these measures may bring about may come at a significant cost to society. Decreasing worker protection may lead to labour and social unrest which, as discussed earlier, may hamper growth. Segments of the population may become

marginalized and income distribution more unequal, again with adverse effects on growth and development.

Finally:

- Expansionary demand-side policies are ineffective to deal with structural unemployment as any decrease in unemployment will be temporary and at the cost of higher inflation. This point will become clear later.

Tips

Policies that attempt to deal with structural unemployment are of a microeconomic nature belonging to the broader class of supply-side policies discussed.

Also, even though it sounds counterintuitive, a growing economy may over the long run suffer from higher structural unemployment. This is because the different income elasticities of demand of the different industries and sectors of an economy will change its structure.

Real wage unemployment (or classical unemployment)

- Real wage unemployment is considered a result of labour unions maintaining the real wage rate (the purchasing power of the money wage rate) too high (above the equilibrium level) for the labour market to 'clear'.

Equilibrium and disequilibrium unemployment

- Unemployment that exists when the labour market is in equilibrium is considered as 'equilibrium' unemployment and is more widely known as the 'natural' rate of unemployment (NRU, see below).
- On the other hand, cyclical unemployment and real wage unemployment are both examples of 'disequilibrium' unemployment as the prevailing wage rate is not the equilibrium wage rate.

The natural rate of unemployment

- The natural rate of unemployment (NRU) is a term introduced by Nobel laureate Milton Friedman, the best known advocate of monetarism.
- The basic idea conveyed is that there may still be unemployment in the labour market even if participants on both sides of the market satisfy their objectives and equilibrium prevails.
- In Fig. 3.26 the curve LD illustrates the labour demand that firms express in the market. It shows how many workers firms are willing to hire at each real wage rate. It is downward sloping as at higher real wage rates they will be willing to hire fewer workers. The curve LF illustrates the labour force available at each wage rate. It shows the number of individuals working or looking for a job at each wage rate. It is slightly upward sloping as at a higher real wage rate more people will be convinced to enter the labour market and search for a job.
- It is the curve AJ that makes this model of the labour market different. It is the 'accept jobs' curve and shows at each wage rate the number of individuals willing to accept a job offer and work. If you are looking for a job you will not necessarily accept the first job offer you get. You may hope to obtain a better job and given the level of benefits collected it may be worth continuing the search. AJ is also upward sloping as the LF is upward sloping but the horizontal distance at each wage rate between AJ and LF decreases because the probability of accepting a job offer will be higher at a higher wage rate.
- The labour market is in equilibrium at Wr'. At Wr' the number of people firms are willing to hire is equal to the number of people willing to accept a job offer. Note though that there is still unemployment even though the labour market is in equilibrium as 'ef' workers are in the

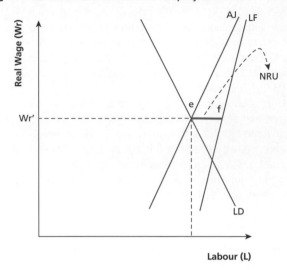

Figure 3.26 The natural rate of unemployment

labour force but without a job. The unemployment that exists when the labour market is in equilibrium is known as the **natural rate of unemployment.**

- Since these 'ef' individuals would not be willing to accept a job offer even if there was one, the NRU is of a voluntary nature. If the wage rate say, because of labour unions was higher above Wr' then part of the resulting unemployment would be of an involuntary nature and part of a voluntary nature. Note though that the voluntary portion at that higher than equilibrium wage rate is not the NRU.
- The NRU is also considered to be of a structural nature as if the AJ curve shifts to the right because of lower unemployment benefits it would decrease.

The Phillips curve

The original Phillips curve

Since the early 1960s and until the mid 1970s economists relied on an empirical result that Alban W. Phillips, a New Zealand economist at the London School of Economics, made in 1958. His work, the Phillips curve, became one of the most famous relationships in macroeconomics. It showed that there was a stable trade-off between the inflation rate and the unemployment rate of an economy.

His original empirical (statistical) work examined UK data on the annual percentage change in money wages and the annual unemployment rate over a period of 96 years (1861–1957). Figure 3.27a shows what he found: that the percentage change in money wages and unemployment were inversely related. If unemployment was low ('tight' labour market) then money wages rose a lot as employers

Figure 3.27 The original Phillips curve

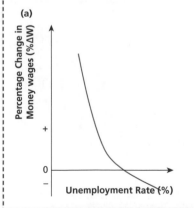

(a)

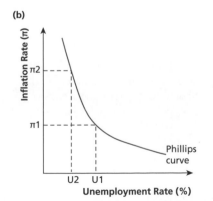

(b)

The original Phillips curve continued

were forced to bid up wages to find employees, while if unemployment was high ('slack' labour market) then money wages increased by a little or even decreased (as firms could hire without having to offer more or even by offering less than last year's prevailing money wage).

Moving from wage inflation to price inflation was the next step. Since wages typically form a big proportion of production costs and since firms in practice often set their price as percentage of their unit costs (a mark-up) it seemed sensible to explore how the annual inflation rate and the unemployment rate were related. Figure 3.27b illustrates what was found: inflation and unemployment were inversely related. If unemployment decreased then inflation increased while if inflation decreased unemployment would increase. The negatively sloped curve in Fig. 3.27b is the original Phillips curve.

This stable inverse relationship seemed to suggest that governments could exploit this trade-off between inflation and unemployment. It was as if the Phillips curve presented policymakers with a menu of choices. They could achieve a lower unemployment rate but at the cost of higher inflation or they could lower inflation but at the cost of higher unemployment.

This statistically determined relationship was compatible with the ruling Keynesian theory. Remember that the Keynesian perspective stressed the importance of aggregate demand in the determination of equilibrium income. If AD rose then real output would increase and thus unemployment would decrease. However, this rise in AD would also lead to inflationary pressures. Thus, as shown in Fig. 3.27b, if using expansionary demand-side policies unemployment decreased from U1 to U2 then inflation would increase from π1 to π2.

The long-run Phillips curve

This is also known as the expectations-augmented Phillips curve or the Phelps–Friedman critique.

- Since the late 1960s the original Phillips curve relationship suffered both empirical and theoretical setbacks. Inflation and unemployment were both increasing in the 1970s. The term 'stagnation' was coined, implying recession together with rising inflation. The original inverse relationship had collapsed and traditional Keynesian analysis found it hard to explain what was going on.
- But beyond this empirical refutation of the original Phillips curve there came a theoretical attack. Ed Phelps and Milton Friedman (both Nobel laureates) independently claimed that in the long run the Phillips curve was vertical at the equilibrium rate of unemployment (the natural rate) and any trade-off between inflation and unemployment could exist only in the short run. This became known as the Phelps–Friedman critique and the theory as the expectations-augmented Phillips curve.
- If a government tried to lower unemployment below this equilibrium ('natural') rate using expansionary policies it would succeed only *temporarily* and at the cost of permanently higher inflation. The short-run trade-off between inflation and unemployment was only because workers suffer from 'money illusion': they form their

expectations about inflation *adaptively* (meaning that they form their expectations about next year's inflation by looking at *past* inflation rates) so they are *slow* to realize that inflation accelerates as a result of the expansionary policies pursued.

- Fig. 3.28b illustrates a labour market in equilibrium with unemployment being at its natural level (distance 'ef' is the NRU). Say that this is at 5.2% and that the economy has been experiencing inflation equal to 1.0% for some time now so that workers again expect 1.0% inflation next year (point A1 in Fig. 3.28a). Assume now that the government adopts expansionary policies to try to lower unemployment to 4.5% *below the equilibrium ('natural') level*. Inflation accelerates now to 2.0%. As a result the real wage rate decreases and firms hire more workers. Unemployment decreases to 4.5% and the economy has moved to point A2. Workers are slow to realize that inflation is actually higher at 2.0% and thus that the real wage is lower. But when their expectations adjust they will demand higher money wages, increasing the real wage for firms back to its original equilibrium level Wr'. Firms will fire workers so unemployment returns to its equilibrium rate at 5.2% (point A3).

Figure 3.28 The long-run Phillips curve (the expectations-augmented Phillips curve or the Phelps–Friedman critique)

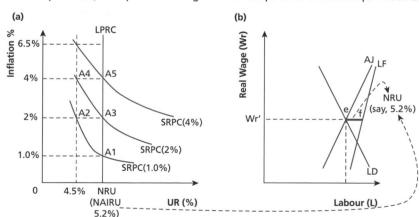

The long-run Phillips curve continued

- If the government insists on trying to decrease unemployment below its natural rate using expansionary demand-side policies it would need to 'engineer' higher and higher inflation rates so that workers would be temporarily fooled and accept job offers. In Fig. 3.28a, inflation would have to accelerate to 4.0% while workers expect it to be at 2.0% for unemployment to drop again and for the economy to move to point A4 before adjusting back to A5.
- The policy implication is clear: governments should *not* try to lower unemployment below its equilibrium (natural) rate using expansionary demand-side policies as it is futile. Any

decrease in unemployment will be *temporary* and at the cost of higher inflation. In the long run, when expectations have adjusted and there is no money illusion, there is no trade-off between inflation and unemployment. There is only one rate of unemployment and it is compatible with any rate of inflation as long as this rate of inflation does not accelerate (and thus temporarily lead to 'money illusion'). In the long run the Phillips curve is vertical at the NRU, which is also known for this reason as the **non-accelerating inflation rate of unemployment** (NAIRU).

Distribution of income

The fifth macroeconomic goal

The fifth macroeconomic goal is to ensure that income distribution is equitable. Equitable does not mean equal.

It means fair. But fairness is an elusive concept and it means different things to different people.

The Lorenz curve and the Gini coefficient

- Income distribution is illustrated through a **Lorenz curve** and the degree of income inequality is measured through the **Gini coefficient**.
- In Fig. 3.29 population (income recipients) is plotted on the horizontal axis in *cumulative* percentages, i.e. from poorest to richest households. Thus at, say, the 20% point we have the poorest 20% of the population and at the 40% point we have the poorest 40% of the population. On the vertical axis we measure the percentage of income received by each percentage of the population.
- The **Lorenz curve** shows the proportion of national income earned by each income group. For example, the poorest 20% in Fig. 3.29 receives only 5% of national income. Note that 100% of the population will of course receive 100% of national income. Also note that the diagonal is the line of equality (perfectly equal income distribution).
- The further away from the diagonal, the more unequal the size distribution of income while the closer to the diagonal the more equal the distribution of income is. If in a country income distribution worsens it means that the Lorenz curve moves further away from the diagonal.
- The **Gini coefficient** measures the degree of income inequality in a population. It is the ratio of the area between the Lorenz curve and the diagonal over the area of the half square in which the curve lies. Focusing on Fig. 3.29, the Gini coefficient is found by dividing area (A) by area (A + B).

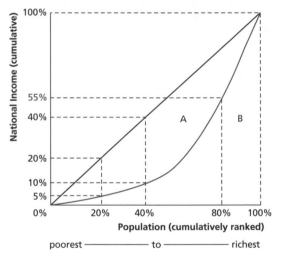

Figure 3.29 The Lorenz curve and the Gini coefficient

- The Gini coefficient can vary from 0 (denoting perfect equality) to 1 (denoting perfect inequality). Typically highly unequal income distributions are distributions with a Gini coefficient between 0.50 and 0.70. Some representative values of this coefficient are: Brazil 0.60, Argentina 0.48, USA 0.40, UK 0.36, Australia 0.35, Sweden 0.25 and Austria 0.23.
- Often what matters is not the level but the direction of change, i.e. whether income distribution is becoming more or less unequal.

Possible benefits and costs of a more equitable income distribution

A more equitable distribution may help accelerate growth and promote human and economic development in many ways:

- The propensity to consume of the poor is higher than that of the rich so redistribution will increase aggregate demand especially for basic goods and services.
- Social tensions are lower and thus governments can more easily undertake important economic reforms which require a high degree of consensus within the population. If people feel that they enjoy the fruits of economic growth then they will be willing to work harder and sacrifice more now in order for them or their children to enjoy more at a later date. They will be willing and able to save more, permitting higher rates of investment and thus growth. Fewer social tensions decrease uncertainty and risks for domestic and foreign investors.
- The very poor will be able to afford access to crucial resources such as education so the amount and quality of productive resources available to a country increases.
- Trust increases among the population so the cost of economic transactions decreases. More economic activity will take place thus accelerating growth.

However, an excessively equal income distribution could lower economic efficiency. It could lower the incentives for hard work and for risk taking. Growth may be undermined.

Direct and indirect taxes

Direct taxes are taxes on income, on profits and on wealth. The burden of a direct tax cannot be shifted onto another entity. Indirect taxes include taxes on goods and on expenditures and they have been discussed earlier. The burden of an indirect tax can be shifted onto a different entity.

Progressive, proportional and regressive taxation

To explain the difference between the above types of taxes it is important to define the marginal and the average tax rate. The **marginal tax rate** is the percentage taken by the government on the last krone or dollar earned. It is the extra tax paid as a result of an extra krone or dollar earned. The **average tax rate** is the ratio of the tax collected over income earned or more generally the ratio of the tax collected over the tax base.

Thus:

- A progressive tax system is one in which higher-income individuals pay *proportionately more* so the average tax rate rises as income rises. In a progressive income tax system the marginal tax rate is greater than the average tax rate (remember that if the average increases it follows that the marginal is greater than the average).

- A proportional tax system is one in which all individuals pay the same proportion of their income independently of the level of their income. In a proportional tax system the average tax rate remains constant as income rises so the marginal tax rate is equal to the average tax rate. A **flat-rate** (proportional) income tax exists in several countries such as Latvia, Russia and Estonia and is considered by many others. It presents many advantages over the progressive income tax systems that most countries have. Disincentives are lower, administrative costs are lower, it is simple and thus more transparent and it is potentially even fairer as loopholes do not exist which usually higher-income households take advantage of.
- A regressive tax system is one in which poorer individuals pay a greater proportion of their income. In a regressive tax system the average tax rate decreases as income rises so the marginal tax rate is less than the average tax rate. Indirect taxes are proportional with respect to expenditure but regressive with respect to income. This is why indirect taxation on food and basic goods is lower or zero.

In Fig. 3.30 the horizontal axis measures the tax base (say, income) and the vertical the amount of tax paid. A proportional tax system is illustrated by any straight line through the origin. In a progressive tax system the slope of the line is increasing while in a regressive tax system the slope of the line is decreasing.

Figure 3.30 Progressive, proportional and regressive taxation

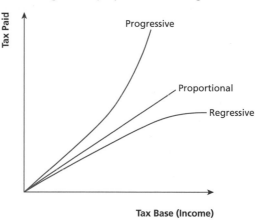

How can income be redistributed more equitably?

Short-run solutions

Usually governments resort to a mixture of progressive income taxes coupled with a system of transfer payments. Transfer payments include pensions, unemployment benefits, disability benefits, subsidies, etc. By taxing higher income households more heavily than lower income households and spending more on transfer payments, national income may be redistributed in an attempt to satisfy the equity goal. Social health insurance is usually part of a package that aims at effectively increasing the income of the lower income strata.

Long-run solutions

In the long run, the most effective route to a more equitable income distribution is by improving the quality and access to education and health services for the most deprived income groups. Job creation policies are also of utmost significance. Lastly, lower corruption and a fair judicial system are also important.

The Laffer curve and tax cuts

HL

- In the early 1980s an American economist, Arthur Laffer, became popularly known because of a diagram that he supposedly sketched on a napkin of a Washington DC restaurant while having dinner. This diagram showed the obvious: that as tax rates rise, tax revenues also increase but only up to a point, beyond which tax revenues collected will start to decline.
- Focusing on Fig. 3.31, with a 0% tax rate the government will collect zero tax revenues so the Laffer curve starts from the origin. As the tax rate increases, tax revenues will also increase but only up to a certain point. There is a tax rate (say, t* in Fig. 3.31) such that if the tax rate increases even more then tax revenues collected will start to decrease. This decrease in tax revenues is because higher and higher tax rates create disincentives for people to work and to invest. At the limit, a 100% tax rate will lead to zero tax revenues for the government as there is no reward to individuals for any productive effort.
- The policy implication is that in countries with high tax rates it may very well be the case that by decreasing tax rates the government will collect more tax revenues as a result of the improved incentive to work and for firms to invest.
- *(optional)* Whether a decrease in tax rates will or will not induce more labour supply depends on the substitution and income effects. If the tax rate decreases then leisure becomes more expensive so individuals will tend to work more. On the other hand, if the tax rate decreases then disposable income increases and since leisure is considered a normal 'good' people will tend to work less. It follows that the effect of a tax cut on labour supply depends on which one of the two effects dominates.

Figure 3.31 The Laffer curve

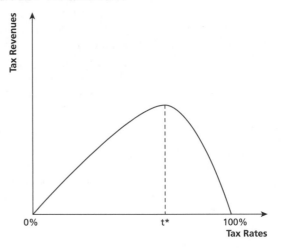

Tip

Try to make sure that the maximum of the Laffer curve you draw is not right above the mid-point 50% tax rate as this could be misleading. We do not know the tax rate after which the disincentives created are so strong that tax revenues start to decrease.

Inflationary and deflationary gaps: an alternative presentation

The inflationary gap

HL

Assume an economy in long-run equilibrium. It is operating at the full employment level of real output which corresponds to the natural rate of unemployment. Remember that this implies that the labour market is in equilibrium, i.e. that the real wage rate is such that it equates the number of workers firms are willing to hire with the number of workers that are willing to accept a job offer. It is also assumed (as the economy is in long-run equilibrium) that expectations have adjusted, i.e. that the anticipated rate of inflation is equal to the actual rate of inflation.

- An increase in AD from AD1 to AD2 in Fig. 3.32 will fool workers who will accept jobs as inflation will accelerate, exceeding the anticipated rate, and thus there will be a *temporary increase in real output to Y'* this temporary difference between Y' and Yfe is known as the **inflationary gap**. As money wages are slow to respond, the real wage rate decreases so firms hire more workers to produce more output and workers accept as they do not realize that inflation has accelerated. The increased output level Y' corresponds to the temporary decrease of unemployment below the NRU that money illusion creates.

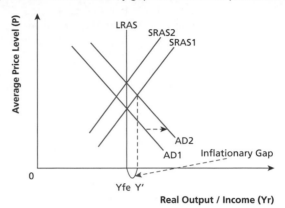

Figure 3.32 The inflationary gap: an alternative presentation

- When expectations of inflation adjust and money wages rise, the real wage increases back to its original level. Production costs for firms increase and so the short-run aggregate supply shifts left from SRAS1 to SRAS2. Output will return to the full employment level and unemployment back to its natural level.

The deflationary gap

HL

Assume an economy in long-run equilibrium operating at the full employment level of output Yfe.

- If now AD in Fig. 3.33 drops from AD1 to AD2 then the equilibrium level of output will decrease to Y'. The difference (Yfe − Y') is known as the deflationary gap.
- This diagram can also be used to show that the equilibrium level of output and the full employment level of output do not necessarily coincide.

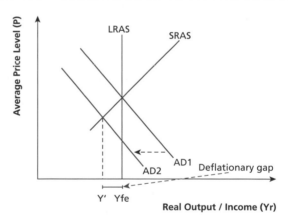

Figure 3.33 The deflationary gap: an alternative presentation

Schools of economic thought: a brief outline

The Classical School

- Given that scarcity is *the* fundamental economic problem, an economy will surely always fully utilize its scarce resources. An economy will thus produce whatever its scarce resources and its technology permit it to produce.
- 'Supply creates its own demand': this is known as Say's law (a French economist) and it means that production creates income and this income will necessarily be used to purchase whatever was produced.
- Overproduction was ruled out, as overproduction implies excess supply which in competitive markets leads to lower prices and thus market clearing.
- Prolonged unemployment also was ruled out as it implies

excess supply in labour markets. Excess supply leads to lower wages forcing the labour market to 'clear' (demand for labour to equal supply of labour).
- Flexibility of prices and wages guaranteed that the product and labour markets would 'clear' (that demand would equal supply).
- The economy would thus tend to operate at or near the full employment equilibrium. Any deviation from full employment would be temporary.
- It follows that there would be no need for the government to intervene. This is known as *laissez faire–laissez passer*.

The Keynesian School

- Demand for output creates the supply of output. It is 'effective' demand that determines equilibrium output and income. An economy's total output depends on the level of 'effective' demand, later referred to as **aggregate demand**.
- There is thus no guarantee that an economy will find itself (will be in equilibrium) at the 'full employment' level of output. Equilibrium may occur below full employment (a deflationary or recessionary gap may exist).
- If the private sector (which includes households and firms) for whatever reason (perhaps just psychological) is unable to express sufficient demand for goods and services in an economy to lead to full employment of resources then the government could raise *its own* spending on goods and services (as well as lower taxation) to increase the level of total demand to the level at which all resources are fully

employed. This is known as expansionary (or reflationary) fiscal policy.
- The inherent **instability** of a market (capitalist) economy led to the observed short-run fluctuations of output around its long-run trend. This instability was a result of consumption and investment being unstable as well as the existence of the multiplier effect and the interaction of the multiplier and the accelerator.
- Instability (the business or trade cycle) required government intervention. Counter-cyclical demand-side stabilization policies were introduced which include fiscal and monetary policies.
- Fiscal policy was considered most effective in times of deep recession.

The Monetarists

Two major developments in the 1970s were responsible for the change in direction in Economics: the great inflation of the 1970s and the deconstruction of the Keynesian interventionist approach by Milton Friedman and the Chicago School (or, more generally, by the Monetarists). Friedman's pro-market ideas began to dominate economic theory and with M. Thatcher in 1979 in the UK and R. Reagan in 1980 in the US they also started to dominate policymaking.

In 1973, the first oil crisis erupted, leading to the quadrupling of the price of a barrel of oil in one day. The effect was 'stagflation', the coexistence of rising unemployment and rising inflation. This was a blow to Keynesian economics as the two were thought to be inversely related through the Phillips curve.

- Monetarists are considered the intellectual heirs of the Classical school of thought.

- Friedman and the Monetarist school tried to show that a market economy is inherently stable and thus there is no need for an active role for the government. Consumption expenditures were not thought to depend on the current level of income and the role of expectations on the business investment spending decision was diminished. Thus private spending was more stable.
- Monetarists first pointed out the possibility of 'crowding-out', thus weakening deficit spending as a tool to reflate a flagging economy.
- Inflation for Friedman was a 'purely monetary phenomenon' with 'too much money chasing after too few goods'. They even considered monetary policy as potentially destabilizing and preferred to rely on pro-market supply-side policies.

The Monetarists continued

- They discredited the Phillips curve inflation–unemployment trade-off, trying to show that in the long run the Phillips curve is vertical at the natural rate of unemployment, a term that Friedman himself coined.
- Extreme Monetarists considered that anything the government can do the market can do better. Government failure was even more likely than market failure.
- Several ideas related to Monetarism are the basic ingredients of the so-called **Washington Consensus**

which pushed stabilization, liberalization and structural adjustment onto developing nations with very debatable results. The East Asian Crisis of 1997–98 may have marked a turnaround in economic thinking. Rising inequalities between and within countries suggest that managing national economies as well as the global economy may be necessary after all. The question of course that still remains is: what kind of managing?

IB Questions: Section 3

SL Long Essays

1a Explain the following types of unemployment
(a) frictional (b) structural (c) cyclical/demand-deficient (d) real wage/classical. (10 marks)
1b Evaluate the effectiveness of the different measures available to governments to deal with the types of unemployment in 1a. (15 marks)

2a Identify the components of aggregate demand and briefly explain two factors that might determine each of these components. (10 marks)
2b Evaluate the likely impact on an economy of a substantial rise in the level of interest rates. (15 marks)

3a Explain the costs of inflation and deflation. (10 marks)
3b Evaluate demand-side policies as a means of reducing inflation. (15 marks)

4a The world economy may be subjected to economic shocks, such as a sudden increase in oil prices and terrorist attacks. With the help of an aggregate demand/aggregate supply diagram explain the possible economic effects of such shocks. (10 marks)
4b Evaluate the main economic policies that governments might use to minimize these effects. (15 marks)

5a Explain the various costs of unemployment. (10 marks)
5b Evaluate the alternative policies aimed at reducing unemployment. (15 marks)

6a Briefly explain the main policy objectives of governments. (10 marks)
6b Discuss the ways fiscal policy might be used to achieve these objectives. (15 marks)

7a With the help of examples explain the purpose of the various supply-side policies. (10 marks)
7b Evaluate the success of these measures in countries where they have been implemented. (15 marks)

8a What macroeconomic policies should a government adopt if it wished to reduce aggregate demand in an economy? (10 marks)
8b Should a government attempt to manage the level of aggregate demand to influence unemployment and inflation rates? (15 marks)

HL Long Essays

1a Explain why a government might find it difficult to maintain a low rate of inflation as the economy approaches full employment. (10 marks)
1b Evaluate the proposition that the priority in economic management should be the maintenance of low unemployment. (15 marks)

2a Explain the relationship between the Lorenz curve and the Gini coefficient. (10 marks)
2b Evaluate the effectiveness of the various methods that governments may use to redistribute income. (15 marks)

3a Explain how interest rates can be used to bring about an increase in economic activity. (10 marks)
3b Discuss the strengths and weaknesses of demand-side policies. (15 marks)

4a What are the possible causes of unemployment? (10 marks)
4b Evaluate possible policies that may be used to lower the natural rate of unemployment. (15 marks)

5a What are the macroeconomic objectives of government? (10 marks)
5b Assume the government chooses to pursue one of these objectives. Evaluate the possible consequences for the other objectives. (15 marks)

6a With the help of diagrams distinguish between demand-pull and cost-push inflation. (10 marks)
6b Explain which policies would be appropriate to deal with these two types of inflation. (15 marks)

7a Explain the difference between demand-side and supply-side economic policies. (10 marks)
7b 'Higher economic growth can only be achieved through the implementation of supply-side policies.' Discuss. (15 marks)

8a Explain the economic problems that high unemployment may cause for a country. (10 marks)
8b Discuss the reasons why governments find the goal of full employment difficult to achieve. (15 marks)

IB Questions: Section 3 continued

HL Short Essays

1 'Macroeconomic equilibrium does not necessarily occur at full employment.' Explain this statement using the concepts of inflationary and deflationary gaps.

2 Explain how a progressive tax system may be used to redistribute income.

3 Explain how an increase in government spending can lead to crowding out.

4 Explain the multiplier effect of an increase in government spending.

5 Explain how the multiplier and the accelerator might be linked to each other.

6 Explain how double counting can occur in calculating national income and how measuring value added can overcome this problem.

7 Keynesians and Monetarists have different views of the likely shape of a country's aggregate supply curve. Using diagrams show how these shapes can affect macroeconomic policy.

8 What are the main problems involved in measuring inflation?

9 Use an AD/AS diagram to analyse the likely effects of an increase in interest rates.

10 Use an AD/AS diagram to analyse the likely effects of an increase in income tax.

11 Examine two reasons why a government might wish to control increases in its expenditures.

12 Explain why the goal of full employment might conflict with the goal of economic growth.

13 What is demand-pull inflation and what can governments do about it?

14 Use an AD/AS diagram to explain how cost-push inflation may occur and outline two ways in which it might be controlled.

15 What are the likely consequences of deflation?

16 Use a Phillips curve to explain the concept of the natural rate of unemployment.

17 Why might knowledge of the shape of a country's Phillips curve be useful to policymakers?

18 Explain two policies that a government might use to deal with the problem of demand-deficient (cyclical) unemployment.

19 What is structural unemployment and what measures might governments take to combat it?

International economics

Free trade and welfare

Benefits of free trade

- It permits specialization of scarce resources, since factor endowments differ between countries.
- The increased specialization permits trading nations to achieve higher levels of output, thus higher levels of consumption.
- Through trade, countries can consume combinations of goods outside their production possibilities frontier.
- Free trade decreases the power of domestic monopolies by exposing them to international competitive forces.
- The increased level of competition increases efficiency and lowers prices of domestic firms.
- It stimulates growth by increasing productive resources, accelerating technological change and spurring competition.
- If real incomes rise then saving rises, increasing the availability of domestic funds for investment.
- It may permit domestic firms to achieve economies of scale by increasing the size of the markets in which they sell their products (especially significant for small nations).
- Diffusion and transfer of technology and ideas across borders becomes faster.
- It presents consumers with a greater variety of goods to choose from.

To illustrate the welfare gains from free trade consider Fig. 4.1.

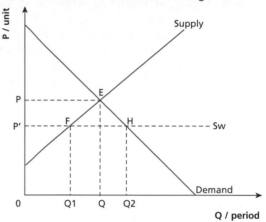

Figure 4.1 Benefits of free trade: market for good 'X'

Initially assume no trade ('autarky case') so the market price of some good X is at P and the equilibrium quantity at Q. If now trade is free and the world price of the good is at P' then the world price would prevail in the domestic market. At the world price P', domestic firms will now produce only Q1 units (instead of Q) and consumers will consume Q2 units (instead of Q). Consumer surplus increases by area (PP'HE) whereas producer surplus decreases by area (PP'FE). Area (EFH) thus represents the net welfare gain resulting from free trade as the consumer surplus gained is greater than the producer surplus lost. Consumers can, in principle, fully pay (compensate) producers and still be better off.

Specialization

Absolute advantage   HL

- The question then becomes: in which goods should each country specialize? According to Adam Smith, mutually beneficial trade is based on the principle of **absolute advantage**. A country may be more efficient in the production of some commodities and less efficient in the production of others relative to another nation. Each country should specialize in the production of the good in which it has an absolute advantage.
- A country has an absolute advantage in the production of a good if it can produce more of it with the same resources (or if it can produce a unit of it with fewer resources).
- If though a country is absolutely more efficient in the production of (both) all commodities then, according to this principle, there would be no reason to specialize and trade.
- On a diagram, the country with the PPF further out on an axis has the absolute advantage in the production of the good measured on that axis. In Fig. 4.2 Country Red has an absolute advantage in the production of good X (it can produce 18 units while Country Black can produce only

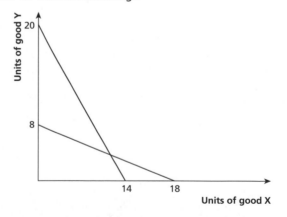

Figure 4.2 Absolute advantage

14 units) while Country Black has an absolute advantage in the production of good Y.
- Country Red should specialize and export good X and import good Y, and vice versa for Country Black.

Comparative advantage

- In 1817, David Ricardo showed that absolute advantage is not necessary. Even if a country is absolutely at a disadvantage in the production of every good compared to another country there is still room for mutually beneficial trade. According to Ricardo only **comparative advantage** is necessary. Each country should specialize and export those goods that it can produce at *relatively* lower cost. Relative efficiency is what mattered.
- A country has a comparative advantage in the production of a good if it can produce it at a lower opportunity cost, i.e. by sacrificing fewer units of another good.
- In Fig. 4.3, Country Red can produce at the most 18 units of good X or 9 units of good Y whereas Country Black can produce at the most 20 units of good X or 20 units of good Y. Country Black has an absolute advantage in the production of both goods as it can produce more of both.
- Since their production possibilities frontiers are not parallel their opportunity cost ratios differ. There is thus room for specialization and mutually beneficial exchange.
- Country Red has a comparative advantage in good X and Country Black has a comparative advantage in the production of good Y. Red should specialize and export good X while Black should specialize and export good Y.
- How do we know that Red has a comparative advantage in good X? First of all by inspection, as its PPF is flatter. On a diagram with two linear PPFs, the country with the flatter PPF has the comparative advantage in the production of the good on the horizontal axis (while the other country has the comparative advantage in the production of the other good).
- Also, by calculating the opportunity cost of producing good X by each country:

For Country Red:

If it produces 18 units of good X it must not produce (i.e. sacrifice) 9 units of good Y, so (dividing both sides by 18) for 1 unit of X it sacrifices 9/18 or 1/2 units of good Y.

For Country Black:

If it produces 20X it must not produce (i.e. sacrifice) 20Y, so (dividing both sides by 20) for 1X it sacrifices 1Y.

- Note that if the PPFs are parallel then there is no room for specialization and mutually beneficial trade (no exports, no imports, etc.).

Figure 4.3 Comparative advantage

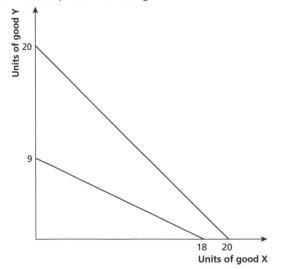

Tips

Since the opportunity cost of producing the good on the horizontal axis is the slope of the PPF (= $\Delta Y / \Delta X$) try to use convenient numbers on your diagram. It is perhaps easier if for the country with the absolute advantage in the production of both goods you assign a slope of (minus) 1 with the maximum quantities of Y and X that the country can produce being equal (like 20 units of Y and 20 units of X). Then for the maximum number of units of Y and X that the country with the absolute disadvantage can produce use two numbers that are multiples such as 9 and 18 (as in Fig. 4.3) or 5 and 15, etc.

Assumptions used to derive the principle of comparative advantage

- Constant costs of production reflected in the linear production possibility curves we draw
- Perfect factor mobility within each country (but immobility between countries)
- No transport costs
- Perfect competition in all markets
- Free trade

Criticisms of the principle of comparative advantage

The above assumptions do not accurately reflect real-world conditions. These assumptions are the basis for the criticisms of the comparative advantage model and its predictions:

- Costs of production need not be constant. They may be decreasing, in which case the gains from specialization may be even greater. Increasing returns to scale in production and the resulting economies of scale are very often the case in the real world.
- Labour and the other factors of production suffer from both occupational and geographical immobility. It may not be costless or even possible for a country to specialize. Real adjustment costs, such as unemployment for certain regions or groups, will result when a country responds to a shift in its comparative advantage.
- Transportation costs in the real world do exist and depending on the weight to value ratio will decrease the scope of foreign trade opportunities. Note though that transport costs have dramatically decreased since the advent of the container in shipping.
- Perfect competition is not common at all. Large firms with monopoly power and scale economies dominate world trade.
- Trade barriers are also a reality which prevents world trade flows from reflecting comparative advantage conditions among nations.

For these and other reasons the actual pattern of **trade flows** does not *fully* reflect comparative advantage.
Still, comparative advantage is a most useful concept in understanding and explaining much of what is going on in the world of trade.

Comparative advantage continued

Factors determining the relative costs of production and thus comparative advantage

- The quantity and quality of factors of production available (i.e. the size and efficiency of the available labour force, the productivity of the existing stock of capital and the rate of investment).
- Movements in the exchange rate (the price of a currency expressed in terms of another) can affect comparative advantage. For example, if the exchange rate rises (appreciates) then exports from a country increase in price. This makes them less competitive in international markets.
- Changes in the relative inflation rates affect export competitiveness. For example if average inflation in Country X is 4% while in Country B it is 8%, the goods and services produced by Country X will become relatively more expensive over time. This worsens their competitiveness and causes a loss in comparative advantage.
- Export subsidies can be used to create an artificial comparative advantage for a country's products: US cotton producers are a good example.
- Non-price factors can lead to the creation or the loss of comparative advantage (e.g. product design, reliability, quality of after-sales support). Export sales of German cars are not easily affected by an appreciation of the euro as their reputation is excellent in foreign markets.

Comparative advantage is a dynamic concept

- Comparative advantage is a *dynamic* concept as it can and does change over time. Governments can and historically have promoted policies that help to create a comparative advantage in specific industries. A government could invest in education, increasing the stock of human capital and thus raising labour productivity and lowering average costs. It could create favorable investment conditions for private firms by ensuring price stability (low inflation), long-run exchange rate equilibrium and more generally a conducive business environment. It could also import technology by attracting foreign direct investment in high-tech sectors.
- An example of a country that did not rely on a static interpretation of comparative advantage but instead *created* a comparative advantage in several other areas is Korea. If it had relied on its original comparative advantage, it would still have been an exporter of rice.

Protectionism

Does it make sense?

- If the benefits from free trade are so many and, as shown in Fig. 4.1, net welfare increases, why do so many countries restrict trade and employ various degrees of **protectionism**? Why is 'managed' trade so common?
- The simple answer is that not all parties involved gain from free trade; some groups are worse off. Free trade creates winners and losers.
- In Fig. 4.1 the increase in the consumer surplus exceeds the decrease in the producer surplus. The winnings of the winners are greater than the losses of the losers but there is no guarantee that the losers will be compensated.
- In addition, the winnings from free trade are spread over a very large number of people, each getting a small addition to his income while the resulting losses are spread over a much smaller number of individuals each suffering a significant cut in his income. It follows that the losers have an incentive to put up a fight against free trade.
- To ensure that the adjustment costs for these individuals are small, governments often judge that some protectionism is necessary.

Non-economic arguments in favour of protectionism

- To ensure that a country is self-sufficient in the production of crucial goods in case of a war (strategic reasons). The weapons and aerospace industry as well as the food sector are often classified as being of strategic importance. The validity of this argument is doubtful at least for countries belonging to wide strategic and/or political alliances.
- To restrict imports of illegal drugs and other harmful substances. Research has raised doubts as to the success of such policies as drug use is widespread in many countries.
- To put pressure on and weaken politically unfriendly countries (embargoes).
- To preserve a way of life or cultural identity as part of a broader social strategy.
- To ensure that certain safety and health standards are met. However, such standards may be a pretence through which domestic producers are protected.

Does it make sense? continued

Economic arguments in favour of protectionism

- **To protect domestic jobs and declining industries**. Calls to protect domestic industries and workers against 'unfair' competition from 'cheap' foreign labour is perhaps the commonest argument heard in favour of protection.

- These calls must be carefully evaluated. Domestic wages could be higher because of higher labour productivity in which case labour costs per unit of output could be lower than abroad. If the higher domestic wages are not a reflection of higher productivity then the domestic industry has a comparative disadvantage. Theory then suggests that labour and other resources should be channelled to other, more efficient uses. Workers and owners of capital, and perhaps whole regions, will have to face real adjustment costs and will resist these changes. Instead of protection, which will reduce the incentive to restructure, other policies could be adopted to smoothen the transition, especially for displaced workers. In the case of developing countries shifting resources may be almost impossible without some government assistance which itself could be too costly to implement. In such a case trade liberalization should proceed gradually.

- **To improve a trade deficit**. The idea is that protectionism will make imports more expensive. Spending on imports will thus decrease, shrinking the imbalance.

  There are several potential problems with this argument. First, it invites retaliation from trading partners as any improvement comes at their expense. Second, restricting foreign products into the country lowers foreign incomes and their ability to absorb our exports. Third and most important, such a policy does not treat the root cause of a widening trade deficit problem. The ballooning trade deficit may be the result of domestic products being uncompetitive and thus unable to penetrate foreign markets (so that exports decrease) while domestic households find it cheaper to buy imports (imports rise). High inflation, structural rigidities, uncompetitive domestic markets as well as poor quality, reliability, delivery, design or marketing may be the real reasons behind a growing trade imbalance, in which case protectionism will not prove helpful but possibly detrimental.

- **To assist certain industries in their initial stages of development** grow and realize their potential. Once they develop the necessary know-how and achieve economies of scale they will be able to meet international competition, at which point the protection should be removed. This is the well-known '**infant industry**' argument.

  It too needs to be carefully evaluated. The argument is sensible and the policy has been used by all developed economies in the past including the US and in varying degrees by all Asian export achievers. It also suffers from potential major drawbacks. How does a government pick a 'winner'? It may be difficult to determine which industry qualifies for such treatment. If a mistake is made will it be possible for the government to withdraw its support? Removing the protection could be resisted by the industry stakeholders resulting in a 'perpetual infant'. There is an inherent risk of making the industry over-reliant on state support, sluggish and inefficient.

- **To help industries facing dumping from abroad**. Dumping exists if a product is sold abroad at a price below average cost. If dumping is proved then **anti-dumping duties** are permitted to ensure a 'level playingfield'.

  However, dumping is not easy to prove. The question arising is, which firm's average costs? It could be that the foreign firms are much more efficient and thus have much lower unit costs of production. Or that the foreign firms are illegally subsidized by their governments, creating an artificial cost advantage. In the former case there is no case of dumping whereas in the latter there is. As anti-dumping duties are automatically imposed when dumping is suspected until the issue is investigated and a verdict is reached, many industries cry 'dumping' to gain time in order to restructure and hopefully become more efficient.

- **The strategic trade policy argument** according to which in a framework of international oligopolies (where few large firms dominate world markets) a government can tilt the balance and the profits away from foreign competitors by using trade policies. The government's assistance can be in the form of subsidies, grants or loans at below market interest rates and tariffs. The classic example is the aircraft manufacturing industry with Boeing and Airbus monopolizing the world market and where each side accuses the other of massive government assistance. In other cases, where there are 'first mover advantages' (implying that firms that are first to succeed dominate the world industry), the assistance could take the form of setting industry standards in favour of domestic firms, as in the case of HDTV in the US.

  The problem with strategic trade policy is that it carries the risk of destabilizing trade disputes and retaliation as it is a 'beggar thy neighbour' policy. There is also the risk of protecting the wrong industries.

- In the case of tariffs, **to provide a government with revenues**. Tax systems in certain developing countries are ineffective, making it difficult for the government to collect sufficient revenue to finance pro-development activities.

  If this is the case then trade liberalization must be gradual to ensure that the provision of basic government services is not interrupted.

Forms of protectionism

Protectionism can take various forms. The most common forms are: tariffs, quotas, voluntary export restraints, subsidies, regulatory barriers (product standards), as well as a host of other measures such as antidumping duties, exchange controls, non-automatic import authorization (import licences), etc. Bear in mind that non-tariff barriers include those barriers that do not directly affect the price of the good.

Tariffs

- A tariff is defined as a tax imposed on imports. It has been the most common form of protection. It may be specific or ad valorem. A tariff will tend to raise the price and domestic production while lowering the amounts consumed and imported. These effects are illustrated in Fig. 4.4.
- Assume the market for some good and let the world price be at P. At P, domestic firms will offer Q1 units per period while domestic consumption will be Q2 units. Imports will be Q1Q2 units per period, the difference (Q2–Q1).
- Let a tariff now be imposed. The tariff will raise the domestic price to P' (note that it will not affect the world price as it is assumed that the country is 'small' in the sense that its production/consumption decisions are insignificant and do not affect the world price). The tariff is thus PP' per unit.
- Domestic production will rise to Q3 units per period while domestic consumption drops to Q4 units per period. The volume of imports shrinks to Q3Q4 units per period.
- The higher price implies that the consumer surplus decreases by area (P'PJC) while the producer surplus rises by area (PABP').
- Area (FHCB) is the tariff revenue collected. This is the case because tariff revenues are the product of the tariff per unit times that number of units imported. The tariff per unit is P'P (= BF) and the volume of imports is Q3Q4 (= FH).

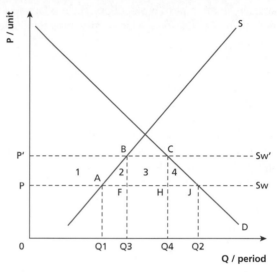

Figure 4.4 Effects of a tariff ('small country' case)

Welfare analysis of a tariff

Δ(producer surplus) = + area (1)

Δ(consumer surplus) = – area (1+2+3+4)

Δ(social welfare) = – area (2+3+4)

But since area (3) represents the tariff revenues collected it cannot be considered a welfare loss as this money can be spent on schools and health care centres.

Thus a tariff leads to a net welfare loss equal to areas (2) *and* (4). Area (2) represents the resulting **production inefficiency** while area (4) represents the resulting **consumption inefficiency**.

Area (2) reflects production inefficiency because the cost of domestically producing Q1Q3 units (which is area Q1Q3BA) is greater than what it would have cost the country to import these units at the world price P (area Q1Q3FA).

Area (4) reflects consumption inefficiency. Units Q4Q2 are now not consumed as a result of the tariff even though these units are valued by consumers more than what it would cost to import them. These units are worth area (Q4CJQ2), which is the sum of how much consumers would be willing to pay for each of these units. They would have cost only area (Q4Q2JH) to import.

Tip

Remember that despite the welfare loss a tariff may make sense. It is a source of government revenues that may be impossible to replace. Also, the adjustment costs for the displaced workers may be prohibitively high.

Quotas

- A **quota** is defined as a quantitative restriction on the volume of imports. Figure 4.5 illustrates the effect of a quota.
- Assume the market for some good (say, lambs) and let the world price be at P. At P, domestic firms will offer Q1 units per period (say 100,000 lambs per period) while domestic consumption will be Q2 units (say 700,000 lambs). Imports will be Q1Q2 units or, in this example, 600,000 lambs.
- Let the government now impose a quota of 300,000 lambs in an attempt to protect domestic producers. No more than 300,000 foreign lambs may enter the domestic market.
- Prior to the quota domestic consumers faced an infinitely elastic supply of lambs (Sw) as they were offered whatever amount they wished at the world price. Now at the world price P, supply will be constrained to whatever amount the domestic producers will be willing to offer *plus* the 300,000 lambs that can now only be imported.
- The new effective supply of lambs is S', which is parallel to the right of the domestic supply curve Sd by the amount of the quota. At each price above P the amount of lambs available to consumers will equal whatever quantity the domestic producers are willing to offer *plus* the 300,000 lambs of the quota.
- At P, the total quantity supplied of lambs will equal Q1 units from domestic firms *plus* the 300,000 foreign lambs allowed and equal to the red distance BF. At that price though, consumers are willing to purchase more lambs, specifically Q2 units. Excess demand equal to FJ units per period will result. The price will thus rise until it reaches P'.
- At this new domestic market price for lambs domestic producers will offer Q3, consumers will buy Q4 with the difference Q3Q4 made up of imported lambs. This is of course the quota of 300,000 lambs imposed.

Figure 4.5 Effects of a quota

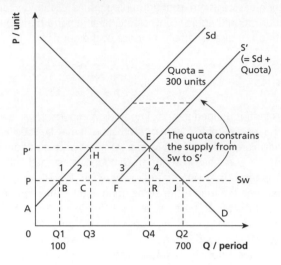

- A quota thus increases the domestic price and domestic production and reduces domestic consumption and, of course, the quantity of imports.

The effects of a quota are thus the same as those of an 'equivalent' tariff with one exception: the tariff revenues area now represents '*quota rents*' which are usually collected by the foreign exporting firms.

Quota rents help explain why quotas are often imposed instead of tariffs even though the associated welfare loss is bigger. Foreigners are 'happy' as they appropriate area (3). Their export revenues (the import bill from the point of view of the importing country) are bigger than if a tariff was imposed and may even be greater than under free trade. With free trade their export revenues were equal to area (Q1BJQ2) whereas after the quota they are area (Q3HEQ4). These possibilities minimize the probability of retaliation.

Welfare analysis of a quota

Δ(producer surplus) = + area (1)

Δ(consumer surplus) = − area (1+2+3+4)

Δ(social welfare) = − area (2+3+4)

Area (3) is known as 'quota rents' and represents money typically earned by the foreign exporting firms which can now sell the product at a higher price.

Again, area (2) represents the resulting **production inefficiency** while area (4) represents the resulting **consumption inefficiency** as explained earlier.

Voluntary export restraints

Voluntary export restraint is a form of protectionism that is a slightly different version of quotas. VERs are agreements between an exporting and an importing country limiting the maximum amount of exports in a given period. The domestic (importing) government *asks* the foreign government to restrict the exports of the good; the term 'voluntary' is misleading since the request is really a demand and it is made clear that unless the foreign government 'voluntarily' complies, more restrictive protectionist barriers will be imposed. Following the 'end' of the MFA (the Multifiber Arrangement), the US and the European Union had asked China to 'voluntarily' restrain its exports of textiles.

Subsidies

- Subsidies lower production costs of firms and thus artificially increase their competitiveness. As a result subsidies will decrease imports and may even lead to exports. The US cotton industry is the recipient of huge government subsidies and ranks number one in world exports. The effects of a subsidy are illustrated in Fig. 4.6.
- Initially assume free trade with the world price of the product at P. The domestic industry will produce Q1 units per period whereas consumption will be at Q2 units per period leading to Q1Q2 units of imports.
- If now a subsidy is granted to the domestic firms then their production (marginal) costs will decrease by the amount of the subsidy. Supply will increase, shifting downward by the amount of the subsidy to S'.
- The world price is not affected ('small country' case) but now at the world price P domestic firms will produce more. Domestic production at P is now at Q3 units per period so the volume of imports will shrink from Q1Q2 to Q3Q2 units.
- Domestic firms will earn P per unit *plus* the subsidy which is the vertical distance HF between the two supply curves, i.e. the new average revenue is Pp.

Figure 4.6 Effect of a subsidy to domestic producers on imports

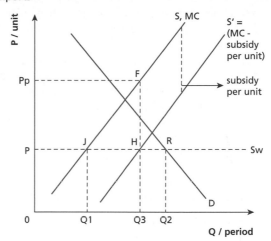

- Total revenues for the domestic industry have thus increased from area (0Q1JP) to area (0Q3FPp). Consumers enjoy the same amount at the same price but the government and thus, eventually, taxpayers are burdened by the cost of the subsidy which is equal to area (PHFPp).

Regulatory barriers

Regulatory barriers may be technical, administrative, or any kind of 'red tape'.

- This is perhaps the most common form of protection. Regulatory barriers include *product standards* (to meet certain domestic requirements), *sanitary standards* (to protect the domestic consumers), *pollution standards*, etc.
- Often these standards are set to protect domestic producers rather than domestic consumers by making it more difficult and thus costly for foreign firms to comply.
- A most famous example is the one related to the city of Poitiers in France. In 1981 the French government ordered that all Japanese video imports were to be inspected and pass customs there. Poitiers is located inland, is far from ports and was staffed with only a few officers ordered to fully inspect each and every truck. The delays were huge and the volume of imports entering France per period was effectively reduced. Following complaints this absurd requirement was withdrawn. Another example is the banning by the EU of US hormone-treated beef in 1989. Even though some studies show that a growth hormone used in US cattle production is a 'complete carcinogen', Americans claim that the ban is nothing more than an attempt by the EU to protect its own cattle producers.

Anti-dumping duties

- Domestic firms may file a complaint that foreign firms are dumping their goods in their market, i.e. selling at below unit costs. A duty (tax) is automatically imposed that raises the foreign firms' price until the issue is investigated and resolved by the World Trade Organization.

- Often, firms file such claims only to buy time to restructure and hopefully become more efficient.

Why have calls for protectionism been increasing?

- A growing number of developing countries (especially in South East Asia and lately China and India) have achieved rapid, export-led growth. Export success by these countries means deep import penetration in Europe and the US. Protectionist response is expected from those groups most affected.
- Large trade imbalances between large trading nations (most prominent example being the US-China case) have strained relationships between these countries and have led to various protectionist measures.
- Exchange rate instability has added risk and uncertainty to trade and since it can lead to sudden shifts in comparative

advantages it may lead to calls for protection for domestic industry. Major trading countries, most notably China, are accused of maintaining their currency artificially undervalued to render their products even cheaper in foreign markets.
- Rising unemployment has always been a reason for increased protectionism. Recessions and unemployment always put political pressure on governments to limit 'job threatening' imports.

Economic integration and trade liberalization

Globalization implies greater interconnectedness of countries in the world. This greater interconnectedness is also expressed in the area of international trade. Economies are becoming more open, meaning that the size of exports and imports as a proportion of GDP is increasing. The volume and value of annual trade flows has been rising in the past decades as a result of trade liberalization.

Trade liberalization, defined as a process of reducing or even eliminating trade barriers, may be achieved through the multilateral route or on a bilateral (more generally, regional) basis.

Trade liberalization through the WTO: the multilateral route

- This refers to the reduction and elimination of protectionism resulting from membership in the **World Trade Organization** (WTO).
- The WTO was set up in 1995 and has 148 member countries, replacing another international organization known as the General Agreement on Tariffs and Trade (GATT). GATT was formed in 1948 when 23 countries signed an agreement to reduce customs tariffs.
- The WTO is an international institution aiming at promoting free trade by persuading countries to abolish import tariffs and other barriers. It has become closely associated with globalization. It *ensures that trade rules are adhered to*, it *settles trade disputes* between countries and it *organizes trade negotiations*. WTO *decisions are final* and every member must abide by its rulings. So, when the US and the EU are in dispute over hormone-treated beef, it is the WTO which acts as judge and jury. WTO empowers its members to enforce its decisions by imposing trade sanctions against countries that have broken the rules.

- The WTO is criticized on several grounds. It is accused of being controlled by the rich nations, especially the US, and that it does not sufficiently consider the needs and problems of the developing world. For example, agricultural products from developing countries do not have free access to the US market but the US insists that the poor open up their markets to US goods and, especially, services. It is claimed that it is too powerful, trying to force nations to change policies, laws and regulations by declaring them in violation of its rules. It is charged that it does not consider the possible adverse effects of trade liberalization on workers, the environment and health, or child labour. Lastly some consider that it lacks transparency in its decision making on trade disputes as it is closed to the media and the public.
- On the other hand, even if the benefits of freer trade have not been shared equally, many believe that the trade liberalization efforts of the WTO have improved living standards across the globe.

The bilateral/regional route: forming regional trading blocs

- The regional approach to trade liberalization refers to agreements between two countries (bilateral) or among a small number of countries to establish free trade between them while keeping protectionist barriers against outsiders.
- Two very well-known examples are NAFTA (the free trade agreement between Canada, Mexico and the US) and the European Union (EU).

Regional agreements can take various forms:

- Two or more countries can form a **free trade area** if tariffs and other barriers among member countries are abolished (or agreed to be phased out) but each member nation maintains its own tariffs on imports from non-member countries. NAFTA is the best-known example.

- A **customs union** is formed if, in addition, a common external tariff against non-member countries is agreed. MERCOSUR, set up in 1991, is an example of a customs union in which Argentina, Brazil, Paraguay and Uruguay are full members.
- If, in addition, unrestricted factor flows are agreed then the member countries have formed a **common market**. Free flow of labour and capital means that individuals have the right to work in any of the member countries without any special permits and that cross-border investment is liberalized.
- Lastly, members may agree to coordinate economic policy, harmonize taxes and even adopt a common currency. In this case they have formed an **economic union**, with the European Union and the Eurozone the only such example.

Evaluation of trading blocs

HL

- What are the *economic effects* of regional trading blocs? The analysis can focus on static and on dynamic effects. *Static* effects include trade creation and trade diversion.
- **Trade creation** enhances welfare. The elimination of internal trade barriers will lead members to import from one another goods and services that were previously produced domestically. This increases efficiency since production shifts away from a higher-cost domestic producer to a lower-cost foreign producer, leading to fewer scarce resources being wasted.
- **Trade diversion** results from the possibility that the remaining external tariff for non-members only may render some member artificially cheaper in the production of a good. Another member will then switch importing from the truly efficient and lowest cost non-member to the artificially cheaper member. This is inefficient since it implies production against what comparative advantage would dictate.
- The relative size of trade creation and trade diversion will vary from case to case and determine whether the agreement enhances or diminishes static efficiency. Thus, whether a particular trading bloc promotes global welfare is an empirical question.

In addition to the above static analysis, the expected *dynamic* advantages should be weighed up.

- On the plus side, a trading bloc expands the size of the market for firms of all involved countries, so faster and higher investment rates will ensue.

- Firms may grow in size especially if their national markets were originally small and so economies of scale may result.
- Seamless borders also permit faster technology transfer.
- Lastly, the bargaining power of members increases and they may thus exercise greater economic leverage than if they acted individually. Again this is more significant for smaller countries.

Are there any potential long-run disadvantages of such trading blocs?

- Firms may grow to such sizes that they suffer from diseconomies of scale. This is rather unlikely though.
- What is more likely is that trading blocs may form by self-interested member producers hoping to benefit from any resulting trade diversion effects.
- Most important, the role of the WTO is undermined. Multilateral agreements which are superior to any regional trading agreement may become more and more difficult to achieve. There is a risk that the world may end up split into major blocs, each a potential 'fortress' to the others. The recent efforts of the three major Asian economies, Japan, China and Korea, to sign free trade agreements with many different countries and regions and the US aggressive strategy of so-called 'competitive liberalizations' whereby it signed a series of trading agreements with many countries on a bilateral basis (using its huge negotiating power) may result in a 'spaghetti bowl' of such agreements which undermine the world trading order.

Exchange rates

The exchange rate of a currency is defined as the price (the value) of a currency expressed in terms of another currency. For example, in December 2007, the euro's exchange rate was $1.45. One needed 1.45 US dollars to purchase one euro.

Foreign exchange markets

- A foreign exchange market is a market in which currencies are exchanged for other currencies. An example is the market where euros and dollars are traded.
- This is a 24-hour, 365 days a year world market that is a good example of a perfectly competitive market: the 'good' is homogeneous as it makes no difference whether a dollar is bought in Frankfurt or Singapore or London; there are very many buyers and sellers of currencies (all major world banks participate, non-financial corporations as well financial corporations such as pension funds, insurance companies, hedge funds, etc.) with no player being large enough to influence the market price of a currency; no entry barriers into the market exist as any new bank or corporate financial or non-financial major can enter and participate, and this market comes closest to perfect information as any new piece of information is available to all participants in real time.
- A distinctive characteristic of this market is that all buyers are at the same time sellers also and vice versa. Also, if the price of currency A expressed in terms of currency B is e then the price of currency B expressed in terms of currency A is (1/e).

Floating, fixed and managed exchange rate systems

- A currency is traded in a **floating (or flexible) exchange rate system** if market forces alone without any government or central bank intervention determine its value. The dollar, the euro and the British pound all float against each other.
- A **fixed exchange rate system** refers to the case where the exchange rate is set and maintained at some level by the government (or the central bank) of a country. China maintained its currency, the yuan (officially the renminbi or RMB), fixed against the dollar between 1994 and 21 July 2005 at RMB 8.28 per dollar.
- A **managed exchange rate system** is one where there is no pre-announced level but either the exchange rate is allowed to float within some upper and lower bound or a system in which authorities intervene when they consider the direction or the speed of adjustment of the currency as undesirable. Since July 2005 the renminbi has been in a managed float with reference to a basket of currencies.

Appreciation and depreciation

- The terms refer to changes in the price (the value) of a currency in a *floating (flexible)* exchange rate system.
- More specifically, a currency **appreciates** if its price increases within a floating (flexible) exchange rate system.
- For example, between 2006 and 2007 the euro appreciated from $1.32 to $1.45. Its price increased, as you could buy a euro for only $1.32 in December 2006 whereas you needed $1.45 in December 2007.
- A currency **depreciates** if its price decreases within a floating (flexible) exchange rate system.
- Using the same example, between 2006 and 2007 the dollar depreciated from €0.76 to €0.69. It became cheaper as one needed €0.76 to buy a dollar in December 2006 while you could buy it only for €0.69 in December 2007.
- It should be clear that if currency A depreciates in terms of currency B it follows that currency B appreciates in terms of currency A.

Figure 4.7 Appreciation of the euro against the US dollar

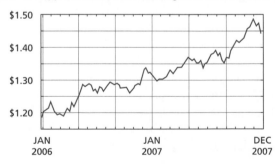

In Fig. 4.7 the appreciation of the euro between January 2006 and December 2007 is shown. Note than in a floating (flexible) exchange rate system the changes are continuous and even though the path (the trend) is upward, reflecting the appreciation, there is a lot of volatility.

Revaluation and devaluation

- The terms strictly refer to *official* changes in the price (the value) of a currency in a *fixed* exchange rate system.
- More specifically, a currency **devalues** if its official price decreases within a fixed exchange rate system. A currency **revalues** if its official price increases within a fixed exchange rate system.

- For example in January 2002 the Argentine peso went from P 1.00 = $1.00 to P 1.40 = $1.00. This is a devaluation of the peso or, equivalently, a revaluation of the dollar. A dollar could have been bought using one peso but after the devaluation one needed 1.4 pesos to buy a dollar.

Labelling a foreign exchange market diagram

- Let us see how to properly label the axes in a foreign exchange diagram. Assume that we are interested in the euro market and that you are focusing on the price of the euro.
- On the vertical axis write 'price of euro'. Then write on the horizontal 'euros traded per period'.
- Lastly return back to the vertical and write 'expressed in dollars, $/€'.
- To avoid errors think of the market for, say, onions instead of the market for euros, in which case the vertical axis would read 'price of a kg of onions, expressed in dollars' while the horizontal would read 'quantity of onions traded per period'.
- More generally, the price of whatever currency you have on the vertical will feature on the horizontal as well as in the denominator of the currencies fraction, as in Fig. 4.8a.
- Since the vertical axis is the price of a euro it follows that the demand curve will be the demand for euros and that the supply curve will be the supply of euros (Fig. 4.8a).

The mirror image is:

- Remember that a trader who is buying euros is at the same time selling dollars and if she is selling euros she is buying dollars.
- Remember also that if the dollar price of the euro is e1, then the euro price of the dollar is the inverse i.e. (1/e1).
- Using December 2007 figures, since the dollar price of the euro was 1.45, then the euro price of the dollar was (1/1.45) = 0.69. On the diagram (Fig. 4.8b) you would write on the vertical axis 'price of dollar', then go to the horizontal axis and write 'dollars traded per period' and lastly, return to the vertical axis to write 'expressed in euros, €/$'. The demand would be demand for dollars, the supply would be supply of dollars and the exchange rate would be euros 0.69 (or 1/e1).

Figure 4.8a Labelling a foreign exchange market diagram

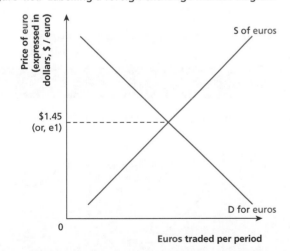

Figure 4.8b Labelling a foreign exchange market diagram

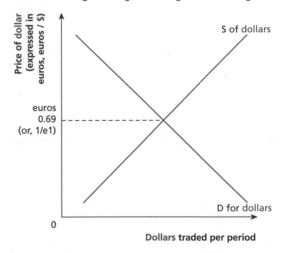

Demand for foreign currency in the foreign exchange market

Imagine the world consisting of only two countries, Japan and Australia. The Japanese currency is the yen (JPY) and the Australian currency is the Australian dollar (AUD). In this simplified setup the question is: who demands Australian dollars in the foreign exchange market? The answer is a Japanese entity (household or firm) which does not have Australian dollars but needs them.

Why would a Japanese entity need Australian dollars? Some basic reasons include:

- A Japanese company planning to purchase Australian wool or iron ore (export of a good).
- A Japanese couple planning to visit Uluru in central Australia where the second largest monolith in the world is located (export of a service – tourism).
- A resident of Japan wishing to make a savings deposit in Australian dollars or to buy Australian government bonds (an investment into Australia).
- A resident of Japan wishing to buy shares in an Australian mining company (an investment into Australia).
- A Japanese company establishing a presence in Australia (an investment into Australia).

More generally, any foreigner wishing to buy Australian goods and services or to make investments in Australia will need to buy Australian dollars. The first two reasons are related to international trade flows whereas the rest are related to international investment flows.

In summary

- The demand and supply of currencies in foreign exchange markets reflect **international trade flows** and **cross-border investment flows.**
- The demand for a country's currency reflects the value of its exports of goods and services as well as the inflow of investments into the country.

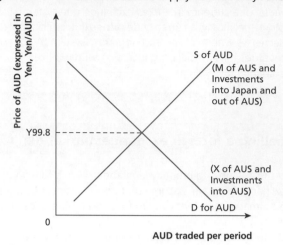

Figure 4.9 What the demand and supply of a currency reflect

- The supply of a country's currency reflects the value of its imports of goods and services as well as the outflow of investments from the country.
- In Fig. 4.9 the demand for Australian dollars reflects the value of Australian exports of goods and services as well as the value of foreign investments (bonds, stocks, etc.) into Australia. The supply of Australian dollars symmetrically reflects the value of imports into Australia as well as outflows of investment capital from Australia.
- In addition, currency speculators may buy a currency not to finance the purchase of a good, service, bond, stock or the acquisition of a foreign company but only in the hope of selling the currency later (even an hour or a day later) at a higher price.

Exchange rate determination in a flexible exchange rate system

- To simplify the analysis let's assume that there are no cross-border investments so that only exports and imports of goods and services (trade flows) create a need to exchange currencies. We'll take the example of the US and the EU15 (the 15 countries in the European Union before the expansion on 1 May 2004). Americans demand euros to buy EU15 goods and services and Europeans supply euros to buy (dollars and thus) American goods and services (Fig. 4.10).
- At the exchange rate e1 the supply of euros e1b reflects the value of imports into the EU15 while the demand for euros is e1a and reflects the value of EU15 exports to the US.
- The EU15 has a trade deficit as M > X and an excess supply of euros exists in the market equal to line segment ab. This excess supply of euros in the foreign exchange market creates pressure for the price of the euro to decrease (to depreciate).

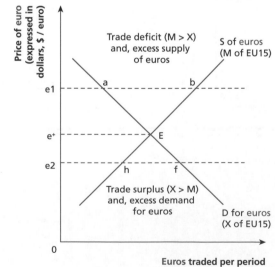

Figure 4.10 Equilibrium exchange rate determination

Exchange rate determination in a flexible exchange rate system continued

- This has two effects: EU15 exports become cheaper and more competitive while imports become pricier and thus less attractive. Eventually the value of EU15 exports will increase and the expenditures on imports will shrink, tending to balance trade flows. This will happen when the exchange rate reaches e*. At e*, demand for euros is equal to supply of euros per period and **trade balance** is restored.
- At the exchange rate e2 the supply of euros e2h reflects the value of imports into the EU15 while the demand for euros is e2f and reflects the value of EU15 exports to the US.
- The EU15 has a trade surplus as X > M and an excess demand for euros exists in the market equal to line segment hf. The excess demand for euros in the foreign exchange market creates pressure for the price of the euro to increase (to appreciate).
- This has two effects: EU15 exports become more expensive and thus less competitive while imports become cheaper and thus more attractive. Eventually the value of EU15 exports will decrease and the expenditures on

imports will increase, tending to balance trade flows. This will happen when the exchange rate reaches e*. At e*, demand for euros is equal to supply of euros per period and trade balance is restored.
- It follows that a trade deficit creates pressure for the exchange rate to depreciate whereas trade surplus creates pressure for the exchange rate to appreciate. The above description presents an idealized view. In the real world a number of problems complicate matters. First of all exchange rates are very much affected by cross-border investments (the buying and selling of bonds and stocks and speculation) and not only by trade flows. Any change in interest rates or in investment sentiment may offset the equilibrating forces described earlier.

Lastly, whether a depreciating currency will increase the *value* of exports depends on the price elasticity of exports. The lower-priced exports will definitely increase the volume of exports per period but whether their value increases depends on the price elasticity of exports.

Why do exchange rates move?

Since we established that the demand and the supply of a currency in the foreign exchange market reflect trade flows and investment flows between countries, it follows that factors that may affect trade flows and factors that may affect investment flows will in turn tend to affect the exchange rate of a currency.

Factors that may affect trade flows: changes in relative growth rates

- A higher growth rate implies that incomes are rising faster. Consumption expenditures rise when incomes rise and household consumption includes spending on both domestic and foreign goods and services. It follows that in a growing economy, imports rise.
- In Fig. 4.11 the price of the Indonesian rupiah is initially assumed at *e1*. If Indonesian growth accelerates then Indonesians' incomes are rising so their consumption expenditures will rise. This means that they will also buy more foreign products.
- Indonesians will thus have to supply more of their currency, the rupiah, in the foreign exchange market to buy the necessary dollars in order to buy more imports Supply of the rupiah will shift to the right to S2 as imports are now greater (M2 > M1).

Figure 4.11 Effect of a growing economy on the exchange rate

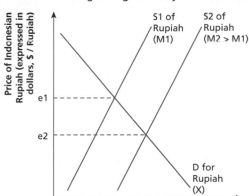

Rupiah traded per period

- As a result, the rupiah will tend to depreciate to *e2*. This is a very interesting result that is seemingly counterintuitive. A growing economy may witness a depreciating currency.

Why do exchange rates move? continued

Factors that may affect trade flows: changes in relative inflation rates

- If inflation in a country accelerates it means that prices in that country are rising on average faster than they did. As a result its products will become less and less competitive abroad.
- Its exports will decrease and so will the demand for its currency in foreign exchange markets. In addition, foreign products (imports) will now seem relatively more attractive to domestic households. Import spending will tend to rise and thus supply of its currency in foreign exchange markets (as they will need more dollars to pay for these imports).
- Figure 4.12 illustrates the effect of higher inflation in Indonesia on its currency, the rupiah. Initially the rupiah is valued against the dollar at *e1*.
- The higher inflation in Indonesia will have an adverse effect on its exports as they will become less competitive abroad and thus decrease, decreasing the demand for the rupiah from D1 to D2.
- At the same time inflation will make Indonesians find foreign products more and more attractive. Imports will tend to increase and thus more rupiahs will be supplied in the foreign exchange market, shifting the supply of rupiahs from S1 to S2. The rupiah will tend to depreciate to *e2*.
- Inflation in an economy will tend to depreciate a currency.

Figure 4.12 Effect of higher inflation on the exchange rate

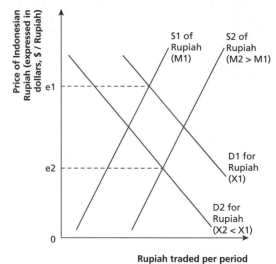

Rupiah traded per period

Factors that may affect investment (capital) flows

- Investment flows are also referred to as **capital flows** and include portfolio investments (the buying and selling of bonds, stocks and other financial assets) and FDI (foreign direct investment which refers to investors establishing a presence in a foreign country either by setting up a new firm or by acquiring a controlling share of an existing domestic firm).
- Much of these capital flows are short term and speculative in nature. Currency speculation is also included in this section. These transactions are included in the capital account of the balance of payments of a country.
- Bear in mind that not all countries have fully liberalized their capital account. This means that foreign investment

may be constrained. Many economies limit the types of foreign investment flows they permit as some of these investments may prove very destabilizing. Short-term speculative capital may suddenly be withdrawn leading to a sudden sharp depreciation and consequently to adverse real effects on the economy. There is a lot of discussion on the desirability of such private capital inflows especially for developing countries.

Factors that may affect investment flows: changes in relative interest rates

- If interest rates in a country decrease then domestic bonds as well as savings deposits in the domestic currency will be less attractive to foreign investors as they will earn less on their financial investments.
- As a result not only will demand for that currency decrease as there will be less demand for that country's bonds, but also there will be an increase in the supply of that country's currency as investors will sell that currency to buy currency and bonds of other countries. The effect of lower interest rates will be a tendency for the currency to depreciate.
- In Fig. 4.13 we assume that the dollar price of the euro is initially at *e1*. Let the European Central Bank decrease interest rates. Now the rate of return on European bonds as well as on deposits in euros is lower so these assets will be less attractive to investors.
- Demand for the euro will decrease from D1 to D2 reflecting the lower demand for European bonds and euro deposits.
- Also, some holders of such assets will decide to sell them, increasing the supply of euros from S1 to S2 as they will switch to more attractive bonds issued by other countries. The euro will tend to depreciate from *e1* to *e2*.
- A note of caution here: if interest rates rise there will be a tendency for the exchange rate to appreciate, *assuming* that foreign investors do not expect the currency to depreciate. For example if interest rates in country A rise then investors will not flock into that country if they expect its currency to depreciate. So interest rates do matter but so does the expectation about the future path of the exchange rate itself.

Figure 4.13 Effect of lower interest rates on the exchange rate

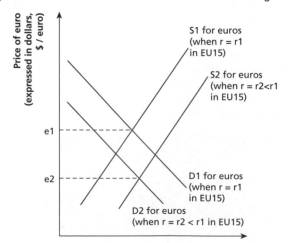

Why do exchange rates move? continued

Factors that may affect investment flows: expectations about future growth

- A growing economy will tend to absorb more and more imports, putting pressure on the exchange rate to depreciate as illustrated in Fig. 4.11. At the same time though there will be other forces in the foreign exchange market that will tend to appreciate the currency.
- If the prospects of this growing economy are good, if, in other words, investors expect it to continue growing then they will want to buy company shares and/or establish a business presence themselves in the country so demand for the country's currency will tend to increase, pushing upward the exchange rate.
- Remember that a growing economy implies growing and profitable firms and plentiful business opportunities which foreigners will also want to take advantage of.
- In Fig. 4.14 the Korean won is illustrated. Initially the equilibrium exchange rate is assumed at *e1*.
- If data and data projections point out strong and continuing growth of the Korean economy and investors around the world perceive the country's economy as a profitable destination then growing interest will be expressed in Korean company stocks and foreign direct investment into Korea will also increase.
- These increased foreign portfolio and direct investments into Korea imply an increase in the demand for won in the foreign exchange markets. Demand for won will increase from D1 to D2 and thus the won will tend to appreciate from *e1* to *e2*.

Figure 4.14 Effect of optimistic expectations about future growth

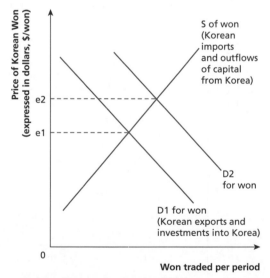

Factors that may affect investment flows: expectations concerning the exchange rate

- Often currencies are demanded in foreign exchange markets not to buy foreign goods or services or to buy foreign bonds, stocks or companies but just to sell it at a later date, perhaps even in a matter of hours, at a higher price and thus make a profit out of the price difference.
- These market participants are known as currency speculators and their demand for the currency is purely speculative. Obviously the driving force behind their demand for a currency is the expected future path of the exchange rate itself.
- In the simplest scenario if they expect the exchange rate to appreciate they buy the currency now and sell it later at a higher price thus making a profit out of the price difference. If others believe and do the same thing then the demand for the currency will increase.
- In Fig. 4.15 currency speculation increases the demand for the Turkish lira from D1 to D2 thus leading it to appreciate from *e1* to *e2*. Expectations can thus often be self-fulfilling.

Figure 4.15 Currency speculation and the exchange rate

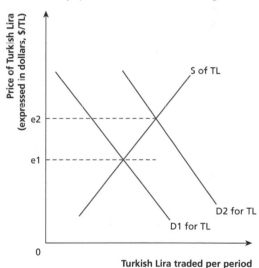

Why do exchange rates move? continued

In summary:

The factors affecting the exchange rate of a currency thus include:

- relative growth rates which affect import absorption;
- relative inflation rates which affect competitiveness of exports and imports;
- relative interest rates which affect capital flows;
- the expected future performance of the economy itself which also affects capital flows;
- currency speculation (buying and selling of currencies to gain from their price movements).

Hence:

- A widening trade deficit will tend to depreciate a currency.
- Strong growth will tend to depreciate the currency as import absorption rises but, at the same time, strong growth and confidence in the prospects of an economy will tend to appreciate the currency as it absorbs investment capital from abroad.
- Higher level of inflation will tend to depreciate a currency as its exports become less competitive abroad and imports more attractive.
- Higher interest rates tend to appreciate a currency as hot monies will be attracted to take advantage of the available higher rates of return on domestic bonds and deposits denominated in the domestic currency.

Tips

In all of the above foreign exchange market diagrams there is no need, for our purposes, to focus on the horizontal axis as we do not care about the 'quantity' of the currency traded per period. It is strongly advised that you always fully label the axes.

Also, 'relative' growth rates (inflation rates or interest rates) imply one country's growth rate (inflation rate or interest rate) compared to the others. For example, in Fig. 4.11 the effect is the same whether growth accelerates in Indonesia or slows down in the US. The effect described in Fig. 4.12 is the same whether inflation increases in Indonesia or decreases in the US. In Fig. 4.13 the effect is the same whether interest rates rise in Indonesia or fall in the US. It is the change in one growth rate (inflation rate or interest rate) relative to the other that matters.

Lastly, short-term capital inflows are known as footloose funds or hot monies. In addition to interest rate differentials these capital flows are also affected by changes in expectations concerning the future path of exchange rates. Since the assessment of exchange rate risk is not the same across investors, such funds are spread among many financial centres. Investors never put all their eggs into one basket.

How does a fixed exchange rate system work?

- Assume a fixed exchange rate system defined as a system in which the exchange rate is set by the government at some desired level, usually against a major currency (say, the US dollar), and is then maintained at that level through central bank intervention in the foreign exchange market. How is the exchange rate maintained at the set level? What can and should the government or the central bank do to maintain the rate at the desired level if for example there are pressures for it to devalue?
- In Fig. 4.16 it is assumed that currency A is pegged against, say, the dollar at e*. As long as demand and supply forces are at D1 and S1 the exchange rate will be at e* so there is no reason for the authorities to intervene.
- Assume now that supply for the currency increases to S2 (perhaps as a result of accelerating inflation and the resulting increased import absorption).
- At e* there will be excess supply for the currency equal to FH per period, putting pressure on the currency to devalue.

Figure 4.16 Fixed exchange rates: how do they work?

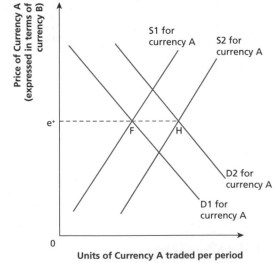

How does a fixed exchange rate system work? continued

- It will be maintained at e* only if somehow authorities manage to increase demand for the currency to D2. How could they do this?
- One obvious option is for the central bank to enter the foreign exchange market and start buying FH units of its currency per period using its foreign exchange reserves (e.g. dollars or euros). Effectively the demand for the currency increases to D2.
- The next line of defence is for the central bank to increase interest rates as **foreign exchange reserves** are limited. The higher interest rates will attract capital from abroad as domestic bonds and deposits denominated in currency A will earn a higher rate of return and thus be more attractive. Higher interest rates though impose a real cost on the economy as growth slows down and unemployment increases.

- The government may also resort to official borrowing from abroad in an attempt to maintain the currency at e*. Borrowing though cannot continue for long as repayment imposes significant future costs on an economy.
- Symmetrically, if there are forces pushing up the currency: central bank will sell the currency, lower interest rates and lend to foreigners.
- It should become clear that this operation resembles in principle the operation of buffer stocks in microeconomics: the central bank should buy the currency if there is excess supply and a tendency for its value to fall while it should sell if there is excess demand and a tendency for its value to rise.

Advantages and disadvantages   HL

Advantages of flexible exchange rates

- Policymakers are free to use monetary policy.
- A trade deficit may be automatically corrected. The currency will depreciate and, assuming proper elasticities, the value of exports will rise and import expenditures will drop. There is no need for the government to adopt contractionary policies which slow down an economy and increase unemployment.
- Exchange rate adjustments through time are smooth and continuous. Currency crises are thus avoided.
- There is no need for the central bank to carry large foreign exchange reserves as there is no need to constantly intervene to maintain the exchange rate at the chosen parity.

Disadvantages of flexible exchange rates

- Uncertainty in the foreign exchange market implies greater risk for traders and investors. This tends to decrease both the volume of trade and the volume of cross-border investments.
- The government lacks the 'policy discipline' that a fixed exchange rate system imposes. A country may thus be more prone to inflation.

Advantages of fixed exchange rates

- Firms engaged in trade can predict with more certainty their export revenues or import bill. Investors avoid exchange rate risk which could lower their return from any investment. Thus more trade and more cross-border investments will result.
- Expansionary demand-side policies that may turn inflationary cannot be pursued by the government. Inflation is not compatible with fixed exchange rates. It leads to trade deficits which exert downward pressure on the currency.

Disadvantages of fixed exchange rates

- The government is deprived of monetary policy. Even the use of reflationary fiscal policy is constrained as budget deficits need to be somehow financed.
- Trade deficits are not 'automatically' corrected. If a trade deficit widens too much it will require a devaluation which can be potentially disruptive.
- To avoid the need to resort to devaluation a trade deficit must be corrected by adopting contractionary policies to lower national income and thus import absorption. This means that growth is slowed down or a recession must be induced so unemployment will increase.
- The central bank must maintain large foreign exchange reserves to be able to intervene in the foreign exchange market and maintain the parity. This involves a high opportunity cost.

Purchasing power parity

- Some economists use the concept of **purchasing power parity** to help predict long-run movements in the foreign exchange value of a currency.
- Purchasing power parity (PPP) is a measure of the **equilibrium value** of a currency – the exchange rate toward which the currency will move over time. The PPP rate is that rate that will equate the cost of purchasing the same basket of goods in two countries.
- If a currency's market exchange rate is presently below its PPP value, PPP advocates will argue that the currency is undervalued and will therefore appreciate in the future.
- For example, consider the basket of goods and services purchased by the typical consumer in both countries. Assume that it can be bought in Europe (EU15) with €100.00 whereas one needs $160.00 to buy it in the US and that the market exchange rate is €1.00 = $1.47; then one may argue that the dollar is overvalued and will tend to depreciate (or equivalently that the euro is undervalued and will tend to appreciate). An American could go to the foreign exchange market and purchase €100.00 with only $147.00 and buy the same basket of goods and services in Europe for which she would need $160.00 to buy in the US. The theory thus suggests that in such a case US imports of goods and services will rise. But, as more dollars will be offered in the foreign exchange market to buy the necessary euros, the dollar will be pushed down (the euro up) until the dollar falls (the euro rises) to €1.00 = $1.60.
- Purchasing power parity theory may be helpful to forecast the long-run value of a currency but its usefulness to predict short-run variations is very strongly doubted. Not only will it take a long time for the equilibrium value as defined to be reached but, in addition, there are many other economic forces that may keep the value away from equilibrium.

Overall, empirical support for purchasing power parity is mixed. PPP often fails. Why? Several reasons complicate issues:

- The basket of goods and services consumed by the typical consumer in each country may differ substantially.
- The basket of goods and services bought by the typical consumer also includes non-traded goods. If, given the market exchange rate, real estate is cheaper in the 'other' country we cannot import buildings and housing from it.
- Trade barriers and transport costs do exist so many goods and services cannot be imported freely.
- Most importantly, exchange rates are highly influenced by capital flows and thus by interest rate differentials and changes in expectations.
- PPP is, however, extremely useful as a conversion factor. Purchasing power parities should be used instead of market exchange rates as conversion factors (to a single currency, usually the US$) of GDP and per capita GDP figures, in order to incorporate cost-of-living differences that will make cross-country comparisons of these variables more meaningful.
- Care should be taken for the PPP value to accurately reflect cost-of-living differences. In December 2007 China's economy (its GDP) 'shrunk' considerably as the price data used for China were from 1980 and did not reflect current living costs. Living costs in China had increased over the period substantially so using the new, more correct data decreased the size of China's economy by almost 40%.

The balance of payments

What is the balance of payments?

- The **balance of payments** is defined as a record of all transactions of a country with the rest of the world over a period of time, usually a year.
- Transactions which lead to an inflow of currency enter the account with a plus sign and are known as credit items whereas those that lead to an outflow of currency enter with a minus sign and are called debit items.

- The balance of payments is divided into two major components, the **current account** and the **capital account**. The sum of these by construction is equal to zero. The balance of payments balances.

Current account

- The **current account** includes visibles and invisibles.
- **Visible** trade refers to exports and imports of goods (their difference constituting the trade balance).
- **Invisibles** include net trade in services such as financial, consulting, shipping, aviation, tourism, insurance, net income from investments (PIDs = profits flowing in and out of a country, interest receipts and payments and dividends) and, lastly, net transfers (including private transfers such as remittances of foreign workers back home and government transfers such as expenses for embassy maintenance and grant aid).
- The sum of visibles and invisibles is the **current account balance**. If it is negative there is a current account deficit whereas if it is positive it is referred to as a current account surplus.

Capital account

- The **capital account** (also referred to as the **financial account** since the 1990s) includes changes in short-term and long-term external assets and liabilities of a country. It records the buying and selling of stocks and bonds, deposits, lending and borrowing as well as FDI (foreign direct investment).
- When a resident of a country buys foreign bonds or stocks, or if she buys a foreign business, this is a debit item as currency flows out of the country and is recorded with a minus sign, and vice versa.
- The capital account can thus be in deficit (if we acquire more foreign assets than foreigners acquired domestic assets) or in a surplus.
- The capital account though also includes official financing (or changes in official reserves) and the inclusion of this item is what forces the balance of payments to balance. It would be impossible over a period of time (say, a year) for more currency to flow out of a country than had flowed in unless somehow this deficit was financed: either by drawing on foreign exchange reserves and/or by official borrowing. If we add the financing of a deficit (the decrease in foreign exchange reserves and/or official borrowing) then the account will balance. Conversely, if more currency had flowed into than out of a country then there would be a balance of payments surplus. The official reserves would have to increase and/or lending would take place for the overall balance of payments to balance.
- If, despite the inclusion of the official financing item, the account does not balance then this is the result of errors and/or omissions. The balancing item ensures that the sum total is zero. If the balancing item is large then this is an indication of poor data collection and statistical services and/or of illegal (drug/arms) sales or purchases.

Correcting imbalances

Current account deficit

- Remember a current account deficit exists if the sum of net exports of goods and services plus net income from investments plus net transfers is negative (it is acceptable, even though not strictly speaking correct, to say that it exists when the value of imports of goods and services exceeds the value of exports of goods and services).
- Whether a current account deficit is or is not a problem first of all depends on its size. To determine the importance of a current account balance we always express it as a proportion of GDP so that the size of the economy is 'scaled out'. Italy's current account deficit in December 2007 was 47.7 billion dollars whereas Greece's was less at 43.2 billion dollars. Only when expressed as a proportion of GDP does one realize that it is Greece that has the problem as its current account deficit is 13.6% of its GDP whereas Italy's is only 2.5% of its GDP (Dec 2007, *The Economist*). Typically a current account deficit is considered serious enough to examine if it is widening and exceeds 5%–6% of the country's GDP.
- Whether a current account deficit is a problem also depends on the reasons for which it exists. More specifically it depends on whether it is temporary or persistent (also referred to as fundamental).
- **Temporary deficits** are short term being either of a transitory nature (e.g. because of a crop failure) or of a reversible nature (e.g. as a result of a booming economy). In the latter case a short-term current account deficit implies an improvement in living standards as the nation is consuming more than it is producing. A strong and growing economy typically records trade deficits as a result of the increased import absorption (assuming of course that growth was not export-led in the first place as in the case of, say, China). Also, a developing economy in the process of establishing certain industries may initially be forced to rely on imported capital goods, leading to trade deficits.
- **Fundamental imbalances** are chronic. They tend to last for a long time and they are the result of structural

Current account deficit continued

problems of the economy. These are indeed serious as they reflect a 'sick' economy. To understand the issue, consider an economy with chronic inflation as a result of highly uncompetitive product markets (with strong oligopolies in many markets being able to raise prices) and rigid labour markets (with powerful labour unions able to increase wages). International competitiveness of exports will be lost and spending on imports will increase as many domestic households will turn to better and cheaper imports. Some claim that this describes Greece with the current account deficit equal to 13.7% of its GDP. Or consider an economy which is growing but as a result of excessive spending by both the government (deficit spending) and by the private sector (low private savings rate). Import absorption and the resulting current account deficit may be unsustainable. Some claim that this is the case of the US.

How can a current account deficit be financed?

Deficits can be initially financed:

- by running down official reserves;
- by official borrowing;
- or by attracting private financial capital inflows.

None of these can continue indefinitely:

- Foreign exchange reserves are limited.
- Official borrowing may lead to a foreign debt problem as it imposes future interest costs.
- Short-term private financial capital inflows may require high interest rates which dampen domestic demand and, most importantly, are very volatile. Such short-term capital may flow out of a country literally at the click of a mouse.

An unsustainable deficit can and will not last forever. Some adjustment process will restore balance. But adjustment may be abrupt and unpleasant. Correcting a current account deficit may require either expenditure-changing or expenditure-switching policies.

Expenditure-changing policies

- These include policies that change the level of aggregate demand and thus the level of national income (real output Y).
- Policies that change the level of AD are the demand management policies already discussed and include fiscal policy and monetary policy.
- Since the level of national income will be affected it follows that imports will be affected and thus the trade balance. For example, to decrease the value of imports of goods and services the government must adopt contractionary policies shifting AD to the left and lowering national income Y. The lower level of Y will lead to fewer imports which will help correct the deficit.
- More generally, the nation's saving rate must somehow rise: the government must run a budget surplus and the private sector must be induced to spend less.

- Note that this policy implies slower growth and thus higher unemployment.

Expenditure-switching policies

- These are policies aiming at switching spending away from imports toward domestically produced goods and services by rendering imports more expensive and thus less attractive.
- A devaluation (or a rapid depreciation) of the exchange rate is one such policy choice. If the price of a currency decreases then foreign goods and services (imports) become more expensive in domestic currency. If the dollar rapidly depreciates then the price of Chinese and other imports will rise in dollars and spending by US households will be switched away from imports. In addition exports will become cheaper abroad and may rise in value. Both effects will tend to correct the foreign deficit.
- A potential problem of rapid depreciation or devaluation is that inflation may accelerate. First of all a rise in export demand will tend to increase AD. Whether this increase in AD proves inflationary depends on whether AD, and thus the economy, is export-driven or whether it mostly relies on domestic consumption (and investment) spending. It also depends on whether the economy is operating close to capacity (full employment) level of output. Remember also that since import prices increase, the cost of living immediately increases. In addition, if domestic firms rely on imports of raw materials and of intermediate products their production costs will rise and could prove inflationary.
- Instead of the exchange rate adjusting, policymakers could render imports more expensive through protectionism. Tariffs, for example, increase the price of imports and lower import spending. Such protectionist policies may first of all invite retaliation and also run against WTO membership rules.
- Note that certain expenditure-changing policy may also end up switching expenditures. For example, a tight monetary policy will decrease national income and thus imports, induce capital inflows which could help finance the current account deficit but also decrease the price level thus leading to increased competitiveness of domestic products compared to imports.

Supply-side policies

- Solutions of a more long-run nature include certain **supply-side policies** aimed at raising the competitiveness of the economy and especially of the export sector. It is more difficult for a more competitive and flexible economy to face a fundamental current account deficit problem.

Current account surplus

Remember a current account surplus exists if the sum of net exports of goods and services plus net income from investments plus net transfers is positive (it is acceptable, even though not strictly speaking correct, to say that it exists when the value of exports of goods and services exceeds the value of imports of goods and services). In general and along the same lines one may argue that if the surplus is small or transitory it is not considered a problem. It is also not considered a problem if it is part of a growth and development strategy that is known as **export-oriented growth**. Still, a persistent current account surplus may involve costs and risks for an economy which should be addressed.

- First of all a persistent surplus implies that the economy is consuming inside its production possibilities. From a static point of view this implies that living standards are lower than they need be but from a dynamic point of view this argument may be turned on its head. Foreign markets can and have proved an engine of long-run growth and development for many countries. The most prominent recent examples include Japan, the four East Asian Tigers (Hong Kong, Taiwan, Singapore and South Korea), Malaysia, Thailand, Vietnam, and of course China and now India.

- More importantly, large bilateral trade surpluses carry the risk of retaliatory protectionist measures by the deficit country. To the extent that the surplus country relies on foreign demand for its growth this is a serious risk which helps explain why China is lately so eager to voluntarily restrain its surge of exports to the US.
- It is also argued that if the current account surplus is the result of trade barriers erected in key markets of the economy then it is not fully exploiting its comparative advantage and is employing its scarce resources inefficiently. Keeping in mind that comparative advantage is not a static but a dynamic concept that countries can, and should try to change, weakens significantly this argument.
- A potentially serious problem associated with a persistent and widening current account surplus is that it puts pressure on the exchange rate to appreciate. This is even more serious if the trade surplus is mostly due to one export (e.g. oil or natural gas). The appreciation means that other exports become less and less competitive in foreign markets and as a result suffer. On the other hand the appreciation puts pressure on firms to cut down on waste and become more efficient.

The Marshall–Lerner condition and the 'J'-curve effect

- When there is a devaluation of a currency (or a sharp depreciation) it is not necessary that the trade balance will immediately improve.
- Devaluation implies cheaper exports and pricier imports. If prices change then quantities will change. But the full response to the price change may for several reasons take some time. The response is limited in the short run as the demand for exports and imports is initially rather price inelastic.

Specifically:

- The value of exports is the product of the volume of exports times their average price. If their average price decreases then their volume will definitely increase. But this increase in the volume (the 'q' of exports) may be insufficient in size to lead to an increase in the value of exports.
- Symmetrically, the equivalent holds for the value of imports. Imports will be pricier following a devaluation but the volume of imports consumed (the 'q' of imports) may shrink only a little in the first few weeks or even months following a devaluation.
- It follows that the extent of the response of the volumes of exports and imports to the change in their price (their elasticity) determines what will happen to the value of exports and imports and thus to the trade balance. It seems that in order for a devaluation to improve a trade deficit the demand for exports and imports must be price elastic. This does not need to be the case. The **Marshall-Lerner condition** proves that the requirement is weaker. It is sufficient that *the sum of the elasticities* is greater than unity.

Statement of the M-L condition

In order for a devaluation to improve a trade deficit it suffices that the *sum* of the price elasticities of demand for export and import exceeds unity:

$$PED_X + PED_M > 1$$

Immediately following devaluation the condition will not hold. Thus, devaluation will initially worsen a trade deficit and only after some period of time will it improve.

Why are price elasticities of demand for exports and imports low in the short run?

- Firms and especially households may not even be aware of the new prices. A sharp depreciation of the dollar will mean cheaper American cars in Europe. Will the average Greek immediately realize that US Jeep Cherokees are now perhaps affordable? Access to new information is never instantaneous.
- But even if it becomes widely known that US cars are now cheaper the typical Greek may need some time to switch away from buying German cars if all her life she bought BMW. Buying habits need time to be overcome.
- Most importantly, it is commercial contracts between exporting and importing firms that slow down the response to a devaluation. Importers may have long-term contracts and business relationships with foreign firms that are difficult to terminate. Importing and exporting firms may be tied into certain buying patterns that are difficult to change because of contracts that they may have signed and also because of trust that they may have built over the years.

The Marshall–Lerner condition and the 'J'-curve effect continued

HL

The 'J'-curve effect

- It was shown, that right after devaluation, a trade deficit typically worsens for some time period before it actually begins to improve.
- In a diagram where time is on the horizontal axis and the trade balance (X − M) is on the vertical, the path through time of the balance of trade following devaluation traces a J-shaped curve. This is known as the J-curve effect.
- In Fig. 4.17 assume an economy with a trade deficit equal to $250 million deciding to devalue its currency. Initially, the deficit becomes larger and larger because the Marshall–Lerner condition is not satisfied: price elasticities of demand for exports and imports are very low and do not exceed unity.
- Only after time t2 in the diagram is the condition satisfied and the trade deficit shrinks below the $250 million mark.
- Note that an inverted J-curve results after a **revaluation** (**appreciation**), where the surplus initially becomes bigger and only later it starts to shrink.

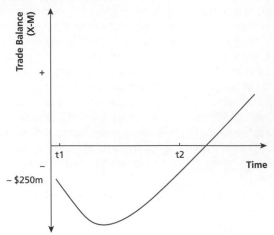

Figure 4.17 The 'J-curve' effect

The terms of trade

Terms of trade: definition and importance

- The **terms of trade** of a country are defined as the ratio of the average price of exports over the average price of imports expressed as index numbers times 100 and measure the *volume* of imports attainable by a given *volume* of exports.
- They are important as they show the volume of foreign goods that can be bought by a given amount of domestic output. They reflect the rate at which one country's goods exchange for those of another country.
- Simplifying, assume that a country exports coffee and imports tractors and that the price of a ton of coffee is $20,000 and the price of a tractor is $10,000. The terms of trade are 2/1 showing that this country can buy (import) two tractors by selling (exporting) one ton of coffee.
- If the terms of trade increase through time it is referred to as a favorable movement in the sense that now the country can attain a greater volume of imports with

the same exports (or, equivalently, the same volume of imports with a smaller volume of exports).
- If the terms of trade decrease (deteriorate or **worsen**) over time this is referred to as an unfavorable movement in the sense that now the country can attain a smaller volume of imports with the same exports (or, equivalently, the same volume of imports with a greater volume of exports).
- An increase in the terms of trade, i.e. a favorable movement or **improvement**, will occur if the average price of exportable goods rises *relatively* to the price of imports and vice versa.

Tip

Volume refers to the quantity of exports or imports. Think of Qx and Qm respectively.

Terms of trade: causes and effects of changes

- One must be careful as to the cause of a change in the terms of trade as it affects the interpretation of the effects. It makes a big difference whether export prices rise as a result of increased demand for a country's exports or as a result of an appreciation of the exchange rate.
- Consider Australia. It predominantly exports commodities (80% of goods exported). The recent surge in world demand for raw materials has led to an increase in the average price of Australian exports. Its terms of trade have increased. What effect would this tend to have on the trade balance, the difference between the value of exports and imports of goods and services? Since both the price and the volume of exports have risen there will be a tendency for the trade balance to improve as export earnings will rise.
- If the terms of trade of a country have increased because of an appreciation of the exchange rate then the effect on the trade balance is more complicated. It depends on the way

the volumes of exports and imports move in response to the price changes. In other words, it depends on the price elasticities of demand of its exports and of its imports.

- An appreciation of the exchange rate implies that the price of exports rises. Exports become less competitive abroad and more difficult to sell abroad. If a country's export prices rise, it will earn more foreign currency only if the volume of exports drops by proportionately less, i.e. if the demand for its exports is price inelastic. If demand for exports (and imports) is price elastic, a 'favorable' movement may lead to a wider trade deficit (or smaller trade surplus).
- Conversely, a depreciation which makes exports cheaper and thus more competitive abroad will tend to narrow a trade deficit if export and import demand tend to be more price elastic. Clearly, the Marshall–Lerner condition enters this discussion.

IB Questions: Section 4

SL Long Essays

1a Explain why countries trade with each other. (10 marks)
1b Given the benefits of trade, evaluate the economic arguments in favour of protectionism. (15 marks)

2a Explain how changes in a country's exchange rate may occur in a floating exchange rate system. (10 marks)
2b Discuss the view that exchange rate changes are the most important factor in determining a country's export sales. (15 marks)

3a Explain three factors which might cause the value of a currency to appreciate. (10 marks)
3b Evaluate the possible effects of such an appreciation on an economy. (15 marks)

4a Describe three possible economic consequences of a persistent current account deficit for a country. (10 marks)
4b Evaluate different methods of correcting current account deficits. (15 marks)

5a Identify the main types of trading blocs and their characteristics. (10 marks)
5b With reference to real-world examples evaluate the advantages and disadvantages of membership in a trading bloc. (15 marks)

6a What are the benefits (gains) from international trade? (10 marks)
6b To what extent is it justifiable for governments to resort to protectionism? (15 marks)

7a Explain why a country's balance of payments on current account may at times be in deficit and at other times in surplus. (10 marks)
7b To what extent does the existence of a current account surplus represent an economic problem? (15 marks)

8a Why do countries practise protectionism? (10 marks)
8b Discuss the likely problems associated with such a policy. (15 marks)

HL Long Essays

1a Explain the various factors which may affect an exchange rate in a floating exchange rate system. (10 marks)
1b Evaluate a government decision to adopt a floating exchange rate system as opposed to a fixed exchange rate system. (15 marks)

2a Explain why an improvement in a country's terms of trade does not always lead to an improvement in its balance of payments on current account. (10 marks)
2b An economy is currently experiencing a deficit on the current account of its balance of payments. The government is considering either allowing the exchange rate to fall or reducing aggregate demand. Evaluate the relative advantages and disadvantages of these two policies. (15 marks)

3a Explain the concepts of trade creation and trade diversion. (10 marks)
3b Evaluate the advantages and disadvantages of joining a trading bloc. (15 marks)

4a Explain the theory of comparative advantage. (10 marks)
4b Given the benefits of specialization evaluate reasons why countries might choose not to specialize. (15 marks)

5a Explain the factors which cause the value of a currency to change under a floating exchange rate system. (10 marks)
5b Evaluate the extent to which an appreciation of a currency may harm an economy. (15 marks)

6a What problems might a country face if it experiences a persistent deficit in the current account of its balance of payments. (10 marks)
6b Evaluate the alternative ways in which such a deficit might be reduced or eliminated. (15 marks)

7a What is a floating exchange rate system and what factors influence the level of a country's exchange rate? (10 marks)

IB Questions: Section 4 continued

7b Do floating exchange rates accurately reflect the relative values of a country's goods and services? (15 marks)

HL Short Essays

1 Outline the principle of comparative advantage. Does it explain modern international trade?

2 A country wishes to improve its comparative advantage in producing manufactured goods. What does this mean and how might it be achieved?

3 Explain two benefits which might arise from international trade.

4 Using an appropriate diagram explain who gains and who loses from the introduction of a tariff.

5 What is a Voluntary Export Restraint (VER) and who is likely to benefit from it?

6 What are the main features of a Free Trade Area?

7 Explain why a current account balance of payments deficit may or may not be a problem.

8 Explain how in theory balance of payments deficits and surpluses on current account are automatically adjusted under a system of flexible exchange rates. Illustrate your answer using demand and supply analysis.

9 For what reasons might a country's exchange rate rise?

10 Using supply and demand curves explain how a government might try to keep the exchange rate of a currency at an artificially high level.

11 A firm is trying to sell in export markets. What factors can influence its competitiveness?

12 Explain the effect of inflation on a country's international competitiveness.

13 Why might a country's current account balance worsen as it approaches full employment?

14 What impact is a substantial rise in the level of interest rates in a country likely to have on its balance of payments?

15 Distinguish carefully what is measured by the 'terms of trade' and the 'balance of trade'.

16 What is meant by an 'improvement' in the terms of trade? Does it necessarily improve a nation's trade balance?

17 How would deterioration in the terms of trade affect the current account of a country?

18 With reference to the Marshall–Lerner condition explain how the depreciation of a country's exchange rate might affect its current account balance.

19 Explain the link between the Marshall–Lerner condition and the J-curve effect.

20 Explain why depreciation of a country's exchange rate might not improve its current account balance.

Development economics

Defining growth and development

Development refers to an *improvement in living standards* in an economy encompassing material consumption, education, health and environmental concerns. Development focuses attention on the individual and on the three dimensions of wellbeing:

- Health: the ability to live a long and healthy life
- Education: the ability to read, to write and to acquire knowledge
- Income: the income needed for a decent life

- The term **sustainable development** focuses attention on *intergenerational* equity along environmental, social as well as economic issues. A widely accepted definition is: 'development which meets the needs of the present without compromising the ability of future generations to meet their own needs'. A development process is considered unsustainable typically when insufficient attention is paid to the environmental consequences and to the resulting changes in the distribution of income. Ignoring these dimensions threatens to reverse any progress made.

- **Economic growth** is a quantitative concept. Growth refers to increases in real GDP (total output) through time. Growth does not necessarily imply development. A country may grow without any development objective being achieved. On the other hand, development typically necessitates growth. Developing countries need to grow to make progress on the development front.

Illustrating growth and development

- The variations in the production possibilities curves of Fig. 5.1 are an attempt to highlight the major difference between the idea of development and growth. Luxury goods and merit goods are on the axes. Potential growth is illustrated in all three cases as there is a shift outward of the production possibilities frontier. Note that the graphs show the production *possibilities* of an economy; they provide no information about preferences and actual output choice.
- In Fig. 5.1a the production possibilities of merit goods, which are assumed to directly contribute to the development process, have remained the same and only the capability to produce 'fur coats', for example, has increased. It can be said that the economy has grown but it has not developed.
- Figure 5.1b illustrates an economy which is now able to produce more merit goods while being able to produce the same amount of 'fur coats' as originally. It has also grown but we can also say that it has developed as its *capability* to produce and offer merit goods is now greater.
- It may be preferable though to use Fig. 5.1c to illustrate the difference in these two terms. This diagram illustrates an economy which has witnessed an increase in its production capabilities, depicted by the shift of the PPF from AB to A'B'. Initially it is assumed that the chosen output mix is at point H. If it now chooses to produce and enjoy the output mix denoted by point J then it has also registered actual growth (as the same amount of one 'good' is produced but more of the other). But since it is not producing more 'merit' goods, development has not taken place. On the other hand, if the new output mix is biased in favour of the production of 'merit' goods, as is the case with point F, then one may claim that this economy has not only registered actual growth but it has also developed.

Tip

This analysis may still be misleading. The diagram may show greater production of health and education services in an economy but it still provides no information concerning their distribution within the population, which may be highly undesirable. For example it may be that only higher-income households have access to education and health services.

Figure 5.1 Growth and development

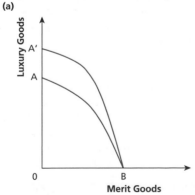

(a)

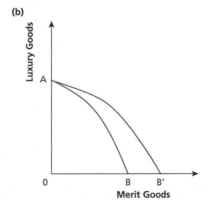

(b)

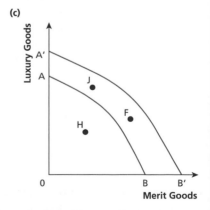

(c)

Characteristics of developing economies

What do developing economies have in common?

The developing economies form a very diverse group, differing in natural resources, historical background, geographic and demographic factors, ethnic and religious make-up, income levels, industrial and political structures. However, they share some common characteristics.

- **Low per capita real income levels**
  Extremely low per capita income levels characterize many developing countries. Low per capita real income levels result in low saving and thus low investments. Low investments lead to low productivity gains and thus low incomes, creating a vicious circle of **poverty**.
  The degree of *income inequality* is generally greater in developing than in developed economies. Income distribution is often highly unequal with the top 20% often receiving *10 to 50 times more* than the bottom 40%.
  The percentage of people in **absolute poverty**, defined as the specific minimum income needed to satisfy the basic physical needs to assure 'continued survival', is also high in developing countries. Large segments of the population suffer from ill health, malnutrition and debilitating diseases; infant mortality rates are also very high.

- **High population growth rates and/or size**
  Many developing economies are still characterized by high population growth rates or, if the population growth rates are not very high, the size of their population may be very high. This may be the result of high birth rates (fertility) coupled with a reduction in death rates (mortality) because of improved health conditions. A major implication of high birth rates is that children under the age of 15 make up almost one-half of the total population. Thus the active labour force has to support a much larger proportion of the population than does the labour force in richer countries.

- **High and rising rates of unemployment and underemployment**
  High unemployment is a common feature of most developing countries. Unemployment, especially in urban areas, may affect 10 to 20% of the labour force. On the other hand, the **underemployed** include those working less than they would like to as well as those who have near zero contribution to total output. In rural areas unemployment suffers from large seasonal variations. Unemployment is a much more complex problem in developing economies and the necessary policy approaches go beyond traditional prescriptions.

- **Dependence on the primary sector**
  Almost 75% of the population of low-income countries is rurally based and the majority of the labour force is occupied in the agricultural (primary) sector. Agriculture contributes around 30% of GDP compared to less than 2% in high-income countries. As per capita income levels rise the structure of demand changes, leading first to a rise in manufacturing and then to a rise in services. The share of services in high-income countries is around 70% of GDP. Of course, variations exist in the structure of output within each income group.

- **Dependence on exports of primary commodities**
  Since a significant proportion of output in low-income countries originates from the primary sector, primary commodities often also form the basis of their exports to other nations. Some countries may significantly depend on a *single* non-oil primary commodity. For example, cotton is the single export crop in Burkina Faso; copper still accounts for two-thirds of Zambia's exports; and uranium accounts for more than 70% of export earnings in Niger. This **commodity concentration** of their exports is a significant barrier in the development process.

Measuring economic development

Using per capita income figures

- The World Bank uses annual **per capita income** to divide countries into groups for analytical purposes.

This is useful and may provide us with some information on the level of development of a country as there is a positive correlation between per capita income and social welfare. Few would question that Norway is more developed than Niger. But growth in per capita income does not necessarily imply improved living standards and may mask very significant differences between countries.

Objections to using per capita income figures

- It fails to incorporate income distribution considerations. Per capita income is a simple average found by dividing national income by the population of a country. It provides no information on whether income is equitably or very unequally distributed.
- It fails to value the environmental degradation often associated with increased production. The pressure on agriculture to produce more food products is responsible for soil erosion and the burning of forests. Industrialization is also often accompanied by massive rural–urban migration leading to heavily polluted and congested cities. Emissions from industry and increased energy requirements also decrease the quality of life.

Using per capita income figures continued

- It fails to include non-marketed subsistence production which may be relatively significant in some low-income countries. Non-marketed subsistence production refers to foods and other goods and services produced by a family for its own consumption. More generally it fails to include the size of parallel (shadow) economies in developing (and developed) countries.
- It fails to reveal the composition of output. Two economies with equal per capita income levels may differ with respect to living standards because of different output mix. A country that spends a large proportion of its GDP on, say, defence, devotes resources there that could have been used otherwise in the production of merit goods such as schools. Figure 5.1 illustrates this issue.
- It fails to include the value of leisure, a most important 'good' an individual may enjoy. It makes a big difference to the worker if the average working week is over 50 hours and he can seldom take a vacation or if the working week is only 35 hours.

- Living standards at any point in time are affected not just by current income but also by the stock of accumulated wealth. The existence of a high-quality and free public school system implies that households with children may devote more of their income to other goods and services.

In addition, there are significant measurement problems that distort comparisons between countries:

- The reliability of the data itself because of poor data collection methods, especially in many developing countries. The necessary infrastructure and personnel to complete such tasks does not often exist.
- The conversion to a common currency. How do you convert Chinese per capita income figures measured in yuan to US dollars? Using purchasing power parity figures is better than using market exchange rates but the PPP can only be an approximation of the actual cost of living.

Other indicators

Since per capita income fails to provide a sufficiently clear picture on the level of development of a country and of its path through time, either it should be complemented by a set of other related indicators, or a composite index should be employed.

Single development-related variables

Related indicators of the level of development of a population include: expectation of life at birth; infant mortality; consumption of protein per capita per day; combined primary and secondary school enrolment; adult literacy rates; percentage of economically active population; energy consumption per capita; percentage GDP derived from each sector; urban population; percentage of adult population with HIV; malaria cases per 100,000; number of doctors or of hospital beds per 100,000 population; newspaper circulation per 1000, etc. No single indicator though is powerful enough to satisfactorily illustrate the complex issue of development.

Composite indices

A number of composite indices have been devised. They integrate economic, social and even political aspects of development. The most widely quoted and used composite indicator is the **human development index** (HDI). The HDI measures average achievements of a population in terms of health, education and access to goods and services. Health is captured by life expectancy and education by the average of adult literacy and school enrolment. Access to goods and services is measured by per capita income. Two major drawbacks of the HDI include:

- Being an average it may conceal important differences within a country. Women, rural populations as well as the very old and the very young often suffer disproportionately but this is not illustrated through the HDI.
- Environmental concerns are not addressed. For example, China's HDI would not have increased as much, had its 'epic pollution' been taken into account in the construction of the index.

Sources of long-run growth

Factors leading to growth

A useful way of remembering the sources of growth is to realize that output *may* grow if the amount of inputs available increases, if the quality of the available inputs increases, if the appropriate available technology improves and if the framework within which economic activity takes place (the institutional framework) improves. Growth may thus follow as a result of:

- More **natural resources** (land) becoming available. This usually implies either the discovery of new mineral or oil deposits or the improvement of existing land. Irrigation, fertilization, improved land management may all improve the quality of existing land and contribute to growth.
- Investment in **physical capital**. New factories, machinery and equipment increase the physical stock of capital. Increased public investments in infrastructure such as roads, ports, communications, power supplies, water and sanitation facilitate and also lower the cost of economic activity.
- **Growth in the labour force.** A larger labour force means more manpower while a larger population increases the demand side of domestic markets. However, a larger labour force may not be able to find employment. In addition, short-term growth may result from better utilization of existing idle resources.

- **Investment in human resources** can exert a most powerful effect on growth as it has a direct positive effect on labour productivity. Improving health services and increasing the stock of **human capital**, defined as the experience, skills and education embodied in the labour force of a country, are considered the best growth and *pro-development* policy choices.
- **Technological progress**. A most influential determinant of growth is technological progress. If labour is the relatively abundant resource then labour-saving technology where higher output levels are achieved with the same quantity of labour is considered 'inappropriate' as it leads to 'jobless growth'. Employing the 'appropriate' technology (which relies on the relatively abundant factor) to accelerate the growth and development process is a most complex issue, especially if environmental considerations are included.
- Devising an **institutional framework** conducive to growth and development. The institutional framework of a country refers to the set of rules and laws, norms and conventions within which economic activity is conducted. It seems that there is no unique set of institutions that singularly promotes growth. Some though have worked better than others. Attempts to transplant a template of westernized institutions into developing countries may not prove fruitful.

Possible costs of growth

Rapid growth may lead to problems that policymakers must deal with to ensure that the process remains sustainable. These include:

- **Environmental costs:** Increased production is often accompanied by pollution and other negative externalities. The technologies employed, the inputs used and inadequate environmental regulations are responsible for the environmental problems that growth may lead to.

- **Rising income inequality:** Growth often leads to increased income inequality which requires government intervention to mitigate as it may prove a barrier to the sustainability of the process. Those not directly or indirectly related to the growth-generating sector of the economy are often left behind. Rural populations, women, the old and the uneducated are the groups that typically suffer the most.

Barriers to growth and development

Factors hindering growth

The following factors are a non-exhaustive list of possible barriers to the process of growth and development.

- **Poor health and low levels of education:** people who are sick or who are not educated and trained suffer from low productivity or, worse, from inability to work at all.
- **Lack of necessary infrastructure:** The Chinese saying 'build yourself a road to get rich' is literally very true for many developing countries. Lack of a road system and of ports decrease the scope of economic activity at the local level and may prevent a country from engaging in export

trade. Going to school, to the doctor or to the market becomes difficult or impossible. Lack of electricity or irrigation or, worse, even a clean water system, condemns the population to increased levels of poverty. Investment, either domestic or foreign direct, will be discouraged.
- **Flight of capital:** if money flows out of a country to safer financial centres or in search of higher rates of return then the ability to finance domestic investments decreases as well as the ability of the government to collect the necessary taxes to finance development projects.

Factors hindering growth continued

- **Corruption and political instability**: Both hinder investment and capital accumulation in a country and make it difficult for a country to embark on long-term necessary reforms.
- **Ineffective institutional framework**: If property rights are not somehow protected and guaranteed the incentive to acquire assets decreases. If banking is ineffective then large segments of the population may have no access to credit. The existence of very many rules and burdensome regulations in an economy makes it costlier to conduct business and also fosters corruption.
- **The world trading system**: many economists claim that the world trading system is biased against the interests of developing countries and especially against the least developed. The role of the WTO has been questioned as well as the trade strategies that many developed countries adopt. Protectionism in the North (in the form of subsidies in agriculture or tariffs, quotas and other barriers in light manufacturing products) has blocked from the markets of the advanced economies the very products where many developing countries have a comparative advantage. Many question the role of the WTO in insisting that developing countries liberalize services and adhering to intellectual property laws.
- Policy advice from developed countries: Structural adjustment loans made by the IMF to many developing countries are believed to have pushed back development in some cases, and the policy reforms formulated by the World Bank, IMF and the US Treasury Department (known as the Washington Consensus) have been heavily criticized.
- **Informal markets**: Much economic activity in many developing countries takes place in informal markets in which businesses and economic activity are not officially registered. This implies that such businesses cannot grow as they cannot borrow from banks, they cannot easily be sold or bought as they lack property rights, and governments cannot collect necessary tax revenues to finance much-needed pro-development projects.
- **High income inequality**: (see below)
- **Indebtedness**: (see pages 129–30)

Types of growth to avoid

- Jobless, where employment opportunities for the poor do not expand
- Ruthless, where income inequality increases
- Futureless, where natural resources are wasted and the impact on the environment is neglected
- Voiceless, where individual empowerment lags behind

Looking beyond growth: sources of development

Factors contributing to development

- **Investing in health and education**: a healthier population not only contributes to the sustainability of any growth process but also enjoys the fruits of growth. A healthier and more educated population will be a more productive workforce. Such investments may be the safest way to achieve a more equitable distribution of income and to increase the participation of people in decision making, both prerequisites for development.
- **Building and strengthening institutions**: improved institutions contribute to growth but also to development as the term also refers to the education, health, judicial and banking system of a country as well as its civil service. Good laws that are enforced also reduce human rights abuses, gender inequality and the degree of corruption in society.
- **Investing in infrastructure**: improved infrastructure not only contributes to growth but improves the day-to-day life of people, permitting them among other things to travel and communicate faster and cheaper.

Educating girls

Educating girls is considered as one of the most significant investments for a developing country as it leads to even greater, gender-specific benefits:

- An educated woman will be qualified to get a better-paid job outside the home.
- An educated mother will have fewer children and be able to spend more on each child.
- An educated mother will have cleaner, better-fed and healthier children.
- An educated mother will tend to seek education for her children.

Income inequality as a barrier to development

- High and rising income inequality makes it difficult to reach consensus among population groups (e.g. workers and owners of capital or rural and urban workers) making necessary institutional and economic reforms difficult for a government to undertake.
- High and rising income inequality increases the probability of civil unrest which increases the risks to both domestic and foreign investments in the country.
- High and rising income inequality increases the likelihood of corruption.
- The existence of very poor means that these people do not have access to education and health resources to become more productive members of society.

Foreign direct investment and the multinational enterprise

- **Foreign direct investment** (FDI) is long-term investment where a firm based in one country establishes a presence in another country. It may refer to either investment in new facilities or acquiring a controlling percentage of the shares of existing local companies. The key characteristic of FDI is that the investor has control of the acquired asset (i.e. the domestic firm or factory).
- A multinational enterprise (MNE or MNC) is a firm which has established production or other operations in more than one country through foreign direct investment.

Why do MNCs invest in developing countries?

The main reasons explaining the presence of MNEs in developing countries include:

- Extraction of natural resources such as oil, copper or bauxite which must be done at location

- Lower labour and other production costs
- Weak regulatory systems of many developing countries
- Avoidance of tariff and other trade barriers
- Proximity to a major market area

Does the presence of MNEs accelerate the process of growth and development?

Arguments in support of MNEs

- FDI can help fill the gap between the target level of investment spending in a country and the actual level achieved.
- FDI can help fill the gap between the target level of foreign exchange and the actual level derived from net export earnings, foreign aid and private remittances. Private foreign capital flowing in will boost foreign exchange and may in the long run generate a flow of export earnings.
- FDI is expected to generate tax revenues.

In addition, multinational enterprises:

- may lead to greater levels of employment providing job opportunities to the local population;
- may provide training and skill creation to the local workforce;
- may help by providing access to management and organizational skills;
- may prove to be a vehicle for faster transfer and diffusion of technology.

Arguments against MNEs

- They may hurt domestic firms by eliminating competition and by importing intermediate products from overseas suppliers instead of buying these from domestic suppliers.
- Repatriation of profits and importation of intermediate products may lead to balance of payments problems as more foreign exchange flows out of the country.
- Their tax contribution may be considerably less than it should be as a result of tax concessions, investment allowances and transfer pricing (which artificially reduces their income).
- The technology employed may be 'inappropriate' if it is capital intensive and employment positions may not be generated.
- Skills of the local workforce may not improve if it is used to fill only the low-skill positions and no training is provided.
- They may generate domestic incomes for higher-income groups with a high propensity to buy imports and a low propensity to save domestically.
- They may worsen the imbalance between rural and urban opportunities and contribute to more unequal income distribution.
- They may use their economic power to influence government policies in directions unfavorable to the development process.

Overall

- The net effects on GDP growth are unambiguous, at least in the short run, but the effects on the long-run development prospects of the host country may not be clear. The terms and conditions of the contracts signed as well as the ability of the domestic government to enforce

these and to regulate the behaviour of these firms are critical in determining whether the long-run effect will be positive or negative.
- In countries where multinational enterprises have contributed directly to its goals and where their activities were not at the expense of domestic production, development has accelerated.

Foreign aid

- Foreign aid is the fourth major source of foreign exchange for the developing world, behind export earnings, investment inflows and migrants' remittances.
- Foreign aid includes any flow of capital to developing countries which is granted on concessionary terms and is non-commercial from the point of view of the donor. Foreign aid includes both outright grants (where no repayment is expected) and loans as long as the interest rate charged is lower than that charged on commercial loans and the repayment period longer.

Types of aid

- **Bilateral aid**: when the flow is from one advanced economy to a poorer nation.
- **Multilateral aid**: when it flows to the developing nation through an international lending agencies and organization such as the United Nations or the World Bank.
- **Tied aid**: The funds must be used to buy imports from the donor country or must be linked to a specific project.
- **Project aid**: This refers to funds used to finance the construction of a particular project (e.g. a dam or a road).

Some aid-related facts

- The annual total flow of aid is roughly $60 billion or approximately 0.25% of the combined GNPs of the advanced economies (one-sixth of annual subsidy payments to rich-country farmers and one-tenth of defence expenditures).
- The share of GDP spent on aid by high-income donors has decreased from approximately 0.5% of GDP in the 1960s to 0.2% at the turn of the century. Only four countries (Denmark, Norway, Sweden and the Netherlands) have met the pledge to devote 0.7% of their GDP to aid.
- Most aid goes to those who need it least; the richer 40% of the developing world's people get twice as much aid per person as the poorer 40%.
- According to the United Nations Development Program (UNDP) development aid is 'inadequate in amount and often inappropriate in form'.

Evaluating the impact of aid on development

The consensus seems to be that the structural adjustment loans of the World Bank and the IMF were not a success. These concessional loans were conditional on countries pursuing economic reforms such as privatizations, deregulation, fiscal restraint, market liberalizations, capital account and trade liberalization (often referred to as the 'Washington Consensus') which in many cases worsened the predicament of people and did not advance development.

Aid can be effective

- When it is narrowly targeted to specific pro-development projects and objectives.
- When it is not 'tied' to buying donor country products.
- Most importantly, when it is reinforced by appropriate domestic policies and institutions in a non-corrupt government environment.

Aid can be ineffective

- When it is given to countries with corrupt governments.
- When it induces countries to postpone improvements of macroeconomic conditions.
- When it replaces domestic savings and trade flows as vehicles for development.

- When it is given on the basis of strategic and political considerations.
- When the technologies transferred and the advice given are 'inappropriate'.

Unfortunately, countries that are in need of aid the most are those least able to use it effectively.

Trade and development

Barriers to primary export-led growth

Primary exports cannot effectively lead the way to economic development. The reasons include:

- Demand for most primary exports is income inelastic and as a result markets for such products in rich countries do not grow fast enough to help accelerate growth.
- Prices received for many primary products have decreased through time. For example, technology and an increase in the number of coffee-producing countries have pushed down the world price for coffee. The terms of trade of countries exporting primary products will deteriorate in the long run.

- Export earnings may exhibit significant year-to-year fluctuations as prices of farm products are affected by the weather and other random factors. Thus, domestic aggregate demand may become unstable and investment spending more risky.
- Primary exports may be dominated by a few multinationals and middlemen so that linkages with the rest of the economy may prove ineffective.
- Agricultural exports have to face the protectionism that advanced economies (the US, the EU and Japan) grant their farmers in the form of subsidies.

The strategy of protection

Import substitution industrialization (ISI)

- In the 1950s it was thought that the problem of development was a structural problem in that developing countries relied too heavily on the primary sector and did not have a manufacturing sector. The creation of an industrial base to substitute domestically produced manufactured goods for imports became known as import substitution industrialization.
- Non-durable, simple manufactured goods (e.g. textiles) were targeted.
- Trade barriers would be erected to protect the newly established domestic firms.
- These barriers would stay in place until the firms grew sufficiently in size and acquired the necessary know-how to lower average costs. Trade barriers were reduced when they were able to compete with imports and survive within the domestic markets.

Evaluation of import substitution industrialization

The problems associated with an inward-oriented strategy include:

- Due to protectionism the domestic industry had its own 'captive' market so it was never forced to become efficient. In some cases poor quality, expensive goods were produced.
- The strategy in some developing countries created a domestic elite which became more and more powerful as the industrial sector grew.
- The protective trade barriers in many cases were never removed.
- The established industries were often 'capital intensive', employing 'inappropriate' technologies and creating minimal employment benefits.

Outward-looking strategies (export-oriented growth and development)

- The structural change brought about by ISI was followed in some East Asian countries (Korea, Taiwan, Hong Kong and Singapore: the four 'tigers') by an attempt to export these simple, non-durable, manufactured goods they had been producing for their domestic market. These, and later other developing countries, adopted an 'outward orientation'.
- In this process, the role of the state varied between countries but, in all of them, it played a significant, complementary role. It provided guidance and assistance to the private firms but only if they achieved specific performance standards typically associated with export targets. These firms were thus forced to produce low price, high-quality goods in order to continue to enjoy any state subsidies or cheaper loans from banks.

- Export promotion is not sufficient to promote development and to ensure the sustainability of the process. The state in these countries invested heavily in education, slowly creating a more productive workforce with higher skills. The state also ensured that the fruits of economic growth were enjoyed by all. These countries thus avoided the costs associated with rising income inequality.
- The first Asian country to initiate such an approach to growth and development was Japan, followed by the four East Asian 'tigers', then Malaysia, Indonesia, Thailand and Vietnam. China and India are the current stars of the export-oriented strategy.

Outward-looking strategies (export-oriented growth and development) continued

Advantages of outward-oriented strategies

- Focusing initially on the production and exporting of simple, manufactured non-durable goods changed the structure of these economies. Employment opportunities increased for the rural migrants, as these industries were mostly labour intensive.
- These export earnings alleviated balance of payments problems as they were used to finance the importation of necessary intermediate and capital goods. There was less danger of the economy running into foreign exchange and foreign debt problems.
- Rising exports increased aggregate demand and fuelled growth in output and incomes.
- Focusing on the large export markets forced firms to grow in size and acquire scale economies. This is especially important for small countries.
- Firms were forced to learn more about manufacturing their products more efficiently. International competition provides the stimulus. The state also invited technical assistance from abroad but it usually limited contracts to no more than three years forcing the domestic firms to learn the necessary technology.
- Operating successfully in world markets permitted firms to acquire the marketing, financial, managerial and, most importantly, entrepreneurial skills. Exposure to world competition permits a local entrepreneurial class to evolve and mature.
- Through varying degrees of state guidance these economies slowly shifted their comparative advantage and production to more sophisticated and complex manufactured products and later to knowledge-based and technology-intensive products. The strategy facilitated **export diversification** which decreased the risks of exporting and created a variety of positive spillover effects for these economies.

Possible disadvantages of outward-oriented growth

- Such growth depends on how fast the rich economies are growing. A recession in the US or Europe will slow down the process if domestic demand is weak.
- It must successfully overcome the hurdles that protectionism in developed countries creates.
- It may lead to worsening income distribution as the rural sector may be left behind.
- The drive to produce cheaply for export markets may lead policymakers to ignore the costs of environmental degradation.
- It forces policymakers to maintain the exchange rate artificially undervalued to provide an extra competitive edge to their exports, risking not only rising protectionist sentiment abroad but also inflation at home.
- It may lead policymakers to postpone the creation of a social safety net that would include state pensions and health insurance as the growth process does not rely on the ability of the population to spend on domestic goods and services.

Indebtedness

The debt crisis

- In 1982 Mexico announced that it was not able to service its debt. Mexico was not alone. Due to the factors listed below, 15 Latin American nations and some sub-Saharan African countries were forced to request emergency aid from the International Monetary Fund (IMF).

The causes of the first debt crisis

The causes included:

- World interest rates increased as a result of the extremely tight monetary policy adopted by the US Federal Reserve Bank to fight off inflation. As a result, interest payments on existing loans (outstanding debt) of these countries increased and new borrowing became more expensive.
- As a result of the higher interest rates the US fell into recession, dragging other countries with it. World demand for the primary exports of these developing countries thus decreased, lowering their prices, their volumes and consequently the export earnings of these countries.
- The higher US interest rates led to an appreciation of the US dollar and thus an increase in the real value of the debt as some of the export earnings of these countries were in other hard currencies.
- Worse still, the funds that had been borrowed by many developing country governments were often misappropriated or wastefully used so that the productive capacity of these economies was not enhanced.

The debt crisis inflicted tremendous pain on the people of these countries and led the IMF and the World Bank to assume a new role. Conditional lending programmes were initiated with recipient countries agreeing to implement Structural Adjustment Policies. There seems now to be a consensus that these policies did not advance the development cause.

Costs of high levels of indebtedness

High levels of foreign debt still burden many developing countries. High levels of indebtedness hold back the development process in many ways:

- Since foreign exchange earnings are drained to service the debt, paying for necessary imports of capital goods and food products becomes more difficult.
- The state is deprived of funds to spend on necessary infrastructure.
- The state is deprived of funds to spend on health care and education. In many sub-Saharan countries the amount spent to service debt exceeds the amount spent on primary education and primary health care combined.
- Debt overhang adversely affects domestic and foreign investment as investors fear higher taxes and the economic instability of these economies.
- Necessary reforms are more difficult for the government to initiate. The economic problems associated with debt servicing make it more difficult to reach consensus within the population.

Structuralist models of development

The Harrod-Domar model

- The Harrod-Domar model highlights the importance of savings and investment for a developing country. It shows that growth of an economy is positively related to its savings rate σ and negatively related to λ, the capital–output ratio:

$$g = \sigma/\lambda$$

- The greater the savings rate σ, the higher the resulting growth rate. The savings rate is the proportion of income saved ($\sigma = S/Y$). A higher rate of saving will increase growth because it permits more investment in physical capital, a source of growth.
- The capital–output ratio (λ) shows how much capital is needed to produce a dollar's worth of output. It is often considered to approximately equal 3 in developing countries, meaning that to be able to produce *every year* a dollar's worth of output three dollars worth of capital were needed to be in place. It reflects the efficiency of using machines. It makes sense that growth will increase if you need less capital to produce the same amount of output, i.e. if λ decreases.
- Since domestic savings in many developing countries were not enough to finance the desired rate of investment, a 'financing gap' resulted. Foreign aid was seen as being able to fill this gap.

Problems with the H-D model

The problems with the H-D model are several and include:

- It equates growth and development.
- Foreign aid financing is not necessarily channelled to the investments with the highest social rate of return.
- Foreign aid may imply **soft loans** which could cause debt repayment problems later.
- It is a model that promises poor countries growth in the short run through aid and investment. Such a mechanistic application of aid has proven ineffective.

The Lewis surplus labour model

- According to Lewis and others (1954), developing economies had a dual structure in the sense that there were two sectors, a large agricultural sector and a small industrial sector.
- The premise on which the Lewis model rests is that in the agricultural sector in developing economies labour was employed very inefficiently, so that by taking workers out of agriculture and employing them in the urban, industrial sector, food production would not decrease while industrial output would increase.
- Rural labour in developing countries was thus an 'untapped' resource.
- Industrialists in the urban sector would have to pay a wage rate somewhat higher than the subsistence average wage rate rural workers got paid to attract them to migrate into the cities and work in factories.
- The profits earned by the industrialists would be reinvested, increasing the need for more labour to be employed.
- As long as surplus labour existed in agriculture, the industrial sector could attract more workers without having to raise the wage they offered because food supply and the cost of food would not rise.
- As the process continues industrial wages will have to rise, forcing the industrial sector to modernize and become more efficient. Increased scarcity of workers in rural areas will have the same effect in agriculture forcing it too to modernize.
- Employment would rise as well as national income and the economy will have transformed.

The Lewis surplus labour model continued

Criticisms of the Lewis model

The appeal of the Lewis model was great as it seemed that just by shifting resources (labour) from low productivity agriculture to industry, self-sustained growth would follow. The process proved to be much more complex. Problems with the Lewis model include:

- Labour in the rural sector may be backward in terms of the technology employed but it may not be inefficient.
- Any surplus may only be of a seasonal nature.

- Profits may be not reinvested but may flow out of the country (**capital flight**) or be spent on imported luxury goods.
- If they are reinvested they may be reinvested in labour-saving technologies thus not increasing employment.
- Income distribution may worsen in the process, with urban industrial workers' earnings outstripping those in the farming sector, creating sustainability problems for the development process.

Microfinance and microcredit

- **Microcredit** refers to very small loans granted to the very poor.
- The pioneer of microfinance is Bangladeshi economist Muhammad Yunus who several decades ago created the Grameen Bank. Yunus won the Nobel Peace Prize for his efforts in 2006. The Nobel Committee adopted the view that reducing the gap between the rich and the poor is necessary to decrease conflict in the world.
- These very small loans can help poor people start a small business or expand an existing one or meet an emergency arising from disease, theft or bad weather.

- Much of this micro-lending is offered to women who tend to spend the money more carefully and productively and are also more likely to pay back the loans.
- Lending money to women has helped empower women. Their participation in such programmes gives them greater bargaining power and permits them to take part in family decision making while it also increases their mobility.
- Microfinance in Bangladesh has over 13 million clients and microfinance now exists in more than 100 countries.
- It is considered to play a significant but rather limited role in the development process of nations.

Fairtrade

- **Fairtrade** is a symbol of 'ethical production'.
- It aims at making consumers in the advanced economics more aware of the plight of farmers and other small producers in developing countries.
- Traders wishing to gain Fairtrade certification must pay producers a price that (a) covers the cost of environmentally friendly and sustainable production and (b) provides a living wage.
- Producers are required to be organized democratically in cooperatives or other types of groups.

- Plantations and factories with the Fairtrade certification must enforce acceptable health and safety standards, provide housing if workers are away from home and not use child labour.
- Educated consumers are willing to pay a higher price because the certification guarantees adherence to ethical production principles.
- Fairtrade contributes to the wellbeing of many small producers in developing countries but the scale is at present too small to make much difference in the developing world.

Nongovernmental organizations

- The term usually describes an array of groups and organizations which pursue some kind of public interest or public good and aim at providing services directly or indirectly to the public. Oxfam, Friends of the Earth and WWF are well known NGOs but there are very many other smaller, grassroots organizations that serve similar purposes.
- NGOs have had an increasing significance in efforts toward sustainable development at the international level.
- They try to affect inter-governmental negotiations that range from the regulation of hazardous wastes and a global ban on landmines to increasing access to AIDS drugs for affected people in developing countries.

- Many work closely with the people they wish to help, which increases their effectiveness.
- NGOs have often exposed the social and environmental externalities that result from the practices of many multinational corporations. Many NGOs act as watchdogs of MNCs. Labour, environmental and human rights records are scrutinized and activists have in many instances forced change upon them.
- Businesses have been forced to 'care' about the effects of their activities, not just on their share price but also on workers, communities and the world at large. Many companies now allocate significant but still inadequate resources to environmental and social affairs.

Changing focus in the field of development economics

- Initially the focus was on growth. Poor countries did not grow because their economies had the 'wrong' structure. Underdevelopment, the term used back then, was considered a structural problem: these economies relied almost entirely on agriculture.
- The way out was for these countries to industrialize. Somehow, a manufacturing sector had to be created. The structure of these economies had to change.
- In the 1980s and early 1990s the emphasis in the field of development economics changed. The shift was on 'getting the policies right'. This approach was considered appropriate across all developing nations independently of their particularities. The right policies included smaller budget deficits, interest rate and exchange rate liberalization, trade and capital liberalization, privatization and deregulation, *regardless* of history and prevailing local conditions. This set of policies is often referred to as the Washington Consensus. The results were not those expected. China and India managed to register impressive growth, reduce poverty and achieve social progress and development but each followed its own variation of policies and implemented these at different speeds. Africa with few exceptions did not make significant progress and much of Latin America suffered from a series of crises.
- It has been realized that achieving growth *and translating it into development* is an extremely complex issue and that each country must try to work around its own constraints and find its own recipe for development. The consensus is that there is no unique set of institutions and no rigid set of policies that all countries can adopt and expect growth *and development* to follow. The Chinese experience with its enormous success, its enormous problems, its particularities and its inherent contradictions is changing economic thinking once again.

The role of markets and the state in the development process

- The debate about the role of the state and the role of markets in the process of development has gone through many stages. A growing consensus is now being formed which considers the roles of the market and the state to be complementary.

Why are markets and prices important?

- Because they provide signals for the allocation of resources
- Because they create incentives
- Because they permit choice
- Because profit-oriented entrepreneurs can spot opportunities and use resources efficiently
- Because competition leads to lower prices and better quality and forces firms to innovate.

Why is an effective state required to achieve development?

- Because infrastructure which is necessary for growth and development is a 'public good' in the sense that the private sector will not provide it.
- Because an appropriate institutional environment is necessary for markets to operate. At the very least the state has to protect property rights and guarantee the rule of law.
- Because basic education and health create very significant positive externalities and would be underprovided if left to the market.
- Because the market cannot guarantee an equitable distribution of income between individuals, groups, regions or time.
- Because the market cannot guarantee effective protection of the environment.
- Because it is necessary to create a stable macroeconomic environment for economic activity to grow.

Markets and the state should be partners in the process of growth and development with the private sector providing the necessary vigour and the state the framework within which economic activity can take place, rectifying market failures and enhancing the resources available.

IB Questions: Section 5

SL and HL Long Essays

1a Explain the various types of aid which a developing country might receive. (10 marks)

1b 'Aid is an ineffective means of promoting the development of poorer countries.' Evaluate this statement. (15 marks)

2a Explain why a firm may benefit from becoming a multinational corporation. (10 marks)

2b Evaluate the effectiveness of foreign direct investment as a means of achieving economic growth and development in a less developed country. (15 marks)

3a Explain how an increase in the quantity and quality of a nation's factors of production can promote economic development. (10 marks)

3b Evaluate the impact of globalization on the economic development of developing countries. (15 marks)

4a Explain two significant barriers to economic growth in less developed countries (LDCs). (10 marks)

4b Evaluate strategies that might be used to overcome the two barriers identified in (a). (15 marks)

5a Explain the main characteristic of a market economy. (10 marks)

5b Evaluate the proposition that economic development is best achieved through the market system. (15 marks)

6a What evidence would indicate to an economist that a country is experiencing economic development as well as economic growth? (10 marks)

6b Evaluate the strategies that may be used to achieve economic development. (15 marks)

7a Explain the difference between inward and outward-oriented development strategies. (10 marks)

7b Which strategy do you consider to be most effective? Justify your answer. (15 marks)

8a Distinguish between domestic and foreign direct investment. (10 marks)

8b Evaluate the importance of saving and investment in the process of economic development. (15 marks)

9a Why do growth rates vary between countries? (10 marks)

9b Discuss the barriers that a less developed country might face in attempting to increase its growth rate substantially. (15 marks)

10a Explain how economists might measure the extent to which living standards vary between countries. (10 marks)

10b Evaluate the ways in which more developed countries might help less developed countries to raise living standards. (15 marks)

11a Describe the main barriers to economic development that countries may experience. (10 marks)

11b Evaluate the view that countries with a more equal distribution of income and wealth are more likely to experience higher levels of economic development. (15 marks)

12a Using examples, explain the difference between economic growth and economic development. (10 marks)

12b Is economic growth always a desirable policy objective for a government? (15 marks)

13a Under what circumstances might a country achieve economic growth without economic development? (10 marks)

13b Evaluate the effectiveness of outward-oriented strategies to achieve economic growth and development. (15 marks)

14a Using examples, describe various sources of funds available to developing countries through trade and aid. (10 marks)

14b Evaluate trade and aid as means of achieving economic growth and development. (15 marks)

HL Short Essays

1 Distinguish between an outward-oriented growth strategy and an inward-oriented growth strategy.

2 Explain which is likely to be higher in a less developed country, Gross National Product or Gross Domestic Product?

3 Explain two ways in which the international indebtedness of developing countries might hinder their growth and development.

4 Explain why economic growth is likely to generate external costs which are a threat to sustainable development.

5 Explain how overdependence on primary products may act as a barrier to economic development.

6 Use a production possibilities curve to explain the distinction between economic growth and economic development.

7 Explain two ways in which multinational corporations might hinder the development of less developed countries.

8 Why might a less developed country find it difficult to maintain stable export revenues?

9 In what ways might a more equal distribution of income contribute to economic development?

10 Distinguish between the forms of aid which a developing country might receive.

11 Poor people in less developed countries often derive little benefit from economic growth. Why might this be so?

12 Explain why primary school education for girls is considered by many economists to be a particularly worthwhile investment for less developed countries.

IB Questions: Section 5 continued

13 A less developed country exports tea and imports most of its consumer durables. Explain why the terms of trade are likely to worsen against this country and discuss the consequences.

14 Outline the possible advantages of a country specializing in manufactured goods instead of primary products.

15 Explain what is meant by the term sustainable development and discuss ways in which governments can encourage it to take place.

Glossary of Syllabus Terms

Absolute advantage (HL) A country is said to have an absolute advantage in the production of a good if it can produce *more* of it with the *same* resources.

Accelerator principle or theory (HL) A theory of investment level determination where the level of investment depends on changes in national income. A (Keynesian school) explanation for the instability of investment in a market economy.

Accounting costs (HL) Production costs for which a firm makes explicit monetary payments.

Actual and potential growth Actual growth refers to increases in real GDP through time; potential growth refers to a shift outwards of the production possibilities boundary.

Ad valorem tax An indirect tax expressed as a percentage of the price of a product, e.g. VAT.

Administrative obstacles (regulatory barriers) Government or administrative regulations or requirements that result in a lower level of imports into a country.

Aggregate demand Total planned spending on domestic goods and services at various possible average price levels per period of time.

Aggregate supply The level of planned output of goods and services at various possible price levels per period of time.

Aid Any flow of capital (grants or loans) from developed to developing countries that is non-commercial from the point of view of the donor and for which the terms are concessional, i.e. interest rate is lower than the market rate and repayment period longer.

Allocative efficiency Exists when 'just the right amount' *from society's point of view* has been produced. It requires that, for the last unit produced, price is equal to its marginal cost.

Anti-dumping duties Taxes (tariffs) that bring the import price of the good that is being dumped closer to the price charged by domestic firms in order to avoid injury to the domestic industry in the importing country.

Appreciation An increase in the exchange rate within a flexible (floating) exchange rate regime.

Balance of payments (BOP) A record of all transactions of a country with the rest of the world over a period of time. It is broken down into the current account and the capital account.

Barrier to entry Anything that deters entry of a new firm into a market, e.g. a patent.

Basic economic questions The 'what', 'how' and 'for whom' questions that all economies must somehow answer.

Bilateral aid Aid from one government to another through some kind of national aid agency.

Breakeven output (HL) That level of output for which the total revenues of a firm are equal to the total costs of production so that profits are zero.

Budget deficit A budget deficit exists if government spending (G) exceeds government (tax) revenues (T).

Buffer stocks A policy aiming at stabilizing the price of commodities (coffee, cocoa, tin, etc.). A target price is chosen and the manager buys and stocks the good if the price tends to fall or sells from stocks if the price tends to rise. See related 'commodity agreements'.

Business/trade cycle The short-run fluctuations of real GDP around its long-run trend.

Capital Produced means of production (tools, machines, equipment, factories, etc.).

Capital account of the BOP Records the portfolio and foreign direct investments into and out of a country over a period of time.

Capital flight Refers to financial capital, exiting a country legally or illegally, and flowing into safer and more profitable financial centres.

Capital flows Investment flows per period of time into and out of a country. These include portfolio and foreign direct investments.

Cartels (HL) Formal collusion of oligopolistic firms agreeing to behave as if they were a monopoly by restricting output in order to fix price at a higher level.

Centrally planned (command) economy Refers to an economy in which the state determines prices and output of goods and services.

Ceteris paribus All other factors remaining constant.

Circular flow model An economic model showing the major interrelationships and flows, real and monetary, between the major 'players' (decision-making units) of an economy.

Glossary of Syllabus Terms continued

Collusive oligopoly (HL) When oligopolistic firms formally or tacitly agree to fix price or to engage in other anti-competitive practices.

Commodities Primary products used as inputs in the manufacturing process and traded in international markets (e.g. coffee, cotton, tin, zinc, copper, etc.).

Commodity agreements Agreements between producers to coordinate commodity exports in order to stabilize prices. Either a production (export) quota system is operated (such as the International Coffee Agreement) where producers (exporting countries) agree to limit the amount exported, effectively forming a 'cartel', or a buffer stock system (cocoa, rubber, etc.) may be operated. Commodity agreements usually collapse because of financing problems.

Commodity concentration of exports When one or very few products are responsible for a large percentage of the export revenues of a developing country, e.g. copper and nitrates for Chile.

Common market A form of economic integration whereby members move forward to establish not only free trade in goods and services but also free movement of factors of production.

Comparative advantage (HL) A country is said to have a comparative advantage in the production of good X if it can produce it at a lower opportunity cost, i.e. by sacrificing fewer units of good Y, compared to another country.

Consumption externality When the consumption of a good imposes costs or creates benefits for third parties for which the latter do not get compensated or do not pay for.

Contestable market (HL) A market characterized by no entry or exit barriers (no sunk costs) thus subject to 'hit and run' entry. As a result, even if only few or one firm exists, it will be forced to price efficiently because of the fear of 'hit and run' entry by potential entrants.

Convertible currencies A country's currency is convertible if it may be freely used in international transactions by citizens of any country.

Cost-push inflation Inflation resulting from adverse supply shocks shifting aggregate supply to the left; usually, rising commodity prices are responsible, especially oil prices.

Cross-price elasticity of demand The responsiveness of the demand for good X to a change in the price of good Y.

Crowding-out (HL) The idea that expansionary fiscal policy was not as effective as Keynesian theory claimed because deficit spending required financing which would lead to increased interest rates and thus reduced private sector spending.

Current account (of the BOP) Records the value of exports and imports of goods and services of a country in a period of time. A current account surplus exists if the value of exports of goods and services exceeds the value of imports. Conversely for a deficit. More precisely, the current account includes visible trade and invisibles. The latter include trade in services, net investment income as well as net transfers.

Customs unions A form of regional economic integration whereby two or more countries abolish tariff (and other barriers) between them and establish a common external barrier toward non-member countries.

Cyclical (or demand-deficient or Keynesian) unemployment Unemployment that is a result of insufficient aggregate demand (and of sticky money wages). Cyclical unemployment rises as an economy moves deeper into recession.

Deflation Refers to the case where the average level of prices is decreasing through time. Deflation implies negative inflation rates.

Deflationary gap A deflationary gap is present if equilibrium (actual) real output falls short of the level corresponding to the full employment level of output as a result of insufficient aggregate demand.

Demand The quantity of a product that consumers are willing and able to purchase per time period at a specific price, ceteris paribus.

Demand-pull inflation Inflation resulting from aggregate demand rising (faster than aggregate supply).

Demand-side policies Policies aimed at influencing the level of aggregate demand in order to affect growth, employment and inflation. They include fiscal and monetary policy.

Demerit goods Consumption of such goods creates very significant negative externalities on society so governments try to decrease or prohibit their consumption. Typical examples include alcohol, tobacco and illegal drugs.

Depreciation (of a currency) A decrease in the exchange rate within a floating (flexible) exchange rate system.

Devaluation (of a currency) A decrease in the exchange rate within a fixed exchange rate system.

Glossary of Syllabus Terms continued

Differentiated product Products which are similar but not identical across sellers in an industry. They are considered by consumers as close but not perfect substitutes.

Direct taxation Taxation on income and wealth.

Diversification (of exports) A policy initiative to move away from commodity concentration of exports. When a country, instead of relying on only a few commodities to export, tries to export a bigger variety of goods and services.

Dynamic efficiency (HL) When a firm enjoys economies of scale, leading to faster rates of innovation (new products and new processes).

Economic costs (HL) Economic costs are the value of all resources sacrificed to produce a good.

Economic development A sustainable increase in living standards that implies increased per capita income, better education and health as well as environmental protection.

Economic union A form of regional economic integration where members of a customs union decide to integrate further by harmonizing taxation and other economic policies and even establishing a common currency.

Economies and diseconomies of scale (HL) Economies of scale exist if average costs decrease as the size (scale) of the firm increases. A firm is facing diseconomies of scale if unit costs rise as it further expands in size.

Elasticity Generally, the responsiveness of an economic variable to a change in some other economic variable. For example, price elasticity of demand.

Entrepreneurship The willingness and ability of certain individuals to organize the other three factors of production and to take risks.

Equilibrium A market is considered to be in equilibrium if there is no tendency for change. This will be the case if quantity demanded per period equals quantity supplied.

Exchange rate The price of a currency expressed in terms of another currency. The number of units of a foreign currency required to buy a unit of the domestic currency.

Exit barriers (HL) Costs that a firm incurs upon exit.

Expectations The present perception of decision-making units concerning the future state of affairs in an economy, a market or the value of an economic variable.

Expenditure-changing and expenditure-switching policies (HL) Expenditure changing: demand management policies that will lower aggregate demand and thus national income thus reducing imports and a trade deficit. Expenditure switching: policies that will try to switch expenditures away from imports and towards domestic products by making imports relatively more expensive and thus undesirable. For example, through devaluation or through the imposition of tariffs.

Export-led/outward-oriented growth A strategy stressing export markets in the belief that the resulting increase in aggregate demand and in foreign exchange earnings together with the faster transfer and diffusion of technology and all other trade-related efficiency benefits will accelerate the growth and development process of developing economies.

Export subsidy A payment granted by a government to domestic firms to strengthen their competitiveness against foreign producers.

Externalities When an economic activity creates benefits or imposes costs for third parties for which these do not pay or do not get compensated respectively.

Factor endowments The quantity and quality of factors of production (land, labour, human capital, physical capital and entrepreneurship) an economy has at its disposal.

Fair trade (organizations) Fairtrade is a certification designed to allow socially conscious consumers to identify goods (usually coffee, cocoa, honey, cotton but also textiles and handicrafts) which meet certain minimum standards. It is a certification of 'ethical production'.

Fiscal policy Refers to the manipulation of the level of government spending (G) and of taxation (T) in order to affect aggregate demand; expansionary FP is the case if government spending (G) rises and/or taxes (T) decrease in order to reflate an economy in or falling into recession.

Fixed exchange rate system When the exchange rate is set at a level or within a range by the government and is then maintained there through central bank intervention (specifically, through buying and selling the currency in the foreign exchange market and/or manipulating the interest rate).

Flat rate tax A tax (usually on income) that is a constant percentage of the tax base.

Floating (flexible) exchange rate system If the exchange rate is determined solely through the interaction of demand and supply for the currency with no government (central bank) intervention.

Glossary of Syllabus Terms continued

Foreign direct investment (FDI) When multinational corporations establish a new firm or acquire controlling interest in an existing one in a foreign country. It is distinct from portfolio investment as in FDI the investor has control over the asset.

Foreign exchange reserves The value of foreign exchange holdings held at the central bank of a country.

Free good vs. economic good Economic goods are goods whose production involves the sacrifice of scarce factors of production. Free goods do not have an opportunity cost (e.g. sea water).

Free market economy Refers to an economy in which markets, in other words the interaction of buyers and producers, determine prices and output.

Free trade Refers to international trade that is not subject to any type of trade barrier.

Free trade area (agreement) An FTA is formed when two or more countries abolish tariffs (and other barriers) between them while maintaining existing barriers to non-members.

Frictional unemployment The term refers to people in between jobs. It is a form of unavoidable unemployment as people are constantly moving between jobs in search of better opportunities. Better and faster information concerning the labour market can lower this type of unemployment.

Full employment The term has come to refer to the situation where there is equilibrium in the labour market and thus any unemployment remaining is not demand-deficient. Any increase in total output beyond that level will prove inflationary and temporary.

Giffen goods (HL) Giffen goods, together with Veblen goods, are an exception to the law of demand. If the price of such goods increases, quantity demanded per period will increase, giving rise to a positively sloped demand curve. A Giffen good has the following characteristics: it is a very strongly inferior good, it is consumed by the very poor and expenditure on such a good dominates total expenditures, e.g. perhaps noodles and rice in western China.

Gini coefficient (HL) A measure of income inequality within a population that ranges from zero (perfect equality) to 1 (or 100) in the case of absolute inequality; Brazil has one of the highest Gini coefficients (about 0.60) whereas Austria has one of the lowest (0.25).

Globalization The process of increasing world-wide interconnectedness reflected in greater trade and cross-border investment flows, the proliferation of multinationals and existence of faster and cheaper communication (internet, cell phones) and transportation.

Goals of firms (HL) Profit maximization is the working assumption but several other behavioral assumptions have also been proposed by theorists. Sales (revenue) maximization, long-run profit maximization, satisficing theories, as well as managerial theories are among the alternatives.

Government failure When government policies aiming at correcting a market failure fail to do so as a result of unintended consequences, measurement problems, biases, etc.

Grant aid These are aid funds that need not be repaid to the donor country.

Gross Domestic Product The value of all final goods and services produced within an economy over a period of time, usually a year.

Gross National Product GNP equals GDP plus income from abroad minus income paid abroad.

Growth Refers to increases in the real GDP (the total output) of a country through time. Can be distinguished into actual and potential.

Homogeneous product A product that consumers consider identical (perfect substitutes) across all firms of an industry.

Human capital The education, training and experience embodied in the labour force of an economy.

Human development Expanding people's choices and the level of wellbeing they achieve: material consumption as well as better health and better education.

Import substitution/inward-oriented growth A growth strategy in which domestic production is substituted for imports in an attempt to shift production away from the primary sector and industrialize.

Incidence (burden) of taxation The term refers to who ends up paying a tax (tax shifting). An indirect tax imposed on a firm may eventually be partially or wholly paid by consumers.

Income elasticity of demand The responsiveness of demand to a change in income.

Income, expenditure and output method Three conceptually equivalent methods of measuring overall economic activity. The output method includes all final goods and services produced within a period of time; the income method adds all incomes that this production process generates (wages, profits, interest and rents); the expenditure method sums all the expenditures made for the purchase of these final goods and services produced.

Increasing, constant and decreasing returns to scale (HL) These refer to production technologies that a firm may face in the long run. Increasing returns to scale exist if a rise of all inputs by 1% leads to a rise in output by more than 1%; constant returns to scale exist if a rise of all inputs by 1% leads to a rise in output by exactly 1%; decreasing returns to scale exist if a rise of all inputs by 1% leads to a rise in output by less than 1%. Increasing returns to scale lead to economies of scale.

Indebtedness Within a development framework the external (foreign) debt of a country. The money a developing country owes to foreigners including governments, multilateral institutions and commercial banks.

Indirect taxation A tax on goods or on expenditure on a 'per unit' basis or as a percentage of the price.

Infant industry argument The argument that the only way a developing country can create a competitive domestic industrial sector is if it blocks all competing imports with prohibitive tariffs until it becomes sufficiently efficient.

Inferior goods Goods for which demand decreases following a rise in consumers' income.

Inflation Refers to a sustained increase in the general price level.

Inflationary gap An inflationary gap is present if equilibrium (actual) real output (temporarily) exceeds the level corresponding to the full employment level of output.

Informal markets Markets in which activity is not officially registered. Also referred to as parallel markets. Street vendors in many cities are typically part of the informal sector of an economy.

Infrastructure Refers to the road system, the rail system, the harbours, airports and telecommunications that a country has and which facilitate economic activity as they lower production and transaction costs.

Institutional factors Refers to the laws and regulations of product, labour and capital markets in a country; more generally to the legal and regulatory framework within which economic activity is conducted.

Interest The reward of the factor of production, capital. The payment made for using borrowed money over a period of time.

Invisible balance Invisibles in the balance of payments include exports and imports of services, net income from investments (profits, interest and dividend receipts and payments) and net transfers (official and private remittances).

J-curve effect (HL) Following devaluation, a trade deficit will typically worsen before it starts improving (thus tracing the letter 'J' through time) as the M-L condition in the short run is not satisfied.

Kinked demand curve (HL) A theory where in a (non-collusive) duopoly if one firm lowers the price the rival firm will follow whereas if it raises price the rival will not follow; it shows that in an oligopoly, even if cost conditions change, prices are 'sticky'.

Labour The human efforts used in the production of goods and services.

Laffer curve (HL) A curve showing that if tax rates rise beyond some point, tax revenues will decrease because of the disincentives to work and invest that are created.

Land Natural resources that an economy is endowed with.

Law of demand As the price per unit of a product rises, quantity demanded per time period decreases, ceteris paribus.

Law of diminishing marginal returns (HL) A short-run law of production which states that as more and more units of a variable factor (e.g. labour) are added to a fixed factor (e.g. capital) there is a point beyond which total output will continue to rise but at a decreasing rate or, equivalently, that marginal product will start to decrease.

Law of supply As the price per unit increases, the quantity that a firm is willing to offer per period rises, ceteris paribus.

Long run (HL) The long run is defined as the time period during which all adjustments are considered possible; in production, it is when all factors of production are considered variable so no fixed factors exist. The firm can thus change its scale of operations in the long run.

Long-run cost curve (HL) A locus of points that show the minimum unit costs a firm will incur to produce a certain level of production when it can change all factors of production.

Glossary of Syllabus Terms continued

Long-run Phillips curve (HL) A vertical line at the non-accelerating inflation rate of unemployment suggesting the idea that there is a rate of unemployment compatible with any rate of inflation as long as this does not accelerate and that in the long run there is no trade-off between inflation and unemployment that policymakers can exploit.

Lorenz curve (HL) A diagrammatic illustration of how national income is distributed within the population of a country.

Luxury goods Usually the term refers to goods with a high income elasticity of demand (greater than 1).

Managed exchange rate system Usually refers to a floating system in which authorities (central banks) intervene whenever they consider the movement of the exchange rate undesirable.

Marginal utility The extra satisfaction a consumer derives from consuming an extra unit of a good.

Market A process or an institution through which potential buyers and sellers of a product interact.

Market clearing price That market price for which quantity demanded is equal to quantity supplied per period. No excess demand or supply exists at such a price.

Market failure When market forces (demand and supply conditions) alone fail to allocate scarce resources efficiently, meaning that either too much or not enough of a good is produced/consumed. Typical cases include the existence of monopoly power; of externalities; of public, merit and demerit goods.

Market success When market forces (demand and supply conditions) alone lead to socially efficient outcomes meaning that 'just the right' amount of a good is produced from society's viewpoint and thus scarce resources are allocated in the best possible way.

Marshall–Lerner condition (HL) A condition stating that devaluation will improve a trade deficit if the sum of the price elasticities of demand for exports and imports exceeds unity. Since this condition is typically not satisfied in the short run the trade deficit initially worsens, giving rise to the 'J-curve' effect.

Maximum price (price ceiling) A price set by an authority (the government) below the equilibrium determined price (the market price) aiming at protecting (low-income) consumers.

Merit goods Goods whose consumption creates very significant positive externalities to society. As a result,

governments often want even the poor or the ignorant to consume sufficient amounts of these goods. Typical examples include basic education, basic health care, museums, etc.

Microcredit schemes Very small loans to the very poor in developing countries that are used to help them start or grow small businesses and meet emergencies. Microcredit pioneer Muhammad Yunus and the Grameen Bank in Bangladesh won the 2006 Nobel Peace Prize.

Minimum price (price floor) A price set by an authority (the government) above the equilibrium determined price, usually in order to protect producers.

Mixed economy Refers to an economy in which economic decisions are determined by both market forces and the state.

Monetary policy The manipulation of interest rates in order to affect aggregate demand and thus inflation, output and employment.

Monopolistic competition Very many small firms, no entry or exit barriers and a differentiated product.

Monopoly One firm, a 'unique' product and high entry barriers.

Multilateral aid Aid dispensed through multilateral organizations such as the IMF or the World Bank.

Multinational (or transnational) corporations (or enterprises) Corporations that have established a presence and manage facilities in more than one country. A result of foreign direct investment.

Multiplier effect (expenditure multiplier) The (Keynesian) idea that a rise in injections (G, I, X) will lead to a greater increase of national income. Fiscal policy is thus a powerful tool to lift an economy out of a recession.

National vs. domestic (output or income) National aggregates focus on the nationality of factors independently of their location, whereas domestic aggregates focus on location independently of the nationality of the factors of production involved.

Natural monopoly (HL) A natural monopoly is said to exist if the available production technology *in relation* to the size of the market is such that two firms cannot profitably coexist; typically, a result of very significant economies of scale.

Natural rate of unemployment (NRU) or non-accelerating inflation rate of unemployment (NAIRU) (HL) The natural rate of unemployment is

Glossary of Syllabus Terms continued

defined as the equilibrium rate of unemployment, i.e. the unemployment that exists at the real wage rate that equates the number of workers that firms are willing to hire with the number of workers who are willing to accept a job offer. It is also the unemployment compatible with any rate of inflation as long as it does not accelerate. The long-run Phillips curve is vertical at this rate of unemployment.

Net investment Gross investment minus capital consumption (depreciation).

Net National Product Gross national product minus depreciation.

Non-collusive oligopoly (HL) When oligopolistic firms compete through price or non-price competition.

Non-convertible currencies Currencies that are not traded freely in foreign exchange markets.

Non-governmental organizations (NGOs) These are organizations usually independent of governments and typically aiming at designing and implementing development-related projects. An example is Oxfam which is concerned with poverty alleviation.

Normal goods Goods for which demand increases following an increase in consumer income.

Normal profits (HL) The minimum reward required by a firm to remain in business that compensates for the risk incurred by the entrepreneur (normal profit is thus an element of economic costs as without it the firm would not secure the factor of production, entrepreneurship).

Normative (economic) statement A value judgement, an opinion; usually spotted by words such as 'ought to be', 'fair', 'unfair' etc.

Official aid Aid from governments or multilateral institutions such as the World Bank.

Oligopolistic interdependence (HL) Interdependence exists when the outcome of any action of an oligopolistic firm depends on the reaction of the rival firm(s).

Oligopoly Few interdependent firms, either a homogeneous or a differentiated product and entry barriers.

Opportunity cost (of an action) The value of the next best alternative sacrificed.

Per capita (GDP or income) or per head The GDP (or national income) of a country divided by its population.

Perfect competition Very many small firms, a homogeneous product, no entry or exit barriers (also, perfect information and perfect factor mobility); few examples, mostly found in the agriculture sector.

Phillips curve (HL) An empirically derived inverse relationship between the rate of inflation and the rate of unemployment: a decrease in unemployment will result in an increase in inflation and vice versa.

Positive (economic) statement An (economic) statement that can (at least in principle) be tested against data. For example, 'unemployment in Australia has decreased since 2006'.

Positive and negative externalities A positive externality arises if an economic activity creates a benefit to a third party for which it does not pay, whereas a negative externality arises if an economic activity imposes a cost on a third party for which it does not get compensated. They can arise either in the production or in the consumption of a good.

Poverty (cycle) A vicious circle in which low incomes leading to poverty are responsible for low savings which are able to finance limited investments leading to low income levels.

Price discrimination (HL) When a firm charges for the same product two or more different prices in two or more markets and the price difference is not a result of production or provision cost differences.

Price-elastic demand Demand is considered price elastic if a change in price leads to a *proportionately* greater change in quantity demanded.

Price elasticity of demand The responsiveness of demand to a change in price.

Price elasticity of supply The responsiveness of supply to a change in price.

Price-inelastic demand Demand is considered price-inelastic if a change in price leads to a *proportionately* smaller change in quantity demanded.

Price support Same as minimum price.

Primary/secondary/tertiary sector The primary sector refers to agriculture, mining, forestry and fishing; the secondary sector refers to manufacturing (industry) and construction while the tertiary sector refers to services.

Private sector The private sector of an economy includes households and firms.

Glossary of Syllabus Terms continued

Production and consumption, positive Externalities arising in the process of production are production externalities whereas if they arise in the process of consumption they are consumption externalities. These could be either positive or negative externalities.

Production costs (HL) The value of resources sacrificed for the production of a good or service.

Production possibilities curve (or frontier or boundary) Shows the maximum amount of good Y an economy is able to produce for each amount of X it chooses to produce if it fully and efficiently employs all of its scarce resources with its given level of technology.

Productive efficiency When production takes place with minimum average (unit) costs, implying that production takes place with minimal resource waste.

Profit maximization (HL) The assumed goal of the typical firm; firms will choose that level of output for which economic profits are maximum, which requires that marginal revenue is equal to marginal cost and that marginal cost is rising.

Profits The reward of entrepreneurship. They are defined as the difference between total revenues and total economic costs.

Progressive, proportional and regressive taxations Progressive tax system: when a higher-income household pays proportionately more than a lower-income household. Proportional tax system: when a higher-income household pays proportionately the same as a lower-income household. Regressive tax system: when a higher-income household pays proportionately less than a lower-income household.

Property rights (HL) Legal ownership rights over an asset. Property rights are part of the institutional framework of an economy.

Protectionism Refers to policies that aim at restricting the flow of imports into a country and/or creating an artificial advantage to exporting firms.

Public goods Goods which are non-excludable and non-rival. Since they are non-excludable consumers have the incentive to conceal their preferences and behave as free riders. Public goods are a case of market failure and typical examples include national defence, traffic lights, lighthouses, etc.

Public sector The state, the government.

Purchasing power parity (PPP) theory (HL) A theory of long-run equilibrium exchange rate determination: in the absence of trade barriers, transportation costs and cross-border capital flows and if all goods were tradable then the market exchange rate would gravitate towards its PPP value, i.e. it would reflect cost-of-living differences.

Quota A quantitative restriction of imports. For example, the government of Egypt may impose a limit on the number of South Korean cars permitted to enter the country. The term is also used to refer to the amount of output a cartel member is assigned when joint profits are maximized.

Rationing system A mechanism employed to allocate goods to consumers. The price mechanism is an example of a rationing system.

Real GDP GDP after adjusting for inflation; real GDP measures the volume of output produced in an economy over a year.

Real wage unemployment Results if, for whatever reason, the real wage rate is above the equilibrium rate; trade unions or sticky money wages are usually blamed.

Recession An economy is in recession if real GDP is decreasing for at least two consecutive quarters (negative growth rate).

Regional economic integration When countries become members of regional trading blocs; more generally, the elimination of trade and investment barriers among a group of countries.

Rent The income for the services of a piece of land collected by its owner.

Resource allocation The appointment of scarce resources to different uses for the production of different goods and services.

Revaluation An increase in the exchange rate (the price of a currency) within a fixed exchange rate system.

Sales (or revenue) maximization (HL) An alternative to the profit maximization firm goal. Revenues are maximized at that output at which marginal revenue is zero.

Scarcity The idea that human wants exceed the ability to produce goods and services from our limited resources to satisfy these wants.

Seasonal unemployment Unemployment due to seasonal variations of demand. For example, when construction workers are unemployed because of extremely cold weather.

Glossary of Syllabus Terms continued

Short run (HL) The time period, during which some but not all adjustments are possible; in production, it is when at least one fixed factor of production exists.

Shutdown rule (HL) A loss-making firm in the short run will shut down and exit only if the price (average revenue) is less than the average variable cost. In the long run it will shut down if it is making losses.

Soft loans Loans granted on concessionary terms. The interest rate charged is lower than market interest rates and the repayment period is longer. Such loans are considered foreign aid.

Specialization When a factor of production is employed in the production of only one good or even a part of a good. Specialization results in increased levels of output.

Speculation The buying and selling of foreign exchange (or more generally an asset) in order to profit from differences in its price.

Structural unemployment Unemployment that persists way past recovery. The result of a mismatch between the skills available from the unemployed and the skills demanded by the (vacant positions in the) labour market as well as of built-in institutional disincentives.

Subsidy A payment made by the government to firms aiming at lowering costs and price and thus raising production and consumption of the product as well as firm revenues.

Sunk costs (HL) Entry costs which cannot be recovered upon exit. Typical example is advertising costs.

Supernormal (abnormal) profits (HL) Anything above the minimum profit required to remain in a certain business.

Supply The quantity that a firm is willing to offer per period of time at a given price, ceteris paribus.

Sustainable development Development that meets the needs of the present generation without decreasing the ability of future generations to meet their own needs. Typically it implies development that does not result in environmental degradation.

Tariff A tax on imports as a result of which the domestic price of the product rises, the level of domestic production rises, the level of domestic consumption drops and the volume of imports is restricted. A tariff also generates revenues for a government.

Technical efficiency (see Productive efficiency)

Terms of trade (TOT) The ratio of the average price of exports over the average price of imports expressed as index numbers times 100. Shows the volume of imports attainable with a unit of exports.

Terms of trade: improving If the TOT ratio rises. It shows that more imports can now be attained with the same volume of exports.

Terms of trade: worsening (or deteriorating) If the TOT ratio decreases. It shows that fewer imports can now be attained with the same volume of exports.

Tied aid Aid that has to be used to buy the donor's products (often unnecessary or low priority and/or more expensive); considered a factor partially explaining the weak link between aid and development.

Total, average and marginal costs (HL) Total costs are the costs incurred for the production of Q units of output; average costs are the costs incurred when producing Q units expressed on a per unit of output basis; marginal costs are the extra costs when producing an extra unit; it is thus the change in costs as output changes. This is the slope of the total cost curve.

Total, average and marginal product (HL) Total product is the output derived from a specific combination of inputs. Average product (of labour) is defined as output per worker. Marginal product of labour is the extra output from one more unit of labour. It is thus the change in output from a change in labour. This is the slope of the total product curve.

Total, average and marginal revenues (HL) Total revenues are defined as the product of the per unit price times the number of units sold. Average revenue is total revenues divided by output. Marginal revenue is the extra revenue from selling one more unit of output. It is thus the change in total revenues from a change in output. This is the slope of the total revenue curve.

Tradable (marketable) permits (or licences) (HL) A market-based solution to the problem of pollution-emitting firms where the government determines the maximum acceptable level of pollution and then issues to firms permits (rights to pollute a certain amount) which are tradable. Firms have the incentive to engage in active trading until a new allocation of permits emerges with the total level of pollution the same but with minimal amount of production sacrificed.

Trade balance The difference between the value of exports and imports of goods (and services) per period. If the value of exports exceeds the value of imports then a trade surplus is recorded; conversely, a trade deficit is the case if the value of imports of goods (and services) exceeds that of exports.

Glossary of Syllabus Terms continued

Trade creation and trade diversion (HL) Trade creation: the increased trade as a result of lower trade barriers in a regional trading bloc where a less efficient member now imports a good from a more efficient member instead of producing it itself. Trade diversion: the inefficient rise in trade within a regional trading bloc whereby a less efficient member imports a good from another member, instead of importing it from a truly more efficient non-member.

Trade flows Exports and imports of goods and services per period.

Trading blocs A form of economic integration where a group of countries decreases trade barriers amongst them while maintaining barriers to non-members. May take the form of a free trade agreement, a customs union, a common market or an economic union.

Transfer payments Payments from the government to individuals that do not reflect contribution to current production. Examples of transfer payments include unemployment benefits and pensions.

Underemployment When individuals are employed but are working less than they would have wanted to or in positions below their skills.

Underprovision and overprovision of merit and demerit goods When market forces lead to less than the socially optimal amount being produced or consumed (case of merit goods) or to more than the socially optimal amount being produced or consumed (case of demerit goods).

Unemployment When individuals who are actively searching for a job cannot find one.

Utility The satisfaction derived from consuming a good or a bundle of goods.

Veblen goods (HL) One of the two exceptions to the law of demand: as the price rises, quantity demanded per period also rises (ceteris paribus) resulting in an upward sloping demand curve. It is a good viewed as a status symbol (a snob good), valued because its high price is beyond other individuals. Related to conspicuous (ostentatious) consumption. Hermès handbags are perhaps an example.

Voluntary export restraints A form of protectionism which is similar to a quota as it also refers to a quantitative restriction but in this case the exporting firms 'agree' to limit the volume of exports of a good, typically to avoid worse protectionism.

Wages The reward of the factor of production, labour.

World Trade Organization An international organization with 150 member countries which aims at further liberalizing trade through conducting multilateral trade negotiations, at regulating trade and which is the arbitrator of all trade-related disputes. It was established in 1995 and grew out of the GATT.

X-inefficiency (HL) Refers to the 'internal slackness' that often characterizes 'entrenched' monopoly firms. Term introduced by Harvey Leibenstein.

Zero economic profits (HL) Imply that total revenues are equal to total (economic) costs. Since normal profits are included in (economic) costs, it follows that a firm earning zero economic profits is making just enough to remain in business (i.e. making normal profits).

Guidance for students on evaluation

Remember: In all questions (d) of the data paper (SL2 and HL3) you are asked to 'evaluate using your knowledge and the information available'. Each of these questions is worth 8 points for a total of 24 out of a possible 60, or 40% of the paper. Since the data paper is 50% of the SL exam and 40% of the HL exam this means that 20% and 16% respectively of the total externally assessed component of your Economics grade is determined by these (d) questions. It seems that it is worth working on them for a while.

To evaluate in (d) questions: Consider it a role-playing game: imagine yourself as a junior economist sitting at a round table discussing an issue with other fellow economists when the person in charge of the meeting turns around and asks you 'what do *you* think, Angelina?' You will need to formulate an intelligent answer *using your background and the specific information available*. Well, this is really what examiners expect you to do when asked to evaluate something in an exam!

Read the question very carefully ensuring that you have precisely understood exactly what you are asked to evaluate. Brainstorm for 2–3 minutes, thinking of the *possible perspectives or points of view* that could be relevant, making very brief notes. Turn to the extract to find the information you will use. Underline phrases from the passage and/or squeeze the information out of the data in diagrams or tables. Terms employed should be defined. Diagrams are not typically expected but they are appreciated. Remember though the trade-offs you face.

Possible perspectives or points of view include:

- **Consumers (buyers)**
  Not all consumers are the same:
  - Households may be poor or rich so distributional effects may exist. For example, in evaluating a higher gasoline tax as a solution to pollution and congestion, the poor may suffer proportionately more, as such a tax is regressive in nature. A rise in income taxes often adversely affects the poor more as they have less opportunity to evade tax, and capital flight is a 'privilege' of the rich.
  - Households may be rural or urban. In the above gasoline tax, the rural population will suffer from the higher gas prices for no good reason as they do not contribute to congestion. Export-led growth is a success story in general but rural populations are often left behind.
  - Consumers may be young or old. This is perhaps a significant distinction if asked to evaluate privatization of health care services in a country as health care services are predominantly consumed by older people.
  - Households may be borrowers or net savers. If you are evaluating a tight monetary policy the effect will be different on each of these households. Think of having a huge mortgage to repay versus having millions in deposits.
  - Remember that firms may be 'buyers'. A tariff imposed on steel may help the steel industry but hurt the auto industry as steel is an input.

- **Producers (firms):**
  Not all firms are the same:
  - Importers vs. exporters and import-competing firms. In evaluating the effects of depreciation it makes a difference whether I sell olive oil abroad or I am a car dealership importing and selling Jeep Cherokees from the US.
  - Small local vs. large multinational firms. Any adverse development in an economy may hurt smaller local firms more than larger multinational firms which sell a wider range of products in more markets.
  - Whether income-elastic or -inelastic products are sold. A recession is easier to survive for a firm selling highly income-inelastic goods or services.
  - Is the firm selling in a competitive, concentrated, protected or contestable market? It often matters.

- **Society:**
  - Efficiency considerations (allocative, technical, dynamic)
  - Distributional (equity) considerations
  - Externalities that may be generated or corrected
  - Whether growth or the development process is affected

- **The state (the government):**
  - Effects on its expenditures and on taxation
  - On debt considerations
  - On possible side effects of policies

- **Other viewpoints:**
  - The short-term and the long-term perspective. These may differ. A decrease in the price of a good will affect total firm revenues differently as PED is greater in the long run.
  - Possible micro and macro effects. The elimination of trade barriers increases competition leading to lower prices and forcing greater efficiency but also holding back inflationary pressures.
  - Developed vs. developing economies. Lower interest rates or taxes to lower unemployment may perhaps be ineffective in the case of a sub-Saharan economy. Spending on education, health and infrastructure could be much more effective.

In evaluating you may:

- Want to question whether, or to what extent, the underlying assumptions of theory hold. For example, if you were asked to evaluate free trade, presumably it is 'good' as the country will specialize where it is relatively more efficient while discontinuing production in areas where it is relatively inefficient as comparative advantage dictates. But the model assumes that factors of production are able to shift from the inefficient sectors to the efficient, which is not necessarily the case. Huge adjustment costs may result. If a country does not have the necessary infrastructure or tax revenues do heavily rely on tariffs then rapid trade liberalization may prove a mistake.
- Always think of the possibility of unintended consequences. A tax to decrease consumption of alcoholic beverages may be ineffective because of

Guidance for students on evaluation continued

a chain of undesired substitutions. Poor households may be forced to switch to cheaper, inferior-quality brands with even worse health effects. Higher income households may not be affected since their expenditures on alcoholic beverages are a small percentage of their income and thus very price-inelastic.

- Consider the difficulties of measurement. A pollution tax equal to the external cost of production theoretically 'solves' a negative externality that has led to a market failure. This though requires that the state can correctly estimate the true size of this external cost. Inflationary pressures require tighter monetary policy, but how much should the central bank raise interest rates?
- The possibility of government failure is always present. Breaking up a monopoly may be the wrong move as the market was perhaps contestable or because a better policy would be to liberalize trade, in which case the benefits from large size would continue to exist.
- Remember that any policy decision has 'winners' and 'losers': identify them.

Do NOT forget:

- to link your answer with the data provided in the extract or the table. Make explicit references to the extract, quoting or using figures. If you do not link your answer to the data provided or if the examiner does not realize that you have done so, you cannot earn more than 5 of the 8 points awarded.

Lastly:

- Avoid being absolute. Why? Because economics is a social science and each economic variable depends on a host of other variables. There is a story that Winston Churchill or Harry Truman once asked for a 'one-handed economist' because of being fed up with his economic advisors telling him: 'On the one hand this, but on the other hand that'. No economist is one-handed in this sense.

Guidance for students on diagrams

Understanding and using diagrams is an essential skill for any economics student. Unfortunately, very many students do not display in their exams sufficient mastery of this skill. Diagrams are often missing even in questions that explicitly require their use; if they are present, they are often sloppily drawn or inadequately labelled; and, even if they are 'picture perfect', they are not an integral part of the argument or the explanation. It's as if the diagram and the analysis are not related.

Keep in mind

- Many students try to remember what a diagram looks like and then they try to reproduce it. They usually fail. A diagram is not a picture. Diagrams are logical constructions. They must be constructed in a step by step, logical fashion.
- Start by drawing the axes and label them immediately.
- You must be very much aware exactly what each axis measures and represents.
- It is often a good idea to use full descriptions for each axis in addition to the letter symbol: 'Quantity per period' is better than just 'Q'.
- Label as you go: label each line (function) you draw right after you draw it.
- You must make sure you understand exactly what each line shows and why it behaves the way it does.

- The order in which the lines are drawn is sometimes vital to ensure a correct result.
- Some intersections are important: e.g. where the MSB curve intersects the MSC curve is the socially efficient outcome; where MR intersects MC is the profit-maximizing output; where aggregate supply is or becomes vertical is the full employment level of output.
- 'Reading' a diagram correctly is very important. What exactly does a demand curve show? Can you show what the average cost of producing Q1 units is equal to in a U-shaped average cost diagram? How much does society value unit Q1 of vaccinations or of whisky?
- You should practise drawing diagrams very many times to make sure that you can draw them correctly and fast. No time should be wasted during an exam to try to remember a diagram.
- Most examiners advise candidates to use a pencil and a ruler for their diagrams. An eraser must be available. Use a soft pencil to easily correct mistakes. You may use a colour pencil but avoid red or green as examiners use these colours.

Remember

The first thing examiners often check in a paper is the existence and the quality of the diagrams in it.

Review questions using diagrams

Higher level

Draw a diagram:

1 To show the effect of a decrease in unemployment on the production possibilities of an economy

2 To show the role of prices in resource allocation in a market economy

3 To show the effect on the demand for Pepsi of a decision by the marketing directors of Coca Cola to decrease the price of Coke

4 To show the effect on the demand for fish of a decrease in the price of chicken following an outbreak of bird flu

5 To show the case where an increase in the price of a good leads to higher firm revenues

6 To show the case where an increase in the price of a good leads to lower firm revenues

7 To show a good characterized by income-elastic demand

8 To show the tax revenues collected by the government and the resulting welfare loss from an indirect unit tax

9 To show the tax incidence on consumers of an ad valorem tax imposed on tobacco products

10 To show the benefit enjoyed by the consumer and the producer as well as the total cost to the government of a subsidy; explain what determines which party benefits more

11 To show the necessary government spending of a minimum price policy

12 To explain why a black market may result when a price ceiling exists

13 To show the law of diminishing marginal returns and how it affects marginal costs

14 To show the relationship between marginal and average costs

15 To show economies and diseconomies of scale

16 To show a perfectly competitive firm making losses

17 To show why the marginal cost curve (above minimum AVC) is the supply curve of a perfectly competitive firm

18 To show under what conditions a loss-making perfectly competitive firm may continue to operate

19 To compare a perfectly competitive industry with a monopoly, also showing the possibility of the monopoly structure charging less than perfectly competitive firms

20 To show the effect on profits of lower oil prices for a monopoly steel producer

21 To show price stability in a non-collusive oligopoly even if cost conditions change

22 To show the case where only a single firm could profitably exist in a market

23 To show that first-degree price discrimination leads to allocative efficiency

24 To show the increased profits that a firm will enjoy if it practises second-degree price discrimination

25 To show the different prices charged in two markets if a firm employs third-degree price discrimination

26 To show why a perfectly contestable monopoly structure could be as efficient as a competitive market

27 To show why an indirect tax could in principle correct the market failure resulting from a polluting steel industry

28 To show how a tax could in principle correct the inefficiency resulting if output and consumption of alcoholic beverages were determined only by market forces

29 To show how a subsidy could improve resource allocation in the market for flu vaccinations

30 To show how a congestion charge (road pricing) could help reduce traffic congestion

31 To show why the effect on smoking of a tax on tobacco could have a different effect on different individuals

32 To show equilibrium unemployment

33 To show the effect on voluntary unemployment of a reduction in unemployment benefits

34 To show the effect on unemployment of a severe recession

35 To show a deflationary and an inflationary gap

36 To show economic recovery

37 To show the effect on the Brazilian economy of a major slowdown in Europe and the US

38 To show how expansionary demand-side policies may prove inflationary and explain, using the same diagram, why a trade deficit could widen

39 To show how tight monetary policy may lower inflationary pressures

40 To show the effect of a sharp and sustained rise in oil prices on the economy of an oil-importing country

41 To show the high output and employment cost of employing tight monetary policy to curb cost-push inflation

42 To show the short-term opportunity cost in terms of increased unemployment associated with policies to disinflate an economy

43 To show the possible effects on tax revenues of a decrease in income tax rates

44 To show the crowding-out effect

45 To show the difference between a progressive and a regressive tax

46 To show that in the long run expansionary demand-side policies will not succeed in lowering unemployment below its natural level

47 To show why Burkina Faso should still specialize in and export cotton to the US even though the US is a much larger economy and has an absolute advantage in cotton production

Review questions using diagrams continued

48 To show the effect on the Norwegian currency (the krone) of a significant current account surplus

49 To show how higher inflation in Mexico will affect the peso

50 To show how an increase in interest rates will affect the external value of a currency

51 To show why a widening trade deficit puts downward pressure on the exchange rate of a currency

52 To show how a coordinated effort by central banks may be needed to help reverse the decline of the dollar

53 To show the operation of a fixed exchange rate system

54 To show what a central bank must do to maintain a currency's external value at a fixed level in the face of inflationary pressures

55 To show the effect of massive capital flight on the exchange rate of a country

56 To show how greater access to the US market may impact on the exchange rate of a developing country

57 To show the efficiency gains as well as the effect on domestic consumers and producers of eliminating a tariff on steel

58 To show the lower import expenditures resulting from the imposition of a tariff on a product

59 To show the rents exporters will enjoy by a voluntary export restraint

60 To show the effects of a quota on consumers of the good

61 To show how a growing economy may not imply higher living standards for the people

62 To show the long-run effect on income distribution of mass education and increased literacy

63 To show the effect on growth of better infrastructure

64 To show the effect of high levels of corruption on an economy

65 To show why the very poor in many developing countries may decide against sending their children to school and why cash payments may be necessary to induce them to do so

66 To show the effect on economic growth of schistosomiasis, hookworm and other deadly diseases endemic in the tropics

67 To show the possible short-run and long-run effects of export-led growth

68 To show the possible implication on income distribution of the Lewis labour surplus model

69 To show the possible implication for income distribution of microfinance

70 To show how eliminating excessive and wasteful regulation may impact on an economy's growth prospects

Standard level

Draw a diagram:

1 To show the opportunity cost of increasing the level of production of a good as well as the concept of efficiency and inefficiency in an economy

2 To show the effect of a decrease in unemployment on the production possibilities of an economy

3 To show how an increase in demand for a product will affect resource allocation

4 To show the effect on the demand for Pepsi of a decision by the marketing directors of Coca Cola to decrease the price of Coke

5 To show the effect on the demand for fish of a decrease in the price of chicken resulting from an outbreak of bird flu

6 To show how a sudden decrease in the demand for a product will lead to excess supply and affect resource allocation

7 To show the possible effect of a rise in per capita income levels on the demand for used cars in a high-income country and a low-income country

8 To show why a price ceiling may lead to black markets

9 To show the necessary government spending from a minimum price policy

10 To show the effect on consumers and producers of a reduction in the guaranteed minimum price for natural sugar

11 To show the different price elasticity of demand between soft drinks in general and Pepsi in particular

12 To show the case where an increase in the price of a good leads to higher firm revenues

13 To show the case where an increase in the price of a good leads to lower firm revenues

14 To show that the price elasticity of supply for natural fibre is different from that of synthetic fibre

15 To show why the price of coffee fluctuates from period to period

16 To show how much farmers earn when a buffer stock policy is in operation

17 To show why an indirect tax could in principle correct the market failure resulting from a polluting industry

18 To show how an indirect tax could in principle correct the inefficiency resulting if output and consumption of alcoholic beverages were determined only by market forces

19 To show how a subsidy could in principle improve resource allocation in the market for flu vaccinations

20 To show how road charging (pricing) could help reduce traffic congestion

21 To show why the effect on smoking of a tax on tobacco will have a different effect on different individuals

Review questions using diagrams continued

22 To show cyclical unemployment

23 To show a deflationary and an inflationary gap

24 To show recession and economic recovery

25 To show how expansionary demand-side policies may prove inflationary and explain, using the same diagram, why a trade deficit could widen

26 To show why the rising popularity of Turkey as a tourist destination may increase Turkey's short-run economic growth

27 To show how higher interest rates may lead to higher unemployment

28 To show why more generous unemployment benefits may increase unemployment

29 To show the effect of a sharp and sustained rise in oil prices on an economy

30 To show how tight monetary policy may lower demand-pull inflation and at what cost

31 To show the high output cost of using tight monetary policy to lower cost-push inflation

32 To show the effects of successful supply-side policies on output and inflation

33 To show the effect on the South Korean currency (the won) of a significant current account surplus

34 To show how accelerating inflation in Argentina may affect its exchange rate

35 To show how a decision by the European Central Bank to increase interest rates may affect the euro

36 To show the possible effect of a widening UK trade deficit on the pound and explain why this may not happen

37 To show what a central bank must do to maintain a currency's external value at a fixed level in the face of infla-tionary pressures

38 To show how a fixed exchange rate system works

39 To show the effects of eliminating a tariff on steel

40 To show how a cotton subsidy to US cotton producers will affect cotton producers and exporters in Burkina Faso

41 To show the lower import expenditures resulting from the imposition of a tariff

42 To show the rents exporters will enjoy by a voluntary export restraint

43 To show the effect of imposing a quota on domestic producers

44 To show the effect on economic growth of mass education and improved literacy in a developing country

45 To show the possible short-run and long-run effects on an economy of an export-oriented growth strategy

46 To show the effect on economic growth of schistosomiasis, hookworm and other deadly diseases endemic in the tropics

47 To show why cash payments to poor farmers in Kenya may be necessary to induce them to send their children to school

48 To show the effect of massive capital flight on the exchange rate of a country

49 To show why growth may not imply economic development

50 To show the effect on growth of successful anti-corruption policies

Index

Index continued

Index continued

Index continued

Index continued

Index continued

Index continued

Index continued